1/5 03/10

NEWCASTLE COLLEGE LIBRARY

02179164

KV-680-162

WITHDRAWN

1/5 03/10

To
you

Superbrands

AN INSIGHT INTO SOME OF BRITAIN'S STRONGEST BRANDS 2008/09

www.superbrands.uk.com

LIBRARY
NEWCASTLE COLLEGE
NEWCASTLE UPON TYNE

Class 658.827

BARCODE 02179164

Chief Executive
Ben Hudson

Brand Liaison Directors
Fiona Maxwell
Claire Pollock
Liz Silvester

Brand Liaison Manager
Heidi Smith

Head of Accounts
Will Carnochan

Managing Editor
Angela Cooper

Assistant Editor
Laura Hill

Author
Karen Dugdale

Other publications from Superbrands (UK) Ltd:
Business Superbrands 2008 ISBN: 987-0-9554784-3-7
CoolBrands 2007/08 ISBN: 978-0-9554784-2-0

To order these books, email brands@superbrands.uk.com
or call 01825 767396.

Published by Superbrands (UK) Ltd.
44 Charlotte Street
London
WIT 2NR

© 2008 Superbrands (UK) Ltd published under licence
from Superbrands Ltd.

www.superbrands.uk.com

All rights reserved.

No part of this publication may be reproduced or
transmitted in any form by any means, electronic, digital or
mechanical, including scanning, photocopying, recording
or any information storage and retrieval system relating to
all or part of the text, photographs, logotypes without first
obtaining permission in writing from the publisher of the
book together with the copyright owners as featured.

Printed in Italy

ISBN: 978-0-9554784-4-4

Contents

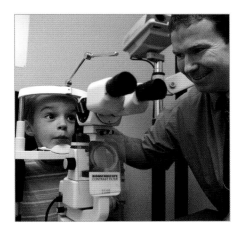

Endorsements

John Noble
Director
British Brands Group

A look through this evocative collection of brands prompts an observation – how old many of them are. Not old in the sense of tired, but in the sense of long-lived. Fifty years ago many of the brands here not only existed, they were leading the field, and it is a tribute to them that they have retained top position to this day.

This is a remarkable achievement. These brands have continued to deliver to consumers through immense change, sustaining their performance and remaining the preferred choice of millions of consumers, decade by decade. As a consequence their reputations continue to grow. Most have already achieved icon status.

The British Brands Group is delighted to support this collection of Superbrands and applauds their staying power. We wish the newcomers every success in emulating their companions and will certainly do what we can to ensure they have the climate in the UK to do so.

Darrell Kofkin
Chief Executive
Global Marketing
Network

Global Marketing Network is totally committed to putting marketing and marketers back in the boardroom, to raising standards in marketing practice worldwide and to supporting the aspirations and rewarding and recognising the achievements of the marketer. We are absolutely delighted to endorse and support the role that Superbrands plays in the advancement of the marketing profession.

A critical element of putting marketing back in the boardroom is the important role that marketers increasingly need to play in building brands that add both sustainable and demonstrable value to the customer, to the shareholder and to society as a whole. We congratulate all those Superbrands that have made it into this volume, and to those people that have been associated with building those Superbrands and for making such an important and outstanding contribution to marketing, thank you for inspiring us all.

Derek Holder
Managing Director
The Institute of
Direct Marketing

We're delighted once again to offer our support to Superbrands 2008/09. The organisations which have made it into the pages of this book have established the finest reputations in their fields. Their quality, reliability and consistency go without saying. A great brand elevates itself above its competitors. The Superbrands that follow are stand-out, iconic, enduring – and profitable.

In tough economic times it's more important than ever to skilfully use the right tools, channels and methods of communication to achieve the long term customer engagement that ensures enduring success. The insights that can be gleaned from the pages of this book are testament to the discipline, the talent and the sheer hard work that go into creating – and sustaining – a Superbrand.

James Aitchison
Managing Editor
World Advertising
Research Center

It's comparatively easy to do well when the times are good. But, as our economy enters uncertain and, perhaps, troublesome times, businesses are inevitably going to face a stiffer challenge. Those that prosper will share something in common: they will be underpinned by a healthy brand, characterised by strong equity and deep consumer relationships.

It's brands like these that the Superbrands programme rightly champions. And it may transpire that the work it does to promote these very best examples from across the UK's brandscape is needed now more than ever before. Because if things do get difficult, we're going to be glad for the insights and inspiration from the role models showcased in this latest volume.

So congratulations to Superbrands from all of us at the World Advertising Research Center for another collection of benchmark brands. Keep up the good work because it's needed – through thick and thin.

About Superbrands

The Superbrands Award Stamp

The brands that have been awarded Superbrand status and participate in the programme, are given permission to use the Superbrands Award Stamp. This powerful endorsement provides evidence to existing and potential consumers, media, employees and investors of the exceptional standing that these Superbrands have achieved.

Member brands use the stamp on marketing materials, including product packaging, POS items, advertising, websites and annual reports, as well as other external and internal communication channels.

Superbrands presents expert and consumer opinion on the UK's strongest brands. The organisation promotes the discipline of branding and pays tribute to exceptional brands through three annual programmes: Superbrands, Business Superbrands, and CoolBrands.

Each programme features a dedicated book, national media supplement and website. By identifying the country's strongest brands and telling their stories, Superbrands provides consumers with a deeper appreciation of the discipline of branding and a greater understanding of the brands themselves.

Each brand featured in this, the tenth annual volume of Superbrands, has qualified for inclusion based on the collective opinions of the independent and voluntary Expert Council and more than 2,200 members of the British public. Full details of the selection process are given overleaf.

Superbrands was launched in London in 1995 and is now a global business operating in more than 55 countries worldwide.

Superbrands Selection Process

The Centre for Brand Analysis

The Centre for Brand Analysis (TCBA) is dedicated to understanding the performance of brands. There are many ways to measure brand performance; TCBA offers tailored solutions to ensure the metrics investigated and measured are relevant and appropriate. Its services aim to allow people to understand how a brand is performing, either at a point in time or on an ongoing basis, as well gain insight into wider market and marketing trends.

Working principally for brand owners, TCBA also provides intelligence to agencies and other organisations. It utilises extensive relationships within the business community and works with third parties where appropriate, to access pertinent opinions, data and insights.

Each year just 500 Superbrands are chosen by the UK public via a YouGov poll. Brands do not pay or apply to be considered. The entire selection process is independently administered by The Centre for Brand Analysis. The key stages of the selection process are as follows:

A comprehensive database of the UK's leading brands is compiled using a wide range of sources, from sector reports to blogs. From the thousands of brands initially identified, approximately 1,350 brands are short-listed.

A voluntary council of experts scores this list, with members individually awarding each brand a rating from 1-10. Council members are not allowed to score brands with which they have a direct association or are in direct competition to.

The lowest-scoring brands (approximately 50 per cent) are eliminated. A nationally-representative group of more than 2,200 UK consumers on the YouGov panel are asked to vote on the surviving brands. Of these, the 500 highest ranking brands are awarded 'Superbrand' status.

When considering brands, both the experts and consumers are asked to bear in mind the following definition of a Superbrand: 'A Superbrand has established the finest reputation in its field. It offers customers significant emotional and tangible advantages over other brands, which (consciously or sub-consciously) customers want and recognise.' All Superbrands must represent quality, reliability, and distinction.

Expert Council 2008/09

Wayne Arnold
Founder & European CEO
Profero

Vicky Bullen
CEO
Coley Porter Bell

Hugh Burkitt
Chief Executive
Marketing Society

Alison Burns
CEO
JWT London

Colin Byrne
CEO
Weber Shandwick, UK & Ireland

Leslie de Chernatony
Professor, Brand Marketing
& Director, Centre for Research
in Brand Marketing
Birmingham University
Business School

Tim Duffy
Chief Executive
M&C Saatchi

Stephen Factor
Managing Director –
Global Consumer Sector
TNS

Peter Fisk
Founder
Genius Works

Cheryl Giovannoni
Managing Director
Landor London

David Haigh
Chief Executive
Brand Finance

Graham Hiscott
Deputy Business Editor
Daily Mirror

Mike Hughes
Director General
ISBA

Paul Kemp-Robertson
Editorial Director & Co-Founder
Contagious

David Magliano
Non-Executive Director
Dyson & Glasses Direct

Mandy Pooler
Director
Kantar

Raoul Shah
CEO
Exposure

Craig Smith
Communications Director
Publicis UK

Linda Smith
CEO
Starcom MediaVest Group UK

Mark Sweney
Advertising, Marketing &
New Media Correspondent
MediaGuardian.co.uk

Alan Thompson
Founding Partner
The Haystack Group

Suki Thompson
Founding Partner
Oystercatchers

Lucy Unger
Managing Partner EMEA
Fitch

Andrew Walmsley
Co-Founder
i-level

Mark Waugh
Deputy Managing Director
ZenithOptimedia

Stephen Cheliotis
Chairman, Superbrands
Councils UK
& Chief Executive, The Centre
for Brand Analysis

**Full biographies for all
council members can be
found on page 144**

Foreword

Angela Cooper, Managing Editor

Superbrands

It gives me great pleasure to introduce this, the 10th edition of Superbrands.

The collection of brands that you will find in this publication span a wide range of sectors, but have the common features of quality, reliability and distinction pulsing through them.

Reaching, and indeed remaining, in the enviable position of being at the top of their markets is a great challenge for these brands. Not only with the current tough economic conditions to contend with but also the increasing demands being placed on them. Many consumers are now concerned about how products go from being a crop in a field to finally being consumed and are increasingly choosing brands that share their views. So how are the Superbrands meeting these challenges? The need for

transparency clearly emerges as key to capturing the trust of the ever-cynical UK consumer. Another theme that runs through the brand case studies in this publication is that of engagement with consumers and the need to communicate through two-way conversations, giving customers the opportunity to get involved in a meaningful way.

The Superbrands organisation also appreciates the need for transparency. We are therefore very pleased to include the complete list of the 500 brands which qualified for Superbrand status at the back of this publication. In addition, you will find an overview of how the top 500 brands are established in the selection process information on page 10.

We are very pleased to have The Centre For Brand Analysis (TCBA) overseeing the selection process. At the back of this publication,

Stephen Cheliotis, chief executive of TCBA and chairman of the Expert Council, analyses the figures from the past three years of results, which gives an interesting insight into the movers and shakers within the top 500.

I would like to take this opportunity to thank the members of the Expert Council, who individually voted on which brands they believe to be worthy of Superbrand status – you can find details of who these individuals are on page 12. I would also like to thank YouGov who carried out the YouGov Consumer Vote, another essential element of the selection process.

Finally, I hope that you enjoy reading this publication and that the brand case studies provide a window into the worlds of some of Britain's strongest brands.

QUALITY

RELIABILITY

DISTINCTION

AUTOGLASS®

Autoglass® is the UK's leading vehicle glass repair and replacement company, serving more than 1.5 million motorists every year. With the widest reaching network in the UK and Ireland, Autoglass® has 121 branches nationwide and 1,300 mobile service units operating 24 hours a day, seven days a week, 365 days a year. Autoglass® is part of Belron® group, operating in 28 countries with a team of over 8,000 highly skilled technicians serving an average of one customer every 3.75 seconds.

Market

Windscreens have evolved over the last 20 years to play an integral role in modern automotive design. Today's cars typically use 20 per cent more glass than in the 1980s and often incorporate complex technology such as rain sensors, wire-heating or satellite navigation components. Take the BMW 3 Series, for example: the latest version has 22 variations, 30 if you include compact models. Specialist skill is required to ensure they are repaired and replaced to the highest safety standards and that's where Autoglass® excels. The company is currently the UK's market leading auto glazing expert.

Achievements

A windscreen accounts for 30 per cent of a vehicle's structural safety and Autoglass® places huge emphasis on training to ensure every screen is fitted safely. It is the only

company in its industry to have achieved accredited status from Thatcham and the Institute of the Motor Industry (IMI) for its National Skills Centre in Birmingham and its Startline Induction and Repair training programmes.

Autoglass® has also won a number of independent awards including two National Training Awards, a Glass Training Ltd (GTL) Commitment to Training award and the Insurance Times Training award. In addition, Autoglass® holds the ISO 9001 quality certification and is exclusively recommended by the AA.

As part of its ongoing commitment to caring for customers, the company's long-standing 'Cracking Car Crime' campaign unites motorists, police forces and local authorities in the battle to beat car crime. The campaign is now in its 15th year.

Autoglass® is committed to the environment and reprocesses the laminate screens it removes, helping to save the energy and resources involved in the manufacture and distribution of new windscreens. The company also promotes windscreen repair over replacement to help reduce carbon emissions and waste.

Product

Quite simply, Autoglass® fixes broken vehicle glass on any make, model or age of vehicle.

The company operates a 'Repair First Philosophy' ensuring that, wherever possible, its technicians will repair a windscreen rather than replace it, so that the existing seal doesn't have to be disturbed; a safe solution that saves time and money.

If the damage is beyond repair, Autoglass® will replace the windscreen. It only uses

1958	1973	1982	1983	1990	1994
FW Wilkinson is founded.	FW Wilkinson becomes Autoglass Ltd, and opens its headquarters in Bedford.	Autoglass becomes part of Belron®, the world's largest vehicle glass repair and replacement company, extending its UK service into all five continents.	Autoglass Ltd merges with Windshields Ltd – an established business founded in 1969 – to create Autoglass Windshields. Two years later, Autoglass Windshields rebrands to Autoglass.	The windscreen repair service is launched.	Autoglass becomes a registered trademark after a seven year IP registration process.

glass manufactured to OEM standards, whether sourced from original equipment manufacturers or other suppliers, ensuring that each replacement windscreen is as good as the original and a perfect fit for the vehicle. It also uses one of the quickest drying bonding systems for safety and customer convenience.

Appointments can be made by phone or online and customers can choose to take their vehicle into their local branch or arrange for a mobile technician to visit a location of their choice.

Recent Developments

Autoglass® recently demonstrated its commitment to raising standards within its sector by becoming the first to introduce the highly regarded Automotive Technician Accreditation (ATA) scheme for the Auto Glazing sector. Under the scheme, technicians can work towards three accreditation levels dependent on knowledge, skills and experience, ultimately leading to Master Auto Glazing Technician status. The scheme provides technicians with recognition of their expertise and customers with additional peace of mind.

In 2007, Autoglass® became the first windscreen repair and replacement company to offer an online booking facility at www.autoglass.co.uk. Thousands of customers each month are now using this interactive option to book an appointment at a convenient time for them.

In 2008, Autoglass® has introduced an innovative new lifting and positioning device – the Little Buddy – to improve the quality and efficiency of its mobile service.

The concept behind the Little Buddy is simple. The device attaches to a vehicle's door glass using a strong sucker while the replacement windscreen is attached to the Little Buddy's telescopic arm. The Little Buddy takes almost the full weight of the glass, allowing the Autoglass® technician to manoeuvre and position the windscreen for a precise and high quality replacement.

As well as delivering greater appointment flexibility and reduced stress on the technician's back, this revolutionary device is also opening the door for women to enter the industry – with the Little Buddy, a single technician can lift and

position screens weighing up to 20kg with precision. Following successful field trials using its own technicians, Autoglass® is investing £600,000 in the Little Buddy devices and has already begun a nationwide roll out.

Promotion

Autoglass® became a household name in the 1990s after entering into the main sponsorship of Chelsea FC and since then, has invested in a number of high profile brand campaigns to ensure that it remains at the forefront of motorists' minds.

In 2005, Autoglass® launched the Heroes radio campaign, using real Autoglass® technicians to explain the benefits of repairing windscreen chips. So far, the campaign has become the most successful in Autoglass® history, helping to boost brand recognition and drive contacts via the call centre and website.

The campaign has scooped a number of prestigious awards over the last two years including: the 2008 Effectiveness Award for campaign with best results at the GCap Radio Planning Awards; the Radio Effectiveness Award for Outstanding Campaign above £250,000 and the Grand Prix for Most Outstanding Radio Planning, both at the 2007 Radio Planning Awards; and was commended for the most effective radio campaign in the 2007 GCap Media Radio Planning Awards.

In April 2008 the firm brought its award-winning Heroes radio concept to TV with a super-heavyweight campaign. The advert shows

real life Autoglass® technician Gavin, the popular voice of the company's radio campaign, explaining the importance of getting windscreen chips repaired and highlighting the quality and safety benefits of the Autoglass® service.

The radio campaign translated well into a televised format and has been successful in communicating the message that Autoglass® can be trusted to provide a friendly, professional and hassle-free service for consumers. During the campaign, the firm experienced record booking levels over the telephone and via the website.

Brand Values

The Autoglass® vision is to be the natural choice through valuing its customers' needs and delivering world-class service. Its brand values are to be caring, expert, professional, innovative and to have integrity.

www.autoglass.co.uk

Things you didn't know about Autoglass®

In 2007 Gavin, the technician featured in the Autoglass® Heroes campaign, beat James Nesbitt from the Yellow Pages adverts to the title of best radio actor of any commercial, as voted by the listeners of Xfm.

The Jaguar range has 29 different variations of windscreen.

In 2007, the Autoglass® 'Repair First Philosophy' resulted in savings of more than 12,000 tonnes of CO_2 equivalent emissions and 4,500 tonnes of waste glass.

Autoglass® doesn't just repair chipped windscreens; it has even repaired a chip on the viewing glass at the tiger compound at Glasgow Zoo.

2002
Carglass Ireland rebrands to Autoglass®.

2005
Autoglass® launches the Heroes radio campaign, using real Autoglass® technicians to explain the benefits of repairing windscreen chips.

2007
Autoglass® becomes the first windscreen repair and replacement company to offer online booking at www.autoglass.co.uk.

2008
Autoglass® launches the Heroes campaign on TV and experiences record bookings in its first week on air. Also in 2008, the Little Buddy is introduced to the Autoglass® workforce.

AVON

Avon is the world's leading direct seller of beauty and related products, with over US$10 billion in annual revenues, and has more than 5.4 million independent sales representatives in over 100 countries. For more than 120 years Avon has been committed to empowering women, through earnings opportunities, offering stylish and affordable beauty products, or by helping to work towards a world free from breast cancer through the Avon Breast Cancer Crusade.

Market

Avon has come a long way since it was established in the US over 120 years ago by a door-to-door bookseller. Today, with more than 42,000 employees, Avon is widely recognised as a leading global brand and a world leader in cosmetics, fragrances and anti-ageing skincare.

Avon is the fifth largest global beauty company, with the UK firmly placed as its fifth largest market, behind the US, Brazil, Mexico and Russia. The UK mass market for cosmetics, fragrance and toiletries, in which Avon operates, was worth around £5 billion in 2007 (Source: Euromonitor 2007).

Avon sells more lipstick, fragrance and nail varnish than any other UK brand (Source: TNS). In the UK, in value terms, Avon is number one in the mass fragrance market, number five in the mass cosmetics market and number five in the mass skincare market (Source: Euromonitor 2007).

Achievements

Nearly one in three women in the UK is an Avon customer with six million women in the UK seeing an Avon brochure every three weeks (Source: IPSOS Mori 2008). Avon provides women with an opportunity for financial independence with flexible earning opportunities. In the UK there are currently 170,000 Avon Representatives, of which 95 per cent are women.

As a company for women, Avon established the Avon Breast Cancer Crusade in 1992. Since then, more than US$500 million has been raised to support breast cancer charities. In the UK, Avon has worked in partnership with charities including Breakthrough Breast Cancer, Macmillan Cancer Support and Breast Cancer Care.

Avon has raised £14 million to date for breast cancer charities in the UK, £12 million of which

has gone to long term charity partner, Breakthrough Breast Cancer. Avon has been pivotal in Breakthrough's growth and development, supporting projects such as the recent Breakthrough Generations Study, which aims to understand the lifestyle factors that may influence the risks of contracting breast cancer. The Crusade also funds four clinical fellows, know as 'Dr Avons'. The Dr Avon programme was the first clinical fellowship programme by a UK beauty company.

In 1989, Avon was the first mass cosmetics manufacturer to stop testing products and ingredients on animals. Today, Avon supports FRAME (Fund for the Replacement of Animals in Medical Experiments), the foundation working to find viable alternatives to animal testing.

Product

More products carry the Avon name than any other brand in the world. For more than a century, Avon's commitment to product innovation has been its hallmark. Avon has invested more than

1886
Established in the US, Avon Products Inc. becomes the world's biggest direct selling beauty company.

1959
Avon UK is established.

1961
Avon launches Skin So Soft, offering the world's first floating bath oil.

1989
Avon becomes the first major cosmetics manufacturer to permanently stop using animals in the safety testing of its products.

1992
The Avon Breast Cancer Crusade is launched in the UK to raise funds to help fight breast cancer.

AVON
BREAST
CANCER
CRUSADE

US$100 million in its research and development laboratory in Suffern, New York. Around 1,000 new products are developed annually to ensure Avon continues to meet the needs of millions of customers.

Avon offers products for the face, eyes and lips, as well as application tools. Best-sellers in the range include SuperSHOCK Mascara, In a Blink Eyeshadow and Liner, Nailwear and Plump Pout Lipgloss. Other Avon make-up brands include: ANEW Beauty, Perfectwear, Arabian Glow and Color Trend.

In spring 2007, Avon enlisted celebrity make-up artist Jillian Dempsey as its global creative colour director to further elevate its style authority and refresh its flagship brand. Fashion designer Cynthia Rowley was also brought on board to bring the emotional and aesthetic appeal of the brand to life. These two industry icons collaborated for the first time to create Avon's limited edition colour collection for autumn 2007, bringing the look of the runway to the everyday.

ANEW – Avon's premium anti-ageing skincare brand – incorporates ANEW Clinical, ANEW Alternative and ANEW Ultimate. ANEW Clinical comprises products to help resurface, firm and plump the skin, providing an 'at home' alternative to surgical procedures. ANEW Alternative combines the ancient properties of Eastern herbs with state-of-the-art

scientific research. The ANEW Ultimate range is aimed at mature skin and boasts Avon's most recent breakthrough in anti-ageing, harnessing the power of skin proteins to help recreate the look of youth in the skin.

New fragrances are launched by Avon every year. Recent introductions include Avon's best ever selling fragrance, formed in collaboration with legendary French couture fashion designer, Christian Lacroix. The two signature fragrances from this collaboration comprise Christian Lacroix Rouge (for women) and Christian Lacroix Noir (for men).

Avon Skin So Soft is the flagship personal care brand, offering a range of choices for all skincare needs. Other Avon personal care brands include Advance Techniques haircare, Naturals, For Men, Bronze family suncare, Active deodorants, Kids, Senses bath and body care and Footworks.

Recent Developments
In March 2007, Avon launched Hello Tomorrow, its first ever globally integrated marketing campaign, which showed an innovative new face of Avon to the world. The global advertising campaign appeared in print and on television in 35 countries. With a dynamic team of stylish professionals on board including Hollywood make-up artist Jillian Dempsey and fashion designer Cynthia

Rowley, Avon is well on its way towards another century of beauty innovation.

Avon launched Hello Tomorrow on International Women's Day, and unveiled a series of initiatives created to advance the cause of women's empowerment worldwide. The Hello Tomorrow Fund was also launched in more than 18 countries, providing funds and support to eligible individuals with ideas that will empower women.

In August 2007, the actress Reese Witherspoon was appointed as Avon's Global Ambassador. In this role, Reese serves as a spokesperson for Avon's Representatives, its beauty brands and is Honorary Chairman of the Avon Foundation.

Promotion
Avon's primary channel for promotion is its brochure, with its range available to order through an Avon Representative or online. Avonshop.co.uk is designed to power incremental sales growth for the brand, reaching new customers without regular access to an Avon Representative.

Avon is fondly known for its iconic 'ding dong, Avon calling' fanfare which first aired on US television in 1954. More recently, Avon's visibility on television has increased dramatically with several advertising campaigns. In addition, recent years have seen Avon invest more than ever in significant celebrity alliances and valuable experts within the industry.

Brand Values
The Avon company vision is 'to be the company that best understands and satisfies the product service and self-fulfilment needs of women globally'. Avon strives to provide accessible, high-quality beauty and fashion whilst offering value for money.

www.avon.uk.com

Things you didn't know about Avon

An Avon lipstick sells somewhere in the world every three seconds.

Famous faces of Avon include Jerry Hall, Sadie Frost, Marie Helvin, Denise Van Outen, Tess Daly and Louise Redknapp.

Across the world, Avon produces a total of 600 million brochures in more than 25 languages each year.

In 2006, Avon sold enough mascara in the UK to reach a height of 412,000 metres if placed end to end, the height of 930 Empire State Buildings.

It is estimated that since 1959, more than four million women in the UK have been an Avon Representative in their lifetime.

1997
Also in 1992, Avon is the first beauty company to bring Alpha Hydroxy Acid (AHA) Technology to the mass market with the launch of its ANEW skincare brand.

Avon becomes the first major beauty brand to sell online, at www.avonshop.co.uk.

2005
Avon opens its state-of-the-art research and development laboratory in Suffern, New York.

2007
Actress Reese Witherspoon is named as Avon's Global Ambassador.

The BBC is the world's best-known broadcasting brand with a remit to inform, educate and entertain. Today's digital BBC plays a key civic role in UK life and as an organisation aims to engender creativity and trust, enriching people's lives with quality programming and services. BBC content is watched and listened to via eight national television channels, 10 national and 45 nations & regions radio stations, and can also be accessed online.

Market

Broadcasting in the UK is undergoing a radical transformation brought about by digital technology. Approximately 20 million households already receive digital multi-channel television and radio services from Sky, Virgin Media and Freeview and 52 per cent of homes have broadband connection. By 2012, every home in the UK will receive digital television. The original

public service broadcasters, BBC, ITV, Channel 4 and Five, are now multi-platform, multi-media brands operating 24 hours a day, seven days a week; each with a significant online presence (Source: OFCOM 2006).

Achievements

In 2007/08 the BBC received 278 programme related awards across television, radio and new media. These included 40 Baftas, 46 Royal Television Society (RTS) awards, 22 Sony Golds for Radio and three Webby awards for its online service, as well as eight International Emmys for television.

The BBC takes its corporate and environmental responsibilities seriously, working towards bringing added value to the licence fee through non-commercial partnerships and improving sustainability. The Business in the Community Corporate Responsibility Index 2008 awarded the BBC gold status for work on managing its social and environmental impact.

Product

The BBC is thought of primarily as a creator of high quality content and programming, whether on radio, television or online. The product offering is a complex mix with 19 major television, radio and online public service brands working towards providing something for everyone.

Today's BBC television and radio brands, particularly BBC One and BBC Two and BBC Radio's 1, 2, 3, 4 and Five Live, attract large terrestrial audiences. The main channels are complemented by digital brands, BBC Three and BBC Four on television and BBC Radio 1 Xtra, BBC Five Live Sports Extra, BBC 6 Music, BBC 7 and the Asian Network on digital radio. The online destination www.bbc.co.uk is also a recognised brand leader in the UK.

The BBC's Nations & Regions services for England, Wales, Northern Ireland and Scotland produce extensive local programming, achieving sizable audiences.

1922	1932	1936	1953	1960	1967
British Broadcasting Company (BBC) is formed by a group of leading wireless manufacturers.	The BBC moves to the world's first purpose built radio production centre, Broadcasting House in Portland Place, London.	BBC opens the world's first regular service of high definition television from Alexandra Palace, north London.	On 2nd June around 22 million people watch the Queen's coronation live on the BBC – a historic event that changes the course of television history.	BBC Television Centre opens and authorisation is given for a new channel. BBC Two launches in 1964.	Colour broadcasts begin on BBC Two and are extended to BBC One in 1969.

The BBC also actively develops new talent and supports training and production skills for the British broadcasting, music, drama and film industries.

The BBC is required to generate additional revenues by exploiting programme assets that have been paid for by public money. BBC Worldwide sells on programmes and footage and is the UK's number one international television channel broadcaster and joint partner in UKTV. The brand's commercial activity is carried out at arms-length and revenues are re-invested back into the core public service.

Recent Developments

The BBC was granted a new 10-year Royal Charter at the end of 2006 that defined expectations of the corporation in a digital, on-demand world; the emphasis changing from a one-way, studio-based broadcaster of programmes, into an audience focused 'anytime, anywhere, anyhow', content brand. Recent changes such as the launches of iPlayer, a free service enabling viewers to catch up on over 250 programmes screened

over the previous seven days, and Freesat – a new national free-to-view satellite service with ITV, which offers up to 200 channels, full interactivity and high definition broadcasts – strengthen this directional shift. In October 2007 the BBC launched its first multi-platform brand, BBC Switch, creating content across TV, radio and online for teenagers.

In 2008, the BBC website homepage was revamped to allow users to customise BBC content and page layout using moveable widgets. An update of the news and sport websites followed, featuring a newly embedded video service, greater emphasis on breaking news and live events and more ambitious use of pictures. Improved functionality and features are aimed at delivering a reinvented online facility through which the BBC can deliver a world-class, on-demand user experience.

BBC Three and children's channel CBBC, both underwent relaunches in 2008 aimed at increasing brand awareness and to present a more cohesive appeal to target audiences.

Promotion

The trademark block letters of the BBC master brand are instantly recognisable and associated with quality programmes and services. It appears on everything from channel identities to radio station literature and also online around the world.

The current master brand logo was redesigned in the late 1990s to give a simpler, less cluttered image and subsidiary brand identities for channels and services are regularly refreshed to reflect market changes and audience research. All 10 network BBC radio stations unveiled new identities in 2008, providing consistency while celebrating the personality of each brand.

BBC's marketing, communications and audience research division aims to help the audience find content they will enjoy from the BBC by producing integrated communications campaigns supported by on-air trails, off-air media and live events.

For example, David Attenborough's Life in Cold Blood, benefited from a high-profile promotional strategy featuring glossy trails with a specially designed audio bed to target different audiences. In the days leading up to transmission the ante was upped, with an animated chameleon character popping across BBC One idents and trails.

BBC Three's relaunch campaign, in 2008, employed digital, viral, outdoor and stunt activity, promoting new programme content that showcased talent and new interactive formats. In the first month following rebranding the channel's share of 16-34 year-olds rose by 44 per cent year-on-year, and weekly reach was up 33 per cent.

Brand Values

The BBC's core public service purpose to inform, educate and entertain is embedded in the organisation's core values. Politically the BBC is constitutionally independent and impartial in all of its extensive journalism and factual content.

www.bbc.co.uk

Things you didn't know about BBC

The BBC is a leading global news brand – 233 million people use its combined international television, radio and online services every week.

There have been more than 15,000 editions of The Archers radio serial to date.

Blue Peter started in 1958 and is the world's longest running children's programme.

1970s	1985	1990s	2007
In the 'Golden Age' of television, programmes include: I Claudius; Pennies from Heaven; Are You Being Served; The Good Life; and Fawlty Towers.	BBC reporter Michael Buerk alerts the world to a famine of biblical proportions in Ethiopia; the resulting televised Live Aid concert raises more than £60 million.	BBC Radio 5, the first new network for 23 years, launches. The arrival of the internet and digital technology marks the start of a new broadcasting era.	Digital expansion continues with the launch of iPlayer, a service enabling people to download television programmes onto their computers.

Birds Eye is the UK's leading frozen foods brand, providing food to 27 million households across the UK each week. Combining heritage with innovation, Birds Eye is trusted to deliver quality food across its ranges, from fish and vegetables to meat and meals. Birds Eye has led the renaissance of the frozen food category, informing consumers that frozen food locks in nutrition, taste and quality, without preservatives.

Market

Following years of decline, the frozen food market is now seeing strong growth as consumers begin to understand the nutritious, economic and environmental benefits of frozen food. This market is growing more than three per cent year-on-year with some sectors such as frozen vegetables and fish growing at around 6.2 and 7.1 per cent respectively (Source: IRI Data to 19th April 2008). At the beginning of 2008, 87 per cent of households bought frozen food, the highest percentage in the last three years (Source: IRI Data to 19th April 2008).

Achievements

As the market leader in frozen food production and boasting iconic products throughout the range, Birds Eye has successfully used its position to inform consumers about the benefits of frozen food and lead the renaissance of the frozen food category. As a result, it has outperformed the category. For example, Birds Eye Frozen Fish has grown 7.1 per cent year-on-year in value

and 3.6 per cent in volume. Fish Finger sales are up 11 per cent and Chicken Dippers have increased by 6.7 per cent. Furthermore, Birds Eye Chicken Grills now have a 49.5 per cent market share (Source: IRI Data to 19th April 2008). These figures reflect the investment by Birds Eye to provide consumers with increased choice and quality.

Birds Eye's new Omega 3 Fish Fingers took Birds Eye's most famous family favourite and added a health benefit, whilst developing consumer taste for more sustainable fish. The launch was Birds Eye's most successful to date, driving incremental sales in the category, and introducing 1.1 million new households to the fish finger sector.

Birds Eye has also worked alongside WRAP (Waste and Resources Action Programme) on the 'Love Food Hate Waste' campaign to champion the benefits of frozen food in combating household food waste, which in turn saves money and resources.

Product

Birds Eye products occupy nearly every freezer across the UK (Source: IRI Data to 19th April 2008). With new products and variations on classic themes, sales have increased, with consumers exploring the new Birds Eye ranges.

Birds Eye products span the major food groups, and the fish, poultry and vegetables

1925

American scientist and explorer, Clarence Birdseye, invents the quick freezing technique. New freezing technology leads to the creation of a significant new food industry in the US.

1938

Birds Eye is launched in the UK.

1940s

Post-war, Birds Eye opens its first UK factory in Great Yarmouth. Birds Eye revolutionises relationships between suppliers and sellers, renting cabinet freezers to retailers.

1946

The first mass pea production takes place with 390 tonnes of frozen peas being harvested.

1950s

Birds Eye holds a 66 per cent share of the frozen food market. Between 1955 and 1960 the frozen food market increases by more than 500 per cent and the market grows to be worth £42 million. In 1955 Birds Eye invents and launches Fish Fingers.

ranges lead the market and set standards in quality and choice. Birds Eye food is preserved naturally by being frozen, and no artificial colours or preservatives are added to any of its products.

Birds Eye's classic family favourites – peas, fish fingers and beef burgers – have been joined by newer innovations that respond to changing consumer needs and desires. Product ranges now include Simply Chicken, Eat Positive meals, Omega 3 Fish Fingers and the Steam Fresh range, as well as Potato Waffles, Big Bite Burgers, Simply Fish, and Sea Side Shaped Fish, among others.

Recent Developments

In 2008 Birds Eye introduced Eat Positive, its newest range of light meals, which responds to current health and enjoyment trends. Offering superior taste and substantial portion sizes, the range comprises four nutritionally balanced meals, which provide a natural source of vitamins and include at least one of the recommended five daily portions of fruit

and vegetables. Each meal also has a natural health benefit that is clearly stated on the packaging, for example highlighting foods that are rich in specific nutrients.

The launch of the new soya bean range, in 2006, offers an easy way for consumers to increase their intake of protein, fibre and vitamins as soya beans are classed as a 'superfood' that also contain antioxidants and have cholesterol-lowering benefits.

Promotion

After its successful 'Truth' campaign, which aimed to drive reappraisal of the frozen food category, Birds Eye launched a new advertising campaign in September 2007 to drive more emotional engagement with the brand and 'put the good mood back into the British family teatime'.

The Good Mood Food advertising campaign recognises the teatime challenges for mothers who are working to a budget and find it hard to think of nutritious meal ideas.

The three elements at the core of Birds Eye's Good Mood Food manifesto are: simple, nutritional facts so mothers can feel better about serving frozen food; enjoyment – giving mothers the confidence to know they're serving food the family will enjoy; tips to provide mothers with more ideas on feeding the family.

To launch this concept, a manifesto ad rolled out on TV, alongside the sponsorship of ITV's flagship family programme, Ant & Dec's Saturday Night Takeaway. Core nutritional facts about Birds Eye classics and innovative new products aimed to reassure mothers

through the media of TV, press and online. Meanwhile a stream of serving suggestions played out through radio, SMS and digital.

In total, Birds Eye has put more than £20 million behind the Good Mood Food campaign and it is reaping rewards with sales up by over five per cent since the advertising began running.

Brand Values

By reflecting values that are close to mothers' needs, Birds Eye aims to emerge as the choice for the health- and price-conscious family, while also being more environmentally sustainable.

Birds Eye believes in using ingredients found in the kitchen cupboard, which is why Birds Eye food is preserved naturally by being frozen and no artificial colours or preservatives are added. Frozen food can also help to reduce food waste, which equates to savings to the family budget as well as environmental resources.

www.birdseye.co.uk

Things you didn't know about Birds Eye

All Birds Eye peas are frozen within two and a half hours of being picked to ensure that all the nutritional content and field freshness is locked in.

Birds Eye has sold more than 15 billion Fish Fingers since their launch in 1955.

Birds Eye has nearly an 80 per cent share of the UK fish finger market and Britons eat more than 800,000 Birds Eye Fish Fingers every day.

Alongside the WWF, Birds Eye was a founder member of the Marine Stewardship Council in 1996.

1960s

The Birds Eye range now consists of about 80 products. During the decade Birds Eye's market share reaches 75 per cent.

1970s

Birds Eye's range grows to more than 150 products. Home freezer ownership increases from 19 per cent in 1974 to 43 per cent in 1979.

1999

Birds Eye ceases fishing for cod in the North Sea due to depleting stock levels.

2007

In September Birds Eye launches its sustainable Omega 3 Fish Fingers, produced from Alaskan Pollock.

bp

BP has been an international household name for decades. One of the world's largest energy companies, it provides fuels for transport, energy for heat and light, and an array of petrochemical products and retail services. These products and services are delivered to customers in more than 100 countries, through a range of internationally respected brands. Together, they have made BP the global force it is today.

Market

BP's specific areas of business include exploration for and production of crude oil and natural gas; refining and marketing of oil products; manufacturing and marketing of petrochemicals; and integrated supply and trading. BP is also an increasingly significant player in alternative energy and biofuels.

The relaunch of the BP brand in July 2000 proved to be a watershed in the company's history. Since unveiling its new 'Helios' mark, BP has striven to establish itself as an environmentally-conscious brand, developing sustainable ways to meet the world's growing energy demands.

Achievements

Every day, millions of people buy fuels, lubricants and consumer items from some 25,000 BP petrol stations worldwide – a sign of the trust placed in the company's collection of established brands, which include ampm, ARCO, Aral, BP, Castrol, BP Ultimate and Wild Bean Café.

BP wins numerous awards on an international scale. In the UK, BP's driver education and carbon offsetting scheme, targetneutral, was a winner in the Website Category at the 2007 Clarion Awards, which recognise the promotion of social inclusion, CSR, sustainable development and ethical debate. Targetneutral was recognised for educating consumers on reducing emissions.

In addition, BP Connect, BP's fuel and large-format convenience store offer in the UK, received the 2007 Multiple Forecourt Retailer of the Year award at the Retail Industry Awards.

Product

Services available at BP petrol stations include premium fuels, convenience items, freshly prepared food and Wild Bean Cafés. In the UK, the company continues to roll out its partnership with Marks & Spencer's Simply Food, providing selected items from the range, alongside BP's own offering.

BP's premium fuel, BP Ultimate, was originally launched in the UK in 2003 after 18 months of extensive research and is now sold in more than 100 cities in 17 countries, bringing cleaner, higher performing fuels to more markets. BP Ultimate fuels clean the engine while the vehicle is being driven, helping to deliver more power, better fuel economy and less pollution. BP Ultimate Unleaded can clean up to four times more effectively than conventional fuels, gradually

1909
The Anglo-Persian Oil Company (as BP was first known) is formed.

1940s
After World War II, BP's sales, profits, capital expenditure and employment all rise to record levels as Europe is restructured.

1954
BP Visco-Static is brought on to the market – Europe's first multigrade oil.

1965
BP finds the West Sole gas field – the first offshore hydrocarbons found in British waters.

1975
BP pumps the first oil from the North Sea's UK sector ashore after purchasing the Forties field – a development financed by a bank loan of £370 million.

1990s
BP merges with US giant Amoco, and the acquisitions of ARCO, Burmah Castrol and Veba Oil turn the British oil company into one of the world's largest energy companies.

removing engine deposits as well as preventing new ones. Tests show that BP Ultimate fuels can reduce emissions of unburned hydrocarbons, carbon monoxide, nitrogen oxides and carbon dioxide (Source: Based on UK test data. Claims vary between countries. The average power benefit for BP Ultimate Unleaded is 3.8 per cent and the average fuel economy benefit is an extra 13 miles per tank tested against ordinary fuels).

BP LPG (liquefied petroleum gas) has revolutionised the gas bottle market with BP Gas Light, a pioneering new lightweight bottle that was first to market in many European territories. The innovative design, developed for the leisure market (caravans and barbecues), has many practical benefits including easier handling – it's half the weight of conventional steel bottles – and the ability to see the level of the gas.

Recent Developments
BP launched a major new education outreach programme, Enterprising Science, in September 2007. Working with the Science Museum, the programme is designed to reach more than 400 secondary schools and around 60,000 students across the UK each year.

It features two main components: Talk Science, a teacher master class created and delivered regionally by the Science Museum for science teachers; and The Carbon Challenge, an in-school road show focusing on the themes of carbon footprints and climate change for 14-16 year-olds.

In 2007, BP extended its successful driver education and voluntary carbon offsetting programme, targetneutral, to new markets and some of its B2B partners. Targetneutral allows customers to calculate their car's CO_2 emissions, and then to neutralise these emissions by paying a fee of around £20. This is then used to support projects that reduce an equivalent amount of CO_2.

Wild Bean Café is BP's youngest brand. In 2007, it was given a new, contemporary look and feel that separates Wild Bean Café more clearly from the rest of the store, creating a distinctive café environment. Some 150 new Wild Bean Cafés were opened in markets across Europe in 2007, supported by a striking advertising campaign.

Promotion
BP makes innovative use of non-traditional media to deepen consumer engagement with its brands, from the breakthrough online game Gas Mania to the Ultimate Green Driving Test, an interactive tool that shows drivers how their different driving techniques impact safety, CO_2 emissions and fuel consumption.

The BP/Ford World Rally Team has won its second consecutive manufacturers' title in the FIA World Rally Championship 2007, the world's most challenging year-long motor sport and a win that boosted promotion of both the BP and Castrol brands.

Brand Values
In all it says and does, BP aims to be performance driven, innovative, progressive and green. Performance driven means setting global standards of performance in every area, from safety and the environment to delivering greater satisfaction for customers and employees.

Being innovative means using the creative know-how of BP's people, combined with cutting-edge technology, to develop breakthrough solutions to business challenges and the needs of BP's customers.

Progressive means BP is always looking for new and better ways to do things. In touch with the needs of its employees, customers and local communities, BP aims to be accessible, open and transparent.

Lastly, green means demonstrating environmental leadership and overcoming the trade-off between providing access to heat, light and mobility and protecting the environment.

These values combine to make up BP's brand theme of 'beyond petroleum' – providing security of oil and gas supply for today's consumers, while developing sustainable ways of meeting ever increasing energy demands.

www.bp.com

Things you didn't know about BP

The first BP logo was created as a result of an employee competition in 1920. At this time, BP petrol stations in the UK were branded red.

BP Solar is one of the world's largest manufacturers of solar panels and is one of the largest commercial users of solar energy in the world.

Aral's car wash, SuperWash, uses nano-shine particles 2,000 times thinner than human hair.

2000
The BP brand is relaunched with the unveiling of a new 'Helios' brand mark.

2004
Aral opens the first public hydrogen station in Berlin.

2005
BP Alternative Energy is launched, a new business dedicated to the development, wholesale marketing and trading of low-carbon power.

2008
BP announces that it can continue to pump four million barrels of oil per day until 2020, even without new finds.

The benefits of water filtration sometimes can't be seen, but BRITA consumers have relied on BRITA to be the custodians of their drinking water for the past 40 years. As the original inventor of jug water filters, and the leader in research and development, BRITA leads the way in quality, and is trusted by consumers. BRITA is the UK market leader in domestic filtration and its success has resulted in a brand synonymous with filtered water.

Market

Over the last 13 years the UK water filter market has seen a period of sustained growth and is now worth more than £100 million a year. Sector prosperity has been driven by improved technology, extending the choice of water filter solutions available on the market, and the environmental benefits of filtered water consumption. The growing consumer demand for improved quality drinking water, fuelled by an increased national awareness of the importance of hydration in terms of health and well-being, has also had a significant market impact. Of the 24.5 million households in the UK, six million (nearly 25 per cent) now use a water filter jug. BRITA is the leading brand in the household water filter sector, a position reinforced by its leading role in product innovation.

Achievements

On an international platform BRITA supports UNICEF's Drinking Water for Children in Vietnam project, a long term pledge that demonstrates its ongoing commitment to

improving the availability of, and access to, clean drinking water worldwide. On a local level, BRITA UK supports projects in and around the location of its head office in Bicester, Oxfordshire. Here, brand involvement focuses heavily on youth sport development ranging from sponsorship of a youth rugby-training scheme to support and promotion of the Oxfordshire Youth Games.

BRITA is also proud to be one of The Sunday Times 100 Best Companies of 2008, an accreditation and award scheme based on positive feedback from its own employees.

Product

Although tap water in the UK is safe to drink, substances such as limescale, chlorine and heavy metals can affect the taste and smell. BRITA filters reduce impurities to deliver purer tasting water with no residual odour.

BRITA has been the market leader in water filter solutions since launching its inaugural water jug back in the 1970s. Continuous design updates have ensured that the style has remained contemporary with relevant features and benefits. BRITA recently launched a range of limited edition colour jugs in

1966
BRITA founder Heinz Hankammer starts to experiment with the demineralisation of water.

1967
BRITA launches its first water filter product, designed to produce demineralised water for car batteries and laboratories.

1970
BRITA's first household water jug is launched.

1992
BRITA UK becomes a subsidiary of BRITA GmbH and moves to a new office and production warehouse in Sunbury-on-Thames.

1999
BRITA launches the first ever water filter kettle – Acclario.

2004
BRITA moves its UK operation to Bicester, North Oxfordshire, investing 15 million euros in a state-of-the-art production facility and new office building.

response to current kitchen design trends. The design and performance of its iconic replacement cartridge has also evolved over time to produce MAXTRA, BRITA's best ever performing cartridge. MAXTRA can be found in the full range of domestic filter products.

In 2006, BRITA further extended its domestic range by collaborating with leading tap manufacturer Francis Pegler to design a water filter tap to offer its most convenient solution – Instant BRITA filtered water on-tap. In addition, BRITA technology, already firmly embedded in smaller household appliances such as kettles, coffee makers and tabletop chillers, was recently extended to a range of fridges which dispense filtered water at the touch of a button.

BRITA's diverse range of filters and products for professional use – in vending machines, coffee machines, catering ovens and steamers – offer dual benefits: they reduce the build up of scale (so maintenance costs are cut) and improve the quality and consistency of water for food and drink preparation.

Recent Developments
Recycling has been at the heart of BRITA thinking for over a decade. BRITA water filter cartridges are 100 per cent recyclable; the components can either be re-used or re-generated, reducing product waste to a minimum. As part of the brand's ongoing commitment to encouraging more consumers to recycle, it recently launched a nationwide in-store recycling scheme with specially designed bins for customers to deposit their used cartridges. The cartridges are then returned to BRITA for recycling. The scheme, which has bins sited in high street retail outlets countrywide including Argos, Robert Dyas, Sainsbury's, Tesco and John Lewis, is the only one of its kind currently operating in the UK and marks BRITA out as the sole water filter brand actively investing in cartridge recycling. To help consumers find their nearest recycling store, the BRITA website contains a store locator.

Promotion
Since the early 1990s BRITA UK has invested heavily in television and press advertising. Its 'BRITA Couple' campaign ran for 10 years, increasing brand and product awareness, and more recently the launch of 'Hands', showcases the brand's leading products, while simultaneously reinforcing the essence of purity long-associated with BRITA filtered water. The campaign has recently been enhanced to promote the brand's recycling credentials through highlighting its distinctive in-store scheme.

BRITA's television campaigns are supported by high-profile press activity, both in consumer and trade arenas. In early 2008 BRITA UK launched a hard-hitting campaign across various women's titles as well as home and lifestyle sectors that focused on the products' environmental benefits. Significant brand presence at major consumer home interest exhibitions throughout 2008, such as Grand Designs Live, The Ideal Home Show and BBC Good Homes increased its profile further.

Online advertising adds a further dimension to BRITA's promotional strategy through its emphasis on topical recycling initiatives. A dedicated customer care team delivers product information and services through direct mailing methods and more recently its 'aquazine' online magazine through its website.

To support its advertising activity BRITA invested heavily in in-store promotion that has, in recent months, included a number of 'shop-in-shop' display units featuring its full product range.

Brand Values
BRITA filtered water is positioned as 'the smart way to enjoy purer drinking water' – to this end, the brand has a focus on providing contemporary and convenient solutions for high quality water at an affordable price. The comprehensive range of its products, all delivering the consistent quality of BRITA filtered water, offers a solution for all requirements and demonstrates the brand's commitment to the well-being of its customers.

As the best-known brand on the market, BRITA is a trusted authority on water filtration – its area of expertise and core focus – and is passionate about innovation, quality and reliability.

www.brita.co.uk

2005
BRITA UK is voted one of the Top 100 Best Companies to Work For by The Sunday Times.

2006
BRITA celebrates its 40th birthday and 25 years in the UK.

Also in 2006, BRITA collaborates with leading tap manufacturer Francis Pegler to design a water filter tap to offer instant BRITA filtered water on-tap.

2008
BRITA is named as one of The Sunday Times 100 Best Companies of 2008. BRITA also launches its unique in-store cartridge recycling scheme.

Things you didn't know about BRITA®

The company is named after the founder's daughter Brita.

BRITA filtered water is drunk by 250 million people worldwide every day.

All BRITA cartridges are 100 per cent recyclable.

Twelve billion litres of BRITA filtered water are consumed in UK homes each year, enough to fill 3,200 Olympic-size swimming pools.

British Gas is Great Britain's leading energy supplier to homes as well as an installer and maintainer of central heating and gas appliances. In addition, British Gas Business supplies energy to over 900,000 business customers. British Gas is unique in having its own nationwide workforce of over 8,000 expert engineers to provide high quality workmanship and service for customers' central heating systems, plumbing, drains, home electrics and kitchen appliances.

Market

Since the residential gas and electricity markets opened to competition in 1996 and 1998 respectively, British Gas has grown to become the largest supplier of both gas and electricity to domestic customers.

British Gas is also active within the home services market where a number of central heating service offerings are available to suit differing customer needs. British Gas offers a wide range of products from yearly maintenance and repair contracts, to a one-off fixed price heating repair service and an installation service for new central heating systems. The nature of the home services market is diverse with energy suppliers, insurers, water companies, outsource service providers and small independents making up the main competitors.

Achievements

British Gas is highly committed to helping its customers to be greener. It has the largest energy efficiency programme of any domestic supplier in Great Britain and, with the British Gas Energy Savers Report, has already helped over 1.8 million people to understand how to save money and energy.

In 2007, British Gas installed energy efficient measures in more than six million households which will save around 3.8 million tonnes of CO_2 over their lifetime. This is equivalent to the annual household emissions of more than 720,000 households. In addition, when completed at the end of 2008 British Gas will have built what will be the world's largest offshore wind farm project, with the capacity to supply clean electricity to around 130,000 homes.

British Gas is committed to providing an exceptional service for vulnerable customers. Through the British Gas Energy Trust, British Gas has already committed over £21.3 million from which over 600,000 homes have already benefited. Such commitment has resulted in British Gas' 'Help the Aged Partnership' being voted the most recognised out of 25 charity-corporate partnerships in the March 2008

nfp Synergy Charity Awareness survey with British Gas being awarded Charity & Business Partnership of the Year for its 'Help the Aged Winter Deaths' campaign which has helped to improve the lives of around 1.9 million older people.

British Gas' commitment to providing development and career opportunities within a supportive culture has been recognised with both British Gas Business and British Gas Services being placed within the Top 50 in the Financial Times Best Workplaces in 2007.

Product

British Gas focuses on developing innovative products and services to meet a wide range of consumer needs within its chosen markets.

In the energy market, British Gas offers a wide range of tariffs to its customers. Those

1948	**1996**	**1997**	**1998**	**2000s**	**2001**
The Gas Act is introduced, creating a nationalised gas industry – 'the gas board' – throughout England, Scotland and Wales.	The market for the supply of gas to domestic customers is opened up to competition.	Centrica plc is created following the demerger of British Gas plc; British Gas' supply services and retail businesses combine with the Morecambe gas fields' production.	The electricity market is opened up to competition – British Gas successfully enters the electricity market.	The range of products offered by British Gas is extended to include home security, plumbing, drains, electrical servicing, kitchen appliance care, as well as telecommunications services.	British Gas now provides care for more than four million heating and kitchen appliances.

4 free energy saving light bulbs for every customer.
Giving Britain the green light to save energy.

British Gas
Your energy experts

looking for peace of mind can sign up to a Price Protection tariff which offers price certainty in a volatile market. British Gas' Market Tracker offers customers an alternative approach by passing on changes in the wholesale market on a quarterly basis.

Keeping energy affordable is a key focus for British Gas, embodied within products such as the online Click Energy tariff and the British Gas Discount Tracker which offers customers the ability to track prices at 10 per cent below the current standard prices. In addition, British Gas has the UK's largest social tariff on the energy market. This £32 million commitment guarantees that up to 750,000 eligible vulnerable customers can receive British Gas' lowest cost standard tariff.

British Gas also offers customers the ability to invest in future green energy production, with a range of products such as Zero Carbon. In addition, British Gas continues to invest in the development of the latest energy efficient and renewable technologies, such as solar panels and highly efficient boilers that produce their own electricity.

British Gas is the first supplier to offer customers the unique and exclusive ability to top up their key meters from home as part of the Pay As You Go Energy service.

As well as being Europe's leading installer of central heating, British Gas provides maintenance and repair contracts which offer a yearly maintenance and safety inspection, as well as breakdown repair. HomeCare 200 is a lead product with approximately 3.8 million customers.

For customers looking for confidence in high quality boiler repairs without a contract, British Gas also offers one-off heating repairs for a fixed price. Alternatively, HomeCare Flexi blends the benefits of both contract and fixed price repair – designed for those customers who want peace of mind at a lower monthly cost with a fixed fee for each repair.

Exclusively for its energy customers, British Gas runs a Priority Response membership scheme. This guarantees a next day latest response for central heating emergencies and an exclusively low pre-published fixed repair fee, carried out by one of its engineers.

Recent Developments

British Gas is focused on providing its customers with the most convenient way to interact with the business. To offer a higher level of customer service, British Gas launched a number of interactive online offerings, such as the Online Energy Saving Planner as well as the new British Gas website – www.britishgas.co.uk – in July 2007.

British Gas has recently launched a number of green programmes which demonstrate its commitment to both the environment and to helping customers to reduce their energy bills.

Green Streets links 64 households in eight cities across Britain and aims to highlight the positive impact that simple energy efficiency products and small behavioural changes can have. The project has received extensive coverage throughout the UK on TV and in the press. After the first two months of the challenge, energy savings of more than 20 per cent were observed, with all of the residents changing their behaviour to help their street towards a £50,000 community prize.

In April 2008, British Gas introduced Generation Green, a comprehensive and engaging educational programme which rewards schools for learning, actions taken and behavioural change. For taking green steps, schools and the wider community can earn 'green leaves' which can be collected and exchanged by schools for a range of green-themed rewards.

In 2008, British Gas promised four free energy saving light bulbs to all of its customers – part of its commitment to make it easy to take small steps to save both energy as well as money and to make a big difference to Britain.

Promotion

In March 2008, British Gas rolled out its 'Your Energy Experts' brand positioning, supported by an advertising campaign covering both terrestrial and digital TV and radio; weekend press; and posters on more than 2,000 roadside and other prime sites across Britain.

The external launch was preceded by significant investment in British Gas' employees with the creation of new training programmes, personalised career plans and recognition schemes to ensure it is harnessing the best of its individuals.

Brand Values

British Gas prides itself on being a modern, leading service brand that is proactive in ensuring its customers receive good service. Underpinning its brand positioning as 'Your Energy Experts' is a promise to use its expertise to help its customers to be greener, make energy affordable and help to keep homes working.

www.britishgas.co.uk

Things you didn't know about British Gas

British Gas expert engineers fix a boiler every four seconds, and check the safety of over 10,000 boilers every day.

British Gas is building what will be the world's largest offshore wind farm project when completed at the end of 2008.

2003
A new platform is developed to act as a framework to guide the brand's repositioning. The brand promise 'Doing the right thing' is manifested both internally and externally.

2005
British Gas creates a new structure with two distinct business units: Residential Energy and Home Services.

2007
British Gas New Energy – a team specifically dedicated to develop carbon saving initiatives – is launched.

2008
The new brand promise to be 'Your Energy Experts' is launched.

As well as being one of the best-known companies in Britain, BT is also a brand recognised and understood throughout the globe. BT's vision is to be dedicated to helping customers thrive in a changing world. This is a converged world, where individuals and businesses increasingly need to connect and communicate whenever and wherever they happen to be, using whatever device they choose.

Market

The UK telecoms market is worth tens of billions of pounds and is characterised by intense competition, whether for traditional voice services, mobile telephony or broadband.

The last few years have seen many of the major communications companies joining together – through mergers and acquisitions – and offering customers more than just one service.

For example, some offer 'triple-play' (broadband, TV and landline telephony) services, others provide 'quadruple-play' – where a mobile phone service is added.

A number of powerful brands, including BT, have set their sights on succeeding in this,

the quickly developing and increasingly competitive multi-services market.

For BT this means that its brand becomes a critical differentiator and is compelled to work even harder for the company than ever before.

Achievements

BT has successfully transformed itself in recent years. It has evolved from being a supplier of telephony services to become a leading provider of innovative communications products, services and solutions. Its customers range from multinational corporations to residential householders, of which there are more than 20 million in the UK.

The company is the driving force behind the success of 'Broadband Britain', investing millions in a nationwide network providing blanket coverage across the UK. At the end of March 2008, there were nearly 13 million BT wholesale broadband connections in the UK.

In September 2007, BT became the UK's first broadband supplier to pass the four million customer mark – an achievement which cemented BT's position as the UK's most popular supplier of broadband. In fact, by the end of March 2008, that number had risen to 4.4 million.

In July 2007, BT was named Company of the Year in the prestigious annual Business in the Community (BITC) Awards for Excellence.

Furthermore, in September 2007, and for the seventh year running, BT was recognised as the world's top telecommunications company in the Dow Jones Sustainability Index (DJSI). DJSI assesses companies worldwide on their performance in areas such as corporate governance, environmental management, community investment, human rights, supply chain and risk management.

Product

BT offers consumers an extensive portfolio of innovative telephony, broadband and mobility products and services.

The company's developments in products and services for consumers are consistent with its focus on meeting the requirements of today's and tomorrow's customers.

1981	1991	2001	2006		2008
British Telecom is created from Post Office Telecommunications and then privatised in 1984.	The company unveils a new trading name, BT, together with the 'piper' brand identity.	BT rebrands its mobile business as O2, prior to its demerger.	Openreach opens for business and is responsible for managing the UK access network on behalf of the communications industry. Also in 2006, BT Total	Broadband – a comprehensive consumer broadband package – is launched. A new brand in digital TV entertainment, BT Vision, is also launched.	BT becomes Official Communications Services Partner of the 2012 London Olympics.

For the fifth time in consecutive surveys, the independent broadband service monitor Epitiro has identified BT Total Broadband as being the best performing, most comprehensive ADSL broadband service in the UK.

In May 2008, BT launched an innovative new option for broadband customers – BT Total Broadband Anywhere – which enables customers to take their broadband with them wherever they go thanks to a free, internet-capable smartphone, the BT ToGo.

Also in 2008, BT cut calling plan prices for millions of customers and made UK weekend call charges a thing of the past for the majority of British households.

By January 2008, BT's nationwide home computing help and advice service, BT Home IT Support, had clocked up more than 10 million minutes of help and advice to the nation in its first 18 months. The service gives customers straight forward, jargon-free advice and support over the phone for a wide range of issues.

Underpinning BT's range of innovative services is its national network. The company is investing £10 billion to transform the network into an IP-based '21st Century Network'. The 21st Century Network will carry all voice, video and data traffic on a single, state-of-the-art network, giving consumers optimum capabilities to be able to communicate wherever they may be, using whatever device they choose. The first customers went live on the network in November 2006.

Recent Developments
At the end of last year BT joined forces with FON to launch BT FON, the world's largest WiFi community. The BT FON service has attracted more than 100,000 members who can connect to the internet for free in thousands of places around the UK and the world.

The roll-out of BT's next generation television service, BT Vision, has accelerated with customer numbers reaching 214,000 at the end of March 2008.

BT Vision, the first widely available TV service of its kind, combines the appeal of TV with the interactivity of broadband. Customers can watch what they want, when they want and not be tied to TV schedules. Customers of BT Vision have access to a vast range of film, sport, music and television programming on-demand, as well as interactive services and all the Freeview channels.

BT has continued to be innovative. For example, the Go! Messenger product, launched in 103 countries in conjunction with the Sony PlayStation Portable (PSP). It allows PSP users to make video and voice calls from their PSP.

Recently the company has unveiled a new range of more energy efficient phones, heralding the start of a £2 million commitment to improve the energy efficiency of its entire home-phone range. More than 90 per cent of the entire home phone range supplied by BT will be more energy efficient by July 2008.

BT's market-leading WiFi service, BT Openzone, has continued to grow strongly, with customers using around one million minutes every day.

Promotion
Since October 2005, BT has been running a major TV and radio advertising campaign pulling together all of BT consumer communications with a consistent theme and tone of voice. The campaign follows a period of running separate campaigns for different BT consumer products. The campaign features a thoroughly modern, albeit everyday family headed by the characters Adam and his partner Jane

using BT products to help them navigate through life's ebbs and flows.

The ads reflect the increasingly converged world of communications we now live in and focus on a range of BT products and services from WiFi to phonebooks, from 118 500 directory enquiries to landline texting.

Brand Values
BT's corporate identity defines the kind of company it is today – and the one it needs to be in the future. Central to that identity is a commitment to create ways to help customers thrive in a changing world. To do this, BT focuses on 'living' its brand values which are as follows:

Trustworthy – doing what it says it will; Helpful – working as one team; Inspiring – creating new possibilities; Straightforward – making things clear; Heart – believing in what it does.

The BT strapline – Bringing it all together – conveys leadership in the way BT enables global business customers to profit from convergence.

www.bt.com

Things you didn't know about BT

More than a million BT customers have now switched to paper-free billing.

Engineers from Openreach collectively climb the equivalent of Mount Everest every single day while carrying out maintenance on telegraph poles.

300 million telephone calls and 350 million internet connections are made across the BT network every day.

Over the past five years, BT has added one new broadband customer every 40 seconds on average.

CLASSIC *f*M

From the moment Classic FM went on-air, media pundits and classical music buffs alike were ready to write off the idea of a commercial station playing classical music. However within months of launch, Classic FM had an audience of more than four million people, with many listeners coming to classical music for the first time in their lives. Sixteen years on, Classic FM attracts six million listeners every week.

Market

Classic FM is the UK's largest commercial radio station, with an audience of six million people every week, including more than a quarter of a million children (Source: RAJAR).

Alongside Classic FM, there are more than 500 radio stations broadcasting across the UK on FM, MW, online or DAB.

Achievements

Classic FM's pioneering approach to its programming, advertising and marketing has won the station many accolades, including more than 10 Sony Radio Academy Awards. Classic FM has been voted UK Station of the Year four times, and has been nominated for the award on six occasions. It has won two Gold Awards for On-Air Station Sound. Other awards include Campaign Medium of the Year and the UK Brand Development of the Year award from the Marketing Society.

Product

Providing an antidote to life in the 21st century is central to Classic FM's core proposition and from launch, the vision was to treat Classic FM not simply as a radio station, but as a brand in its own right. This philosophy has driven forward a number of new and successful ventures over the years, making Classic FM one of the strongest brands in radio.

Key to Classic FM's success as a truly multi-platform brand has been its ability to identify and pioneer new ways of engaging consumers. Online continues to be a core part of this. Classic FM's revolutionary online service – MyClassicFM.com – boasts seven audio streams, all of which allow listeners to control exactly what they hear, by giving them the ability to rate and ban tracks. In addition, an eighth stream, Classic FM TV, features short-form classical music videos.

Other features, such as the Listen Again player, the internet-only programme Arts Daily, the music download service and a range of podcasts, are giving users unique and compelling content and new reasons to visit the site.

A free premium service for registered users provides a monthly newsletter. This has driven the station's customer relationship management programme to new heights, with 450,000 people currently signed up to receive email news from the station.

Working with Universal Classics and Jazz (UCJ), Classic FM's CD label continues to go from strength to strength, with annual sales topping the 500,000

1992
At 6am on 7th September, Classic FM launches with Handel's Zadok the Priest. Four months after launch, the station is attracting 4.2 million listeners a week.

1994
Classic FM is named UK Station of the Year at the Sony Radio Academy Awards.

1995
Classic FM Magazine launches and quickly becomes the UK's best-selling classical music title on UK news stands.

1999
Classic FM launches its Music Teacher of the Year Awards.

2000
Classic FM is named UK Station of the Year for the third time and also collects the award for On-Air Station Sound.

2001
The Royal Liverpool Philharmonic Orchestra becomes Classic FM's Orchestra in the North West.

mark. As well as a range of compilation albums, Classic FM and UCJ have joined together with HMV to create The Full Works, a range of more than 100 CDs of the greatest classical works played in full.

The first issue of Classic FM Magazine rolled off the press in 1995. It is now the UK's best selling classical music title on news stands, with average monthly sales of up to 41,591 (Source: Audit Bureau of Circulations).

Classic FM has developed a range of highly successful books, which tie in to programming on the station. The Classic FM Friendly Guide to Music has been a notable success and was the best-selling classical music book in the UK in 2007.

Most recently the station has also launched the Classic FM Yamaha Red Recorder Pack, which is the first in a range of branded musical instruments.

Recent Developments

Despite its success in bringing new audiences to both classical music and commercial radio, Classic FM has not rested on its laurels. In spring 2008, the station launched its most significant change in programming output in its 16-year history.

Simon Bates hosts Classic FM's morning show from 8am until noon. It consistently rates as the biggest programme anywhere on commercial radio. At the other end of the day, Margherita Taylor is the voice of Smooth Classics at Six. Broadcast every evening between 6pm and 9pm, the show features three hours of relaxing classics.

Every evening Classic FM underlines its commitment to playing classical pieces in their entirety, with The Full Works, presented by John Brunning on weekdays and Natalie Wheen at weekends.

Other weekend presenters include Myleene Klass, the composer Howard Goodall, Katie Derham, David Mellor and Lesley Garrett. Meanwhile, Laurence Llewelyn-Bowen presents the weekly Sunday Spa.

Blur bassist Alex James follows on Sunday mornings at 11am for the major new 100-part series, The A to Z of Classic FM Music. The weekly programme is the biggest commission in the station's history and aims to provide the definitive guide to classical music.

Off-air, music education is a subject close to the station's heart. The annual Classic FM Music Teacher of the Year Awards seek to recognise those classroom music teachers

who make a real difference to the musical life of their students. Classic FM's involvement with the Schools Proms meanwhile, celebrates the very best of the UK's vibrant musical scene.

Classic FM has its own charity, Classic FM Music Makers, which funds a range of music education projects, including Music Quest, which is delivered by The Prince's Foundation for Children and the Arts.

All of these activities – both on-air and off-air – are scrutinised by the Classic FM Consumer Panel, an independent body composed of Classic FM listeners and chaired by Lord Eatwell.

Promotion

Classic FM has concentrated on two different target markets in order to grow its audience base. Traditional above-the-line brand advertising using outdoor, cinema, TV and broadsheet press, has been used to talk to a national audience.

Alongside this, strategic partnerships have been forged with music and art organisations to promote the brand to people at a local level. These partners include the London Symphony Orchestra, the Royal Liverpool Philharmonic Orchestra, the Philharmonia Orchestra, Welsh National Opera, the Canterbury Festival and the Barbican Centre's Mostly Mozart festival.

Brand Values

Classic FM remains committed to its aim of presenting classical music to an ever-increasing audience by being modern, relevant, involving and accessible. These values have delivered Classic FM the largest commercial radio audience in the UK. This unique upmarket audience comes to Classic FM because the brand offers them an emotional benefit – an antidote to the stress of modern life.

www.classicfm.com

Things you didn't know about Classic FM

The sound of birdsong intrigued audiences and the media across the summer of 1992. It was, in fact, the test transmission of Classic FM. Even Brian Johnston ruminated over it whilst commentating on Test Match Special.

Classic FM sponsored Queens Park Rangers during the first high profile season of England's new elite Premier League.

Classic FM shares more audience with BBC Radio 4 than any other radio station.

The first piece of music ever played on Classic FM was Handel's Zadok the Priest.

2003

The station launches Classic FM Arts & Kids Week. The following year, Classic FM signs its first composer-in-residence, Joby Talbot, formerly of The Divine Comedy.

2005

Research commissioned by Arts Council England shows that Classic FM is instrumental in bringing new audiences to the concert hall.

2006

Classic FM launches the Classic FM Presents label. Its first release is of British tenor Alfie Boe.

2007

Classic FM is named UK Station of the Year at the Sony Radio Academy Awards – for a fourth time.

Registered Trade Mark

The Coca-Cola Company is the world's largest beverage company and the leading drinks brand worldwide, and in Great Britain, Coca-Cola and sugar-free diet Coke are the country's two biggest soft drinks. Coca-Cola is also the world's most valuable brand, heading the 2007 Business Week/Interbrand Top 100 Brands survey with a brand value of US$65.3 billion.

Market

Coca-Cola is the biggest soft drinks brand in the UK. Grocery sales in 2007 saw the brand reach £960 million in Great Britain, compared to £225 million for its nearest rival (Source: ACNielsen). Furthermore, the brand's year-on-year sales has increased by 2.3 per cent in the year from 2006 to 2007, while sales for its nearest rival have increased by just 4.1 per cent (Source: ACNielsen).

In general, the soft drinks category has seen strong growth in the year to December 2007, with sales of soft drinks up 2.8 per cent to more than £6 billion. This growth is partly being driven by the health and wellness trend sweeping Britain, which has seen the soft drinks market innovate and offer consumers more choice in sparkling and still beverages.

Diet and light drinks have seen particular innovation and growth, as well as fruit juices, waters, performance and energy drinks.

Achievements

The Coca-Cola brand is still at the pinnacle of global brand recognition. Looking ahead, The Coca-Cola Company aims to continue to give consumers a range of choices and create demand that will maintain the brand's unique position and continue to grow the market for soft drinks.

Product

There are three core products in the Coca-Cola family – Coca-Cola, diet Coke and Coca-Cola Zero. Innovation is placed at the heart of The Coca-Cola Company, whether evolving products in response to changing consumer needs, or developing new ways to communicate with its customers.

Recent Developments

The first time that The Coca-Cola Company added functional benefits to one of its sparkling beverages was in October 2007 with the launch of diet Coke Plus. This was in response to the growing demand from women for drinks that offer functional benefits, but don't compromise on taste. Aimed at loyal diet Coke drinkers, it is available in two variants – diet Coke Plus with Vitamins and diet Coke Plus with Antioxidant. The product has been well received, and was awarded The Grocer magazine's soft drink launch of the year 2007.

The limited edition Coca-Cola with Orange was launched in July 2007, supported by a £2.5 million media campaign. The aim was to drive excitement in the category following the launch of Coca-Cola with Lime in summer 2006.

1886	**1893**	**1915**	**1919**	**1984**	**2006**
Coca-Cola is invented by John Styth Pemberton, a pharmacist in Atlanta, Georgia. Asa Candler acquires the business in 1888.	The famous signature 'flourish' of Coca-Cola is registered as a trademark for the first time. By 1895, Coca-Cola is available in every US state.	The famous Coca-Cola Contour bottle, made from Georgia green glass, makes its first appearance and has a unique 3D trademark to protect Coca-Cola from a growing army of imitators.	The business is sold to Ernest Woodruff. In 1923, his son Robert becomes president of the company, declaring that Coca-Cola 'should always be within an arm's reach of desire'.	The launch of diet Coke takes place – the first brand extension of Coca-Cola in Great Britain.	Coca-Cola Zero becomes the third brand in the Coca-Cola family in Great Britain.

Promotion

Coca-Cola has always been renowned for memorable marketing. The 1971 'Hilltop' TV commercial, featuring the song 'I'd like to buy the world a Coke', is not only one of the most famous-ever advertisements, but it also broke new ground for being one of the first truly global advertising campaigns.

Coca-Cola continued this tradition in 2007 with the global launch of a new three minute commercial entitled 'Happiness Factory – The Movie'. The commercial was the sequel to the original 'Happiness Factory' advert and, to mark its launch, Coca-Cola became the first brand to host a global red carpet movie premiere in virtual world, Second Life. A viral of the groundbreaking advert was seeded across social networks, reaching 7.5 million 12-24 year-olds, while 20,400 people watched the video on YouTube.

2007 also saw the return of the award-winning diet Coke break advertising, which first aired in 1996, and the arrival of Francois Xavier – the new 'hunk' to appeal to today's diet Coke drinkers.

The 2007 football-focused Coca-Cola Zero ad campaign aimed to highlight 'great things in life without the usual downsides'. One execution saw brand ambassador Wayne Rooney dribbling a ball past a series of obstacles including razor sharp trip wire and a giant spiked boulder, taking a tongue-in-cheek view of the lengths defenders go to in order to stop forwards.

To bring to life The Coca-Cola Company's most successful advertising campaign to

date, 'The Coke Side of Life', The Coca-Cola Company also ran an impactful marketing campaign entitled 'Summer on The Coke Side of Life'. This saw Coca-Cola Great Britain working with some of the world's best-known designers and artists including Sir Peter Blake, the godfather of British Pop Art, to create a unique collection of images that capture The Coke Side of Life philosophy.

Sir Peter Blake created a 20ft high artwork, inspired by Coca-Cola, which was completed live on London's South Bank to celebrate summer. The piece, which took the form of a spectacular image emerging from the neck of the bottle, became a landmark on the South Bank during August 2007.

Coca-Cola Great Britain's 'Talent From Trash' campaign aimed to use the power and widespread appeal of football to motivate and encourage football fans and their families to recycle household waste in order to win cash for their Football League Club's youth programme. Football fans were encouraged to make a daily pledge on the Talent From Trash website and in return, could receive up to £18,000 for their club.

2007 also saw Coca-Cola Great Britain introduce a limited edition, collectible Original Glass Bottle, which was sold exclusively in Harrods, to celebrate 'Peace Day' – an annual day of global ceasefire and non-violence, established by the international Peace One Day project. The 'Peace' bottle is inspired by the spirit of optimism and aims to encapsulate the positive values and vision shared by Peace One Day and Coca-Cola.

Brand Values

The enduring brand values of Coca-Cola have stood the test of time and aim to convey optimism, togetherness and authenticity. Coca-Cola is not political, but aims to bring people together with an uplifting promise of better times and possibilities. These values make Coca-Cola as relevant and appealing to people today as it always has been, and underpin the fierce loyalty, affection and love that generations have felt for the brand and the product. The Coca-Cola Company's reputation for strong marketing ensures that this connection remains as powerful as ever.

www.coca-cola.co.uk

Things you didn't know about Coca-Cola

The Company markets more than 400 brands worldwide, with 20 in the UK alone, providing over one billion servings of sparkling and still beverages every day.

Coca-Cola is thought to be the second most widely understood word in the world after 'OK'.

The launch of Coca-Cola Zero was the biggest for Coca-Cola Great Britain since launching diet Coke 22 years earlier.

Coca-Cola has been an official partner of the Olympic Games since 1928 – the longest running sport sponsorship in history.

In UK grocery stores, sales of diet Coke now exceed Coca-Cola.

Coca-Cola was originally sold as a soda fountain drink – produced by mixing Coca-Cola syrup with carbonated water.

'Coca-Cola', 'Coke', 'diet Coke' and 'Coke Zero' are registered trade marks of The Coca-Cola Company.

COSMOPOLITAN

British Cosmopolitan launched in 1972, and has since remained one of the dominant magazine brands in the UK. Having recently celebrated its 36th birthday, Cosmo attributes this success to the brand DNA, consistency of its voice and the constant ability to innovate and evolve for its generation. Cosmo believes that relevance counts for more than heritage because a consumer purchase of a magazine is an act of trust – "You know something I don't".

Market

The magazine market has come a long way since Cosmopolitan launched in February 1972.

Today, despite the unprecedented levels of competition, Cosmo consistently delivers an average circulation more than 450,000 every month and was one of the best performing women's titles in the ABCs for July-December 2007, recording circulation increases in the last two reporting periods.

At more than 1.8 million, Cosmo's readership is 52 per cent greater than its nearest competitor. What's more, 813,000 readers are unique to Cosmo, choosing not to read any other competitor magazine (Source: NRS July-December 2007). The Cosmo reader accounts for £1 in every £11 spent on beauty and £1 in every £9 spent on fashion in the UK (Source: TGI April 2006-March 2007). Cosmo also generates the highest retail sales value of all monthly magazines in the market.

Achievements

In February 2002, Cosmopolitan celebrated its 30th birthday and was praised highly in the comment of the day in The Times leader column: "Cosmo is bigger than a magazine; it is a brand, an empire, a state of mind."

Since 1972, Cosmo has established an enviable campaigning heritage on a variety of issues, from equal pay and sexual health to motivating political engagement on the rights for rape victims. Considered an authority on a wide range of subjects, Cosmo's spokespeople are widely used by the press for comment.

Cosmo has been recognised with a number of prestigious awards, including the British Society of Magazine Editors (BSME) Innovation of the Year in 2003, for the magazine's Rapestoppers Campaign. The magazine has also been awarded the BSME Women's Magazine Editor of the Year in 1991, 1993, 1999 and 2001, as well as the Periodical Publishers Association Consumer Magazine of the Year in 1992. In both 2004 and 2006, Proctor & Gamble awarded Cosmo its Beauty Award for the magazine that has best supported the beauty & grooming industry and then in 2007, the P&G Beauty 'Consumer' Award.

Product

For the British reader, Cosmo aims to be a life and relationship bible. Through its pages the reader is able to observe life and, more importantly, change her life. The USP of Cosmo is to 'Inspire women to be the best they can be'. As a result, readers can feel engaged, empowered and able to achieve anything they want.

Cosmo's core business is the magazine, but an extended family includes Cosmopolitan Bride and cosmopolitan.co.uk. The brand has also diversified into other areas, such as licensed merchandise carefully selected to fit with its personality. The Cosmopolitan

1972	2002	2004	2006	2007	2008
British Cosmopolitan launches with an issue price of 20p. The first issue – supported by Saatchi & Saatchi – sells out in three hours.	Cosmo launches a travel-size format, offering consumers more choice.	Cosmo appoints London ad agency CHI for the first ATL campaign since launch.	The Cosmo website launches – cosmopolitan.co.uk.	Louise Court is appointed as editor, as Cosmopolitan celebrates 35 years.	The Cosmo Online Fashion Awards are launched and cosmopolitan.co.uk is redesigned.

Collection includes handbags, swimwear, bedding, soft furnishings and beauty accessories. Cosmopolitan has also produced a significant number of books on relationships, sex, beauty and emotional well-being. Most recently, Cosmo has published 'The Best of Cosmopolitan: The 70s and 80s' – a series of era-defining articles and images chronicling the history of the magazine.

Recent Developments

Cosmopolitan.co.uk is an online life, love, sex and relationships bible and was relaunched in April 2008 with a major new design, which aims to enhance and expand the Cosmopolitan magazine reader's experience, creating a powerful online community of women. The redesigned site sees the introduction of new daily content, clear navigation, and greater user interaction.

Users can upload images of their partners to compete in Boyfriend Wars, share their secrets in the Cosmo confessions booth, put problems to the public vote with Moral Dilemma and watch excerpts from behind-the-scenes at Cosmo cover-shoots on Cosmo TV – alongside the customary mix of fashion and beauty that Cosmo is famous for and, of course, the Naked Male Centrefolds.

2008 also saw the launch of the Cosmo Online Fashion Awards. Judged by a panel of celebrities, together with Cosmopolitan's readers and fashion experts, the awards celebrate the best in online fashion retailing.

In such a dynamic marketplace, a business strategy that keeps the brand fresh, modern and relevant is essential. Recent innovations have included the launch of a brand-new editorial property – the 'Ultimate Women of the Year Awards for fun, fearless females'. More than just average celebrity awards, Cosmo rewards the 'most fun, fearless females' in all walks of life, from celebrities to readers, bound by their inspirational qualities.

The Cosmo Beauty Awards, launched in 2003, have become an ultimate buying guide for the consumer and are used extensively by the trade as a powerful brand endorsement of best in class.

In 2006, Cosmo celebrated the 10th anniversary of the Naked Centrefold, a famous editorial and event property that supports Everyman – the testicular and prostrate cancer charity – raising research funds and awareness.

Louise Court became Cosmo's editor in January 2007, injecting the magazine with her own brand of humour, whilst continuing to 'inspire women to be the best they can be'.

Promotion

Cosmopolitan remains the industry benchmark in magazine publishing. To its readers, Cosmo is as relevant today as it was in the 1970s, 1980s and 1990s. In the 2000s, Cosmo has developed a travel-size version to offer choice and convenience at the newsstand.

Working with key beauty and fashion houses that share the same brand synergy, Cosmopolitan creates effective partnerships that can raise its brand awareness in relevant markets, beyond the newsstand.

As a truly multi-platform media brand, Cosmopolitan can connect with its readers over and above the magazine, through online, events, surveys, reader polls, subscribers, e-subscribers, text and email.

Brand Values

The Cosmopolitan mission is to celebrate fun, glamour and passion for life, inspiring young women to be the best they can be. It achieves its aim of being a magazine for a 'fun, fearless female' via eight core editorial pillars: relationships & sex, men, real-life stories, beauty & fashion, careers, emotional health & well-being issues and campaigns. Of these editorial pillars, relationships is unique to Cosmo and is the crucial element that enables a trusted and more intimate relationship with the brand's readers.

www.cosmopolitan.co.uk

Things you didn't know about Cosmopolitan

Cosmopolitan is the world's biggest magazine brand, with 59 international editions, published in 34 languages and distributed in more than 100 countries. It is sector leader in 43 markets.

Cosmo reaches more than 100 million readers every month, worldwide (Source: www.hearstmagazinesinternational.com).

Cover stars have included Jerry Hall, Elizabeth Taylor, Farrah Fawcett, Paula Yates, Bob Geldof, Boy George and Claudia Schiffer, Madonna and Yasmin Le Bon, Beyoncé and J.Lo.

CRABTREE & EVELYN®

Crabtree & Evelyn, originated from a single, family run store in Boston, founded in 1972. Long before the 'natural' and 'wellness' movements became popular in the cosmetics & toiletries industry, it was producing ranges featuring fruit, flower and plant essences. Innovation is key in creating each new generation of products and Crabtree & Evelyn continues to draw upon its rich heritage and accumulated knowledge of plants and botanicals, while making use of emerging technologies.

Market

The UK toiletries market is valued in excess of £4.5 billion and industry analysts anticipate a continued growth in the region of 2.1-2.9 per cent between 2008 and 2010. This is largely due to an expanding customer base from all age groups. Skin care is the sector expected to show the best rate of growth as technological advances promise the youthful appearance craved by all.

Market sectors in which Crabtree & Evelyn competes are buoyant as consumers increasingly seek products to indulge and restore themselves. The company operates in health & beauty, producing fine fragrance, bath and shower gels, soaps, home spa solutions, body lotions and creams, as well as the recent introduction of hand and foot treatments and home fragrance, in the form of atomisers, candles, diffusers and oils.

Achievements

Crabtree & Evelyn's strategic goal has been to establish its name as one of the most familiar and respected personal care brands in the world. Today it has a presence in 40 countries. Products are sold in approximately 350 stores worldwide, with 40 branded stores in the UK. Selected products are also available in department stores and specialty retailers throughout the world.

A significant milestone for Crabtree & Evelyn was the launch of its first ever patent-pending product, Hand Recovery, in 2002. This benefit-driven product, along with Hand Therapy, has been an instant hit and has gained a loyal customer following. The Hand Recovery and Hand Therapy duo are now available within four ranges – Gardeners, La Source®, Goatmilk and Jojoba.

The recently launched India Hicks Island Living range contains both home and body products as well as indulgent products such as scented candles, fragrance diffusers, hand wash, body cream, bath salts and other treasures. The signature Spider Lily fragrance from the India Hicks Island Living collection won the UK's most prestigious trade beauty accolade – the CEW (UK) award for Best New Women's Fragrance in the Prestige/Limited Distribution category – in April 2008.

Product

In bath and body care, Crabtree & Evelyn products are aimed at mood elevation, as every interaction should leave consumers feeling happier about their day.

In bringing new mood-enhancing products to customers around the world, Crabtree & Evelyn looks to the English virtuoso John Evelyn for inspiration. His personal motto, 'explore everything, keep the best', inspires the company to this day to take 'only the best' formulations and products to market.

Crabtree & Evelyn continues to launch new products using the best ingredients and fragrances from around the world. Each one aims to be mood elevating, making the lives of consumers a little more pampered and happier.

Recent Developments

Crabtree & Evelyn is constantly improving its product range by launching innovative new products to create cohesive collections, in addition to its proven strengths of quality and originality.

1972	1977	1980	1990	1994	2002
Products are first sold trading under the Crabtree & Evelyn name.	Crabtree & Evelyn's first store opens in Philadelphia, USA.	Crabtree & Evelyn opens its flagship store in London.	The Evelyn Rose, developed by David Austin, launches at the Chelsea Flower Show.	A range of Crabtree & Evelyn toiletries is specially designed for British Airways Concorde and First Class passengers.	Crabtree & Evelyn launches its first patent-pending hand care product – Hand Recovery.

It built on a long-standing tradition of botanically based products with the launch of the Naturals Collection – a range of 'good for you' beauty remedies that blend together the highest grade botanical extracts, oils and mineral complexes to deliver high performance benefits and textures without parabens, mineral oil, synthetic dyes, sodium lauryl sulphate and sodium laureth sulphate.

For the first time in the company's history, 2007 saw the introduction of a brand ambassador to convey Crabtree & Evelyn's core values and modern outlook. This led to a partnership with British style icon India Hicks. India is the creative force behind the development of the India Hicks Island Living range. Launched in the UK in 2007, the range is inspired by India's island life and the natural beauties associated with living in such surroundings.

Winter 2008 will see the launch of a complete new collection, which will combine the best elements of classic aromatherapy with modern, innovative formulations.

Promotion

In 1994, Crabtree & Evelyn designed a range of toiletries for British Airways Concorde and First Class passengers. Since then, sampling on airlines and in hotels has proved to be a successful way of introducing customers to the brand. Currently, Hilton Hotels worldwide provide their customers with toiletries that have been designed exclusively for the chain by the brand.

The Crabtree & Evelyn Privilege Card Program rewards regular customers by offering discounts, incentives, gifts-with-purchase, and various other promotions and offers. A further incentivised VIP status complements a large database of customers.

In addition, Crabtree & Evelyn provides a customised gift service programme, catering to meet the needs of its customers' special requirements when buying a gift for business associates, family or friends.

Brand Values

Crabtree & Evelyn is known throughout the world for its distinguished range of products and single-minded dedication to quality and design. The brand aims to provide the best ingredients through sourcing without geographic boundaries.

The brand and its products aim to create sensory experiences that delight, comfort, enchant and indulge through mood-elevating products.

Crabtree & Evelyn's philosophy is to continually strive for excellence across all areas of the business, with the aim of consistently offering customers the very best products united with outstanding customer service. The brand believes that its loyal customers trust the brand to take the best fragrances and ingredients from around the world to produce mood elevating luxurious products to make their lives a little better every day.

www.crabtree-evelyn.co.uk

Things you didn't know about Crabtree & Evelyn®

One La Source Hand Recovery product is sold somewhere in the world every minute.

Evelyn was the first perfume to be based on a single, specially created rose. Using headspace technology, it took eight years, 30,000 seedlings and hundreds of cuttings to identify the perfect specimen.

Selected Crabtree & Evelyn products hold the Royal Warrant from HRH the Prince of Wales in recognition of its services as a supplier of fine toiletries.

The brand's name was inspired by the 17th century renaissance Englishman John Evelyn, who wrote one of the first important works on conservation.

The Evelyn Rose, launched in 1990 at the Chelsea Flower Show, was developed by David Austin in honour of John Evelyn.

2005	**2006**	**2007**	**2008**
Crabtree & Evelyn USA signs an agreement with Hilton Hotels Resorts & Spa North America to supply in-room amenity products.	Crabtree & Evelyn announces its first spokesperson and creative partnership, with India Hicks.	Crabtree & Evelyn launches its first co-branded line, India Hicks Island Living, with brand features in key publications such as Vogue, Allure, Red, Elle and Glamour.	CEW (UK) names India Hicks Island Living, Spider Lily Eau de Toilette 'Best New Women's Fragrance' in the Prestige/Limited Distribution category.

DURACELL®

Duracell® has been a leader of the UK battery market for nearly 90 years. In this time, its market has changed significantly to keep pace with the technology of the day, from early flashlights to the multitude of portable devices now available. Recent innovations have been in the rechargeable and portable power markets.

Market

The battery market is currently worth £316 million (Source: IRI/GFK last 12 months February 2008) in the UK alone with Duracell® holding a 51.3 per cent value share of the total general purpose battery market (Source: IRI/GFK w/e 29th December 2007); the brand is the clear leader within this multi-million pound market.

In recent years, there has been a substantial growth in AA and AAA batteries or 'cells', primarily fuelled by sales of high-tech gadgets such as digital cameras, MP3 players and other devices (Source: Euromonitor 2008) which require portable power solutions. The battery market continues to grow as consumers demand more from their power solutions and Duracell® continually leads the category with an extensive product profile and on-going technical development.

Achievements

Since the arrival of Duracell® into the UK during the 1970s, the popularity of alkaline batteries has risen while older, less efficient zinc batteries have been in decline.

By the early 1990s, Duracell® had successfully eliminated virtually all mercury from its batteries and made dramatic improvements to performance. In the three decades of Duracell® history, the life expectancy of an AA cell has more than doubled, while remaining much the same in terms of size and design.

In 1988 Duracell® introduced a way to monitor the lifespan of a battery by printing 'best before' dates on all packs and batteries. By 2002 the 'best before' date was extended to seven years.

Then in 1990, Duracell® introduced the first on-pack battery tester,

followed in 1996 by the unique Powercheck™ battery tester on the actual cell to determine how much life the battery had left.

2003 saw the launch of Duracell® Solutions, as each of the five major cells were assigned a colour to help consumers select the correct battery sizes.

Duracell® has continued to lead and innovate in the category with the significant upgrade of Duracell® Plus and Ultra batteries in July 2008 and the ongoing development of its Rechargeable range.

The last two years have seen Duracell® products achieving consistent Product of the Year (POTY) recognition. In 2007, an independent survey of 10,049 consumers chose PowerPix, the specialist digital camera battery, as the best innovation of the year in the battery category. In 2008, the Duracell® Mini Charger won the POTY award after 12,008 consumers were surveyed and, for the second year running, Duracell® products have been recognised by consumers as 'products which genuinely enhance their lives'.

Product

Over the past 40 years, Duracell® has built a reputation for manufacturing and supplying superior batteries that consistently lead the market in performance, quality and innovation. Duracell® recognises that different devices demand different levels of power and offers a range of products to ensure consumers can select the right battery for the right device.

The two pillars of the portfolio include Duracell® Plus, its core line, and the

---

1920s

Scientist Samuel Ruben and a manufacturer of tungsten filament wire, Philip Rogers Mallory join forces to form Duracell® International.

1950s

Ruben improves the alkaline manganese battery, making it more compact, durable and longer lasting than anything before it.

Eastman Kodak introduce cameras with a built-in flash unit that need the added power provided by alkaline manganese cells but in a new size, AAA – this puts alkaline cells on the map.

1964

Duracell® introduces its AAA battery. Soon, the consumer market for Duracell® batteries rockets.

2000s

Duracell® continues to lead the way with product innovation, reflected in the Duracell® Plus and Ultra batteries.

Duracell® undertakes significant research into the rechargeable and portable power markets to extend its power portfolio.

longest lasting Duracell® alkaline ever, Duracell® Ultra (Duracell® AA/AAA used in any device). In 2008 the core alkaline range has had a significant performance upgrade. Duracell® Plus now has an advanced longer life (compared to the previous Duracell® Plus), while Duracell® Ultra has been upgraded so that no other alkaline battery lasts longer (based on the average testing from devices used most). To complement this innovation in technology and power delivery, the Duracell® range has also received a packaging makeover to highlight the upgrade. The eye catching new 'planet' design aims to be highly engaging for consumers and ensure simple communication of the products, their benefits and the brand presence of Duracell®.

In addition to the core product portfolio, Duracell® is also committed to excellence within the rechargeable sector. As a brand, Duracell® has made full use of its extensive research and development skills to bring to market a range of rechargeable products. The full range includes both family sized

and compact chargers, including the premium one hour charger which charges four AA or AAA cells in one hour.

Duracell® also offers a range of speciality batteries for watches, electronic, security, photo lithium and photo devices.

Recent Developments

Duracell® has recognised the growth in on-the-go devices with a built-in power source. To meet the needs of such devices, the Pocket Charger has been introduced to the range. This provides power to many well know devices including iPod, BlackBerry and a variety of mobile phones from standard AA cells. Meanwhile, the Instant Charger offers similar functionality via a Lithium-ion rechargeable battery – with the added benefit of being recharged from any USB equipped laptop or computer.

In traditional rechargeable technology, Duracell® has recently launched Duracell® Active Charge, a range of cells which not only pre-charge like traditional cells, but can also be fully recharged for energy efficient, long-lasting power. The Active Charge cells retain their charge for longer, meaning more power and less charging time for consumers.

Promotion

As an active partner in the summer music festivals, the Duracell® Powerhouse has for the past three years appeared at the top UK summer festivals. Playing music into the early hours after the bands finish. Duracell® Powerhouse reinforces the brand's connection with music and the key music consumers who are known for their use of high-tech digital devices. Music download also forms a key part of the brand's music partnership. Following the success of its iTunes partnership in 2007, which gave away a free music download with every promotional pack purchased, Duracell® has made the campaign more accessible to all music consumers in 2008 by partnering with Universal Music.

Duracell® is also famous for the Duracell® Bunny – the iconic face of the brand for more than 30 years, recognised by millions of consumers worldwide. He has become a cult advertising figure and over the years has taken on different characters to show the 'Power of the Bunny', illustrating that a Bunny powered by Duracell batteries can continue functioning for longer than ordinary zinc carbon batteries before its battery runs down.

Duracell® recognises the opportunities within the market and is the first major brand in the UK to invest in a significant above-the-line print advertising campaign for rechargeable cells, driving awareness amongst consumers.

Brand Values

Duracell® is the UK's best selling battery brand (Source: IRI/GFK w/e 29th December 2007) and remains at the forefront of technological innovation within the market. Duracell® has market leading consumer recognition and brand positioning. By producing reliable, long-lasting portable power solutions that meet the demands of the modern day consumer, Duracell® remains the trusted market leader.

www.duracell.com/uk

Things you didn't know about Duracell®

One of the biggest Duracell® 'batteries' ever seen is 25ft long and has travelled the length and breadth of the country on several occasions, firstly promoting Powercheck™ and then Duracell® Ultra.

Despite the hundreds of battery sizes available, just five account for 95 per cent of all batteries sold – AA, AAA, C, D and 9V.

As one of the UK's leading power and gas companies, E.ON generates and distributes electricity, and supplies power and gas to around six million customers, as well as offering central heating and boiler care through its Home Energy Services business. E.ON is also at the forefront of an energy revolution, currently in the process of exploring and utilising more sustainable energy provision in response to the very real challenge posed by climate change.

Market

In recent years the energy sector has seen significant increases in wholesale costs, impacting on residential and business prices throughout the UK. The competitive marketplace, with an emphasis on price, innovation and service, now sees consumers regularly switching suppliers and customer choice taking a more pivotal role.

The company which is now known as E.ON, launched in 1989 under the Powergen name, has become one of the UK's leading energy providers. It is part of the E.ON group, the world's largest investor-owned power and gas company.

With climate change, sustainability and ethical responsibility all growing concerns amongst energy consumers, E.ON has been at the forefront of this shifting market focus. E.ON offers green tariffs for both domestic and business consumers and provides a wealth of energy efficiency advice and services to help its customers use energy more wisely.

Achievements

Energy plays an essential role in ensuring quality of life for both present and future generations. Supplying energy reliably, and at affordable prices, is critical in helping people maintain and improve their standard of living.

E.ON is working on more sustainable ways of providing and delivering energy; for example, increased investment in renewable energy and offering advice and services on energy efficiency.

Corporate Social Responsibility is also one of the brand's core values. It partners cities and communities and works closely with schools and charitable organisations on projects across the UK that educate, support and engage; from tackling fuel poverty to helping children adopt healthy, energetic lifestyles.

In 2008 E.ON was formally recognised for its sponsorship of The FA Cup, winning three Hollis awards for Charity and Community,

1989	1998	2002	2005	2006	2007
Following the privatisation of the UK's electricity industry a new generating company, Powergen, is launched.	Powergen evolves to become one of the UK's leading integrated power and gas companies, generating and distributing electricity, and retailing power and gas.	Powergen becomes part of E.ON. Powergen remains the consumer and SME facing brand, as the rest of the business rebrands to E.ON in 2004.	To start the transition to E.ON, Powergen introduces the strapline 'A company of E.ON'. Associated advertising is adapted to reflect this change.	E.ON signs a four-year agreement to become lead sponsor of The FA Cup and sponsors The FA Women's Cup and The FA Youth Cup.	The transition to E.ON is completed, as the mass market retail business Powergen is rebranded.

Best Brand Sponsorship and the prestigious award for Best Overall Sponsorship. E.ON also won Best Sponsorship of a Sport Event or Competition at The Sports Industry Awards 2008.

Product
E.ON offers a range of products and services based around its primary function: energy provision. It was one of the first brands to introduce a capped product to the market, with the most recent being Price Protection Until 2009. Its Go Green tariff is part of a package of sustainable products that combine conventional energy with renewable energy sources, aimed at reducing carbon dioxide emissions and promoting more considered energy use.

E.ON is one of the leading green energy generators in the UK. Its current portfolio, including 21 wind farms and one of the UK's largest dedicated biomass power stations at Lockerbie, generates enough green energy to power all the homes in a city the size of Manchester.

E.ON has also designed a specific range of tariffs for its elderly, vulnerable and fuel poor customers, and is currently the only supplier to provide two products for the over 60s, StayWarm and Age Concern Energy Services – in addition to a £100 million CaringEnergy scheme, designed to help improve the energy efficiency and income of vulnerable UK households.

Recent Developments
As it aspired to a global identity under the E.ON brand, Powergen communications incorporated the look and feel of E.ON until December 2007 when the company completed its rebrand to E.ON, re-enforcing its commitment to the UK market.

Moving forward, the aim of changing energy consumption for the better is at the heart of E.ON's recent See it and Save

campaign. By making energy more tangible for consumers – the advertisement shows a man able to physically see how much energy he consumes – the campaign aims to provide customers with more control over their energy use, and their household budget. The promotion sees the brand engage with its customers in a new and more direct way.

E.ON's commitment to the installation of Smart Meters in residential homes (part of a two-year £12 million investment in metering technologies) is a further example of this recent shift of brand focus; encouraging more responsible energy use to help reduce overall energy consumption and the UK's total carbon emissions.

Promotion
Prior to Powergen's rebrand to E.ON in 2007, its sponsorship of the ITV weather was the longest running TV sponsorship of its time and was part of the rebrand campaign. E.ON has now moved its sponsorship to the Five Homes & Property suite of TV programmes and has invested in higher profile advertising campaigns.

As lead sponsor of The FA Cup and the official Energy Partner to The Football League, sport sponsorship has enabled E.ON to communicate and raise awareness of the brand across the UK. When E.ON sponsored Ipswich Town Football Club, its season-long 'Save Your Energy for the Blues' carbon reduction programme was, again, a UK first and made Ipswich Town the world's first carbon neutral football club.

As Powergen moved to E.ON, the company promoted a progressive stance on renewable energy through its Wind of Change advertising campaign. Featuring a sleepy British coastal town invigorated by an energetic optimistic wind that lifts the spirits of all those in its path, the campaign aimed to reflect a 'wind of change' being brought by E.ON.

The brand's Go Green campaign played along a similar environmentally aware message, introducing the company's new green energy tariff and inviting consumers to let nature in, by way of a combined 100 per cent green dual fuel energy. This move from the more conservative corporate advertisements, towards a new through-the-line campaign (running across television, press, poster, direct mail and online) is an example of the brand's continuing strategy.

Brand Values
E.ON's vision is to change energy for the better, from where it is sourced to how it is delivered to consumers. Citing climate change as the biggest challenge faced, not only by energy providers, but by society in general, E.ON's key brand values of optimism and visionary thinking equip it to face the changing market with confidence, responsibility and an increasingly ethical stance.

www.eon-uk.com

Things you didn't know about E.ON

The E.ON group is the world's largest investor-owned power and gas company; in the UK it employs approximately 16,000 people.

E.ON runs an Energy in the Community Employee Volunteering programme. Last year almost one in five of its UK employees took part in the scheme, leading to nearly £480,000 being given to good causes. E.ON also offers matched funding for employees who raise money for community groups and charities.

E.ON's distribution business, Central Networks, provides a supply to 4.9 million customers in central England through 133,000km of underground and overhead cables, via 97,000 substations.

E.ON's green development portfolio could displace the emissions of almost two million tonnes of carbon dioxide each year.

Fairy was rated as Britain's number one cleaning brand by The Times in February 2007 and has been a regular household feature since the name first appeared in 1898 on a bar of soap. Today the brand represents a range of products renowned for their cleaning ability and caring nature. More than 13 million UK households buy 150 million bottles of Fairy each year, which equates to 57 per cent of the total market (Source: ACNielsen May 2008).

Market

The dish cleaning market contains sink and dishwasher sectors, with Fairy leading the total category in household penetration, volume and value sales (Source: ACNielsen May 2008).

The value of the dish washing sector continues to increase three per cent per annum, driven by the launch of premium products such as Fairy Active Bursts and Fairy Clean & Care, as well as the growth of Fairy Antibacterial products, which deliver superior performance for the consumer; the future is bright for Fairy with a wealth of new product development in the wings.

Achievements

Fairy has grown in recent years to be in the enviable position of becoming the UK's top selling household brand (Source: ACNielsen May 2008). Following the launch of its dishwasher range, it is the only national brand to offer a complete range of products in both the sink and dishwasher categories.

This followed Fairy becoming the UK's fastest growing non-food brand in Grocers in 2006, when turnover topped £120 million

behind the launch of Fairy Active Bursts for dishwashers (Source: Nielsen).

Further to this, turnover has been driven significantly via recent developments, such as Fairy Powerspray and the latest premium washing up liquid range, Fairy Clean & Care.

Fairy Liquid has always been associated with being kind on skin, so it was an important accolade for the brand to become the only product to be awarded top cleaning results by Which? magazine's Best Buy survey, while remaining mild enough to be certified by the British Skin Foundation.

Product

During the 1950s, most people used powders and crystals to wash dishes. After conducting vigorous tests, Fairy launched a dish washing product, Fairy Liquid. By the end of its first year six out of 10 people in the UK had bought it.

The Fairy brand has stood for 'sparkling performance' for more than 100 years. Fairy's dishwashing brand, an iconic household emblem, has maintained market leadership for over 50 years which the brand attributes to unbeatable performance and value: lasting up to 50 per cent longer than the next best selling brand (Source: Independent Laboratory Testing).

Now the Fairy range consists of Fairy Liquid Original as well as four additional scents: Apple Quake, Lemon Twister, Pink Petals and Fresh Lavender.

Fairy Pure Clean with Antibacterial Action combines Fairy Liquid's cleaning performance with natural herb and citrus extracts, which provide the additional benefit of controlling the growth of germs on sponges and cloths. The product is endorsed with a gold seal from the Royal Institute of Public Health and is available in Eucalyptus,

1898	**1930**	**1987**	**1997**	**2003**	**2006**
Fairy Soap launches through Thomas Hedley & Sons.	Procter & Gamble acquires the brand and Fairy Baby trademark.	Lemon-scented Fairy Liquid is introduced alongside Fairy Original. Two years later, a Fairy non-biological laundry product launches for sensitive skin.	Fairy Liquid with antibacterial agents is introduced.	Fairy Powerspray launches, for tough, burnt-on stains, adding £9 million to the category.	Fairy Active Bursts launches and sales top £120 million.

Lime & Lemongrass, Pink Grapefruit and Garden Mint variants.

The Fairy range has also grown to encompass new areas, such as dishwasher products – Fairy Active Burst dishwashing tablets, Fairy Rinse Aid with Active Drying Power and Fairy Machine Cleaner – as well as Fairy non-biological laundry products.

The newest and breakthrough addition to the Fairy family is Fairy Clean & Care, the washing up liquid that moisturises hands while leaving dishes 'squeaky clean'. Packaged in a new bottle shape with the aim of adding a touch of glamour to the home, the thicker and pearlescent liquid is available in three scents: Aloe Vera & Cucumber; Silk & Orchid; and Almond Oil.

Recent Developments

Fairy has been a familiar face in kitchens for generations, so it was a bold move in 2000 for Fairy to change its signature white bottle to fit in with modern kitchens and times. The new transparent bottle was ergonomically designed, making it easier to control. The formula was also changed to make the product more concentrated.

To maintain the momentum of innovation, 2003 saw the launch of Fairy Powerspray, designed to remove tough, burnt-on food from dishes to make washing up easier.

In 2006 Fairy introduced Fairy Active Bursts for dishwashers, a revolutionary all-in-one detergent plus liquid product, requiring no unwrapping prior to use to provide unbeatable cleaning and convenience. The successful launch has seen Fairy Active Bursts become the second best selling dishwashing product

within its launch year (Source: Nielsen 2008), with consumers voting it Dishwasher Product of the Year in 2006 and 90 per cent of independent repairmen recommending the product (Source: GSAT 2006).

The dishwasher range continued to grow in 2007 with the launch of Fairy Pure Clean detergent, Fairy Rinse Aid and Fairy Machine Cleaner.

2008 saw the biggest launch of Fairy liquid ever with the introduction of the pampering range, Fairy Clean & Care.

Promotion

Fairy Liquid TV advertising campaigns first began in the 1950s. This soon led to a host of celebrity endorsements, including actress Nanette Newman with the much loved and remembered line 'Hands that wash dishes are as soft as your face with mild green fairy liquid'.

Brand communication now dominates the category, highlighting unbeatable performance through cleaning messages and value due to mileage performance. Fairy aims to put the customer first, operating a free phone advice line and money back guarantee. Furthermore, Fairy refuses to produce products for other brands or retailers.

In recent years, Fairy's advertising has seen chefs Ainsley Harriott, Anthony Worrell Thomson and Gary Rhodes front the brand together. TV executions show the chefs in the kitchen, talking about the brand in a light hearted manor. This is backed up with print and outdoor work.

In recent years the use of glamorous spokespeople such as Jodie Kidd, Helena

Christiansen and Louise Redknapp has enabled Fairy to talk to a younger audience.

Fairy has also driven a more dynamic brand position in recent years through its False Economy versus Fairy-Conomy campaign, highlighting the value benefits of its longer lasting formula to the consumer's pocket and the environment, with less bottles required. The campaign has been a success, voted second most memorable by consumers (Source: Adwatch September 2006).

Meanwhile, the brand's Fairy Active Bursts product was launched through its unique 'All in One' positioning with the 'no need to unwrap' benefits. This led ad spend and awareness in the dishwashing detergents category in 2006.

Fairy supports a number of charities and has been the UK's number one fundraiser for the Make A Wish children's charity over the last four years through its winter campaign. Its corporate social responsibility policy also means that it donates products for use during natural disasters, such as the 2007 South Coast oil spillage, as it is recognised by the RSPB as the best product for cleaning birds following oil spills.

The launch of the new sensorial product, Fairy Clean & Care, has marked a revolution in the way washing up liquid is advertised. The campaign carries the theme of beauty through TV, print, beauty print specials and the Feel Good Factor PR campaign, featuring the glamorous Lisa Butcher as the face of product.

Brand Values

Fairy has always been a family orientated brand with strong links to the kitchen and the role of mealtimes within families. It is also associated with environmental and sustainable organisations such as the RSPB, WWF, Energy Saving Trust and Wastewatch. Its products are concentrated in order to produce less packaging waste and bottles are recyclable. The dishwasher range is designed to be used in short cycles and at lower temperatures. Fairy is also part of the Future Friendly programme, aimed at inspiring and enabling people to live more sustainable lives.

www.fairy-dish.co.uk

Things you didn't know about Fairy

Since the 1960s the UK has bought more than 4.8 billion bottles of Fairy Liquid, enough to circle the earth 2,400 times.

579 bottles of Fairy are produced per minute – more than 10 million gallons of Fairy Liquid in a year.

One bottle of Fairy washed 14,763 dirty plates – a world record.

2007

Fairy Active Bursts is awarded Dishwasher Product of the Year and the Rinse Aid and Machine Cleaner products are also launched.

2008

Fairy launches Fairy Clean & Care in a new bottle design; the range provides the dual benefits of helping to keep hands soft and moisturised while leaving dishes 'squeaky clean'.

Since its launch in 1960, Galaxy® has seen strong growth that continues to strengthen year-on-year. Such success is built on the consistency of its positioning of magic, femininity and indulgence. Galaxy believes that true chocolate indulgence is about the whole eating experience, which is why everything about Galaxy chocolate, from the taste, to the shape, to the packaging, is designed to make indulging in a Galaxy moment as pleasurable as possible.

Market

The UK confectionery market, valued at over £4 billion, has seen a slowing rate of growth. Chocolate confectionery accounts for the bulk of sales in the market, with the remaining share taken up by sugar products. With brands leveraging the indulgent positioning of their products, the premium market has seen considerable development, while occasions such as everyday sharing have also been targeted.

The UK chocolate confectionery market remains dominated by Cadbury, Mars and Nestlé, and new product development (NPD) is firmly centred on brand extension rather than bringing new names to the consumer.

The UK block chocolate market is worth more than £680 million, with Galaxy block chocolate worth £180 million, a 12 per cent share of the total market (Source: IRI 2008).

The Galaxy brand represents the largest growth in the block category over the past five years, with this trend accelerating recently to reach an 18 per cent year-on-year growth in 2006 (Source: CAGR IRI w/e 30 Dec 2006/IRI 52 w/e 30 Dec 2006).

Achievements

If Galaxy were a stand-alone company, it would be the fourth-largest confectionery manufacturer in the UK, behind Cadbury Trebor Basset, Mars Snackfood UK (Galaxy's parent company) and Nestlé UK. The brand's entire product portfolio is worth £220 million, with Minstrels worth £51 million and Ripple £26 million (Source: IRI Infoscan Total Market 2006). In the past three years the Galaxy brand has grown by 24 per cent (Source: IRI 2008).

As part of Mars Snackfood UK, the Galaxy brand is ultimately part of Mars Incorporated,

1960	**1987**			**1995**	**2000**
Galaxy is launched in the UK and Ireland.	The 'Why have cotton when you can have silk?' Galaxy advertising campaign is launched.	Also in 1987, Ripple and Minstrels are rebranded as part of the Galaxy product family.	1987 also sees the lauch of Galaxy ice cream.	Galaxy Caramel is launched.	The Galaxy Amicelli and Galaxy Silk collections are launched.

which employs 39,000 people in more than 65 countries. Its products are consumed in more than 100 countries and the company has global annual sales of US$18 billion.

Product

Galaxy offers three main products: Galaxy block chocolate, which is marketed simply as smooth and creamy milk chocolate; Minstrels bite size, which are defined as smooth and creamy pieces of Galaxy milk chocolate encased in crispy shells; and the Ripple bar, described as smooth and creamy Galaxy milk chocolate with a rippled centre.

There have been many brand extensions to Galaxy, not only in bar format – such as Galaxy Caramel – but other confectionery products such as ice cream, seasonal Christmas products as well as Easter egg variants. In addition to this, the Galaxy range

of drinks includes Galaxy chocolate flavoured milk, Galaxy Thick Shake and Galaxy Instant Hot Chocolate Drink.

Recent Developments

Galaxy teams are constantly working to create new and innovative ways with Galaxy chocolate.

In 2007, the brand launched three new large block variants: Smooth Dark; Roasted & Caramelised Hazelnut; and Raisin, Almond & Hazelnut. These have a new shape and use a new recipe that is designed to create an even smoother taste. The new products also feature new premium packaging. To support the launch, a large-scale marketing campaign was undertaken. This encompassed TV advertising and product sampling.

Promotion

Twenty years ago, Galaxy's 'Why have cotton when you can have silk?' TV communication propelled Galaxy into the hands of consumers. Having provided a strong platform for the Galaxy brand, the chocolate was able to achieve 16 years of strong sales success in the market. In 2003, the brand was refreshed and relaunched to focus on indulgence and women's relationship with chocolate. The relaunch and subsequent consumer activity has aided continued growth for the brand. These activities included links with a number of key female indulgent occasions such as films or reading.

The first collaboration between Galaxy and films was Down With Love in 2002, followed by the highly successful Bridget Jones partnership in 2004 and another female oriented title, The Devil Wears Prada, in 2006.

The link with reading started in 2005 with different associations with female magazines and bookstore samples. In 2006 Galaxy

linked up with the Richard & Judy Summer Book Club and in 2007 and 2008 Galaxy was the title sponsor of the British Book Awards. The brand has undertaken a multimedia campaign, including TV, press, online and PR, to support this key link with reading.

Brand Values

With a target audience of women between the ages of 25-45, Galaxy stands for 'me time', indulgence, femininity and sensuousness. The Galaxy brand understands the ritualistic nature of chocolate eating, and as a brand aims to provide an entire Galaxy experience, rather than just chocolate.

www.masterfoods.com

Lose yourself in a good book with Galaxy Minstrels.

Things you didn't know about Galaxy®

Galaxy was listed at number 26 in Checkout magazine's annual Top 100 Grocery Brands report for 2007, using data from ACNielsen.

Galaxy chocolate has sales which total those of Ferrero, Green & Black's, and Lindt combined (Source: IRI Infoscan, TNS Worldpanel/Usage Panel).

The average number of Minstrels in a 42g packet is 15.

2003
The Galaxy brand is relaunched.

2004
Galaxy sponsors the film Bridget Jones's Diary and goes on to sponsor The Devil Wears Prada in 2006.

2005
Galaxy's relationship with reading is established and the following year begins its sponsorship of the Richard & Judy Book Club.

2008
Galaxy is the title sponsor for the British Book Awards for the second year running.

Good Housekeeping

Good Housekeeping launched in 1922 and has remained one of the UK's most enduringly successful magazines for 86 years. Good Housekeeping is an international brand with 16 editions around the world including publications in China, Russia, Indonesia, Chile and Central America – selling more than six million copies worldwide every month.

Market

There are more than 3,000 magazines in the UK market, eight of which compete directly with Good Housekeeping.

In 2007 the Women's Interest magazine market was more competitive than ever with increased above-the-line and added value activity, and total sales of 2.3 million copies a month. However, Good Housekeeping has managed to maintain its leadership of this mature market, outselling its competitors with copy sales of more than 460,000 (Source: ABC July-December 2007).

Furthermore, Good Housekeeping boasts the largest subscription base of a magazine in the women's interest market, with 48 per cent of its readers currently subscribing to the title on a monthly basis. Recent orders have seen subscriptions hit 223,288 copies, representing a 6.3 per cent increase year-on-year.

Achievements

In June 2006 Good Housekeeping celebrated its 1,000th issue. Also in 2006, Louise Chunn became editor of the magazine and in 2007 was short-listed for Editor of the Year at the prestigious British Society of Magazine Editors Awards and Periodical Publishers Association Awards.

An ability and willingness to adapt to the needs of its readers has been a major factor in its success. Under Louise's direction, Good Housekeeping has successfully combined a touch of modernity – such as including articles on living with HIV and featuring a male cover star, Jamie Oliver – with the magazine's 86-year heritage of real life content, good health, good food, road-testing the latest products for the home and campaigning on a variety of issues.

In February 2008 Good Housekeeping launched the Get Walking campaign with fitness expert Joanna Hall. The challenge sees 10 volunteers from the UK embark on a 24-week walking programme in a bid to boost their fitness and lose weight, while raising money for a charity of their choice.

The Too Good To Waste campaign launched in October 2007, in response to figures revealing that every year 6.7 tonnes of food purchased is thrown away. The campaign aims to provide advice on waste avoidance shopping, managing leftovers, composting and encouraging readers to lobby local councils for food waste collections.

Product

There is more to Good Housekeeping than just 'good housekeeping'. It aims to be a lively, inspirational and essential part of women's lives in the 21st century. It also aims to be the one magazine readers trust by providing expertise and attention to detail delivered in a positive and accessible way, giving readers access to the 'best of everything'. It is important to Good Housekeeping to give readers a wealth of information and advice,

1922	1924	1994	2000	2006	2008
British Good Housekeeping is launched.	The Good Housekeeping Institute (GHI) is established to provide unbiased advice on the best consumer products available.	Good Housekeeping achieves its highest ever ABC figure – selling 518,435 copies a month (Source: ABC July-December 1994).	The GHI launches an accreditation scheme.	Good Housekeeping celebrates its 1,000th issue in June and Louise Chunn is appointed as editor.	The launch of www.allaboutyou.com takes place.

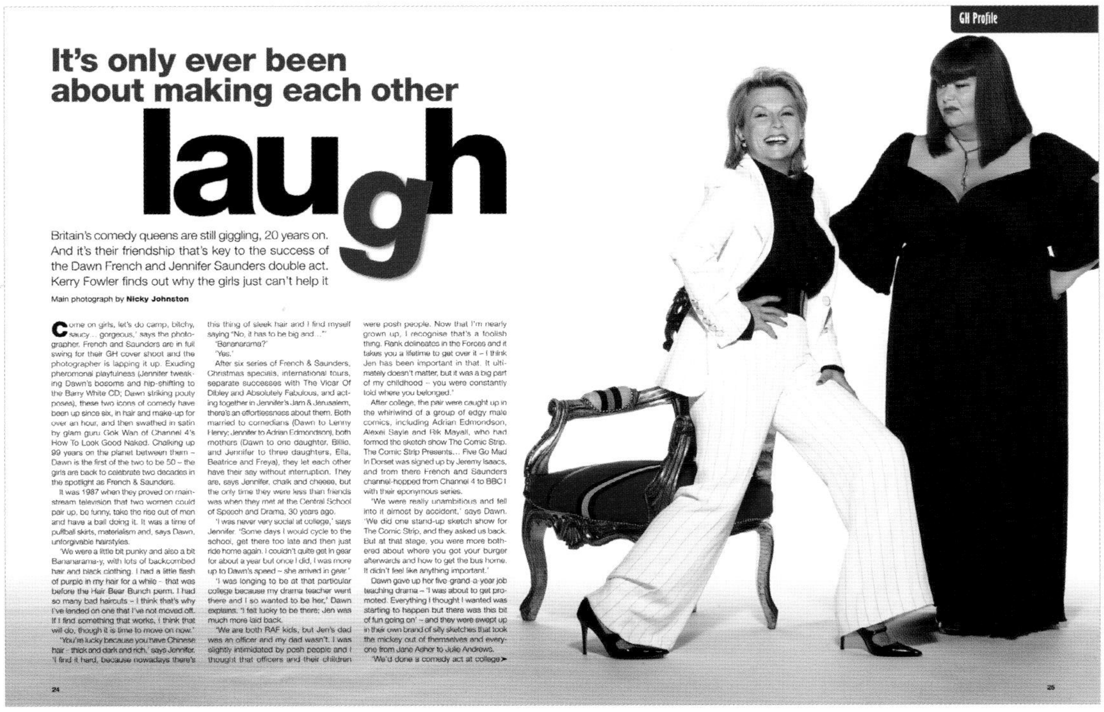
It's only ever been about making each other laugh

Britain's comedy queens are still giggling, 20 years on. And it's their friendship that's key to the success of the Dawn French and Jennifer Saunders double act. Kerry Fowler finds out why the girls just can't help it

Main photograph by Nicky Johnston

GH Profile

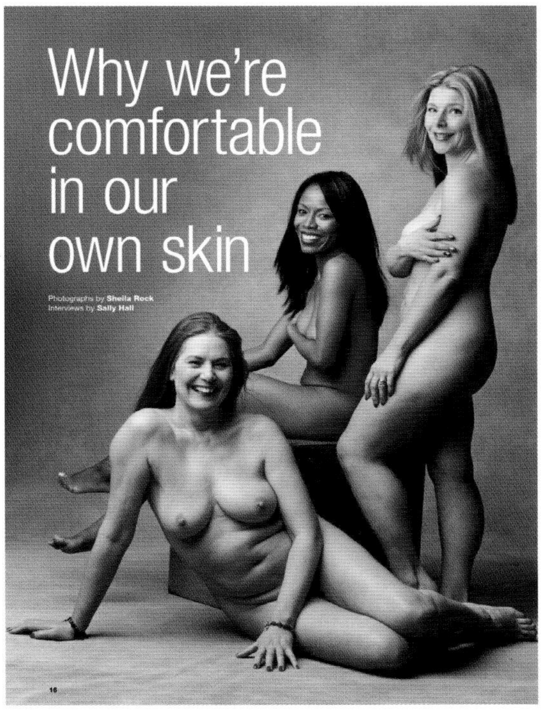
Why we're comfortable in our own skin

keeping them up-to-date and balancing practical solutions with achievable inspiration in a no-nonsense format.

Good Housekeeping is the only women's interest magazine with an independent consumer research centre, the Good Housekeeping Institute (GHI), established in 1924. The GHI was founded to provide readers with unbiased, independent research findings on consumer products.

In 2000, the GHI launched an accreditation scheme which allows manufacturers and retailers of food and non-food products to apply for access to use the GHI Approved logo. This reflects the benchmarks for quality that the GHI has been setting since 1924. Only after a consumer product has passed a series of rigorous Consumer Quality Assessment tests can the GHI Approved logo to be used for marketing, PR and advertising purposes during a 12-month period. The GHI currently has more than 40 accredited products, bringing the trust and authority of the Good Housekeeping brand to a wide-reaching consumer audience beyond the pages of the magazine.

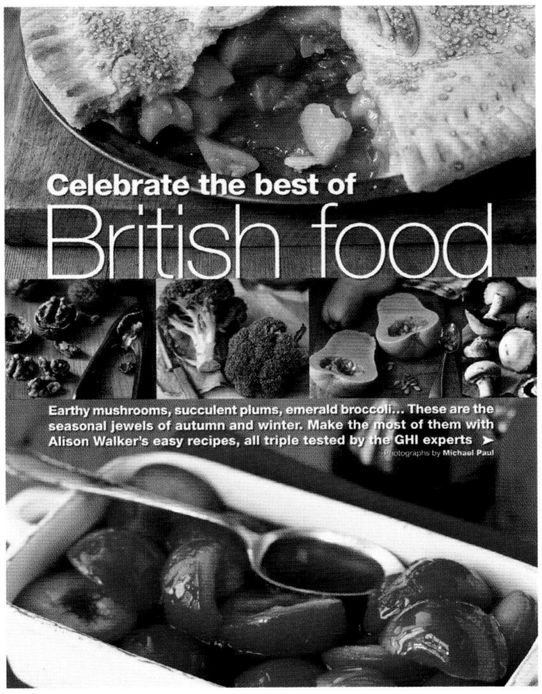
Celebrate the best of British food
Earthy mushrooms, succulent plums, emerald broccoli... These are the seasonal jewels of autumn and winter. Make the most of them with Alison Walker's easy recipes, all triple tested by the GHI experts

Bringing the Good Housekeeping brand to life further, more than 20 reader events are organised annually, ranging from gardening evenings to cookery demonstrations and beauty workshops to fashion shows. More than 10,000 readers have the opportunity to meet the people who work on the magazine and share in their expertise every year.

Recent Developments

In 2003 Good Housekeeping launched its own range of branded products, the Good Housekeeping Essentials range. Established to add value to everyday life, every item is selected for its innovative and user-friendly design and tested and approved by the GHI. To complement the bakeware and utensil ranges already available, a woodware range was launched in June 2005 and a cookware range was launched at the end of the year.

The Good Housekeeping Food Awards were launched in 2004 and are run on an annual basis. Readers are invited to vote for their favourite food, ingredients, restaurants and supermarkets.

A new content rich and community driven website, www.allaboutyou.com, was launched in April 2008. Representing the key editorial pillars of the magazine, the site provides an extensive database of tried and trusted recipes.

Promotion

Core to Good Housekeeping's promotional strategy is to work closely with its editorial teams, to reinforce the brand values and ensure that readers' needs are met, with focus groups and reader panels providing valuable insight into the magazine's readership.

The magazine also endeavours to work closely with third parties to enhance its position both at the newsstand and within the existing subscriber base. Good Housekeeping has seen a steady and consistent subscription growth over the years and in more recent times has tested innovative direct marketing techniques, with significant growth through online channels. Good Housekeeping is also one of the most popular subscription gift pack magazines to be sold through UK retailers such as WHSmith, Tesco, Borders and Waterstone's.

Brand Values

The Good Housekeeping brand is built upon the values of trust, expertise and authority, aiming to be progressive, whilst maintaining its integrity as a consumer champion.

www.allaboutyou.co.uk

Things you didn't know about Good Housekeeping

Good Housekeeping sells one copy of the magazine every six seconds in the UK (Source: ABC July-December 2007).

Good Housekeeping was the first magazine to publish a 'handbag' size. The reduced size was run during the paper shortages of World War II, when the information in Good Housekeeping was deemed by the Government to be vital for the war effort.

Good Housekeeping was the first women's magazine in the UK to interview Hillary Clinton.

Over 45,000 recipes have been developed in the GHI since launch. It would take someone, eating three meals a day, more than 40 years to try all of the recipes.

Cover stars have included Oprah Winfrey, Jane Fonda, Twiggy, Jamie Oliver and, in May 1937, George V.

Highland Spring is the leading UK-produced brand of bottled water. It is also the number one sparkling and number one kids' bottled water brand (Source: Zenith/ACNielsen). It was the first bottled water in the UK to have its catchment area certified organic by the Soil Association and for more than 20 years Highland Spring has been protecting its land in the Ochil Hills, Perthshire – protecting the water, to protect its consumers.

Market

Packaged water is one of the fastest growing and best performing soft drinks categories, growing by 30 per cent in the past five years (Source: Zenith 2008).

Despite a slight volume decline in 2007, largely attributed to the UK's poor summer weather, the bottled water market has never been in better shape. Almost 27 million adults in the UK are now drinking bottled water, an increase of 11 million since 2000. With more people understanding the health benefits associated with good hydration, the market is expected to see further growth in the coming years (Source: TGI Q4 2007).

An additional factor influencing volume sales in 2007 was the trend away from large multi-packs in multiple grocers. Volume sales of small multi-packs increased by 1.6 million litres in 2007 and Highland Spring's 500ml 12-pack was the best performing product in the market (Source: ACNielsen December 2007). Highland Spring was the only top three brand to see growth in 2007, outperforming the market by 4.2 per cent (Source: Zenith Bottled Water Report 2007).

The children's bottled water sector, pioneered by Highland Spring in 2001, is now one of the fastest growing bottled water market sectors today, reaching 13.3 million litres.

Achievements

Despite a market decline of four per cent to 2.185 billion litres, Highland Spring's sales grew by 0.2 per cent in 2007, extending its lead over the third largest brand, Volvic, while edging closer to market leader Evian.

Highland Spring remains the leading UK-produced brand of bottled water, number one in doorstep deliveries and number one in the cash and carry sector. The company produces more than one million bottles of water per day and in 2007 recorded a sales turnover of £51.4 million. In the same year it was also the highest scoring ethical bottled water company, as rated by the Good Shopping Guide (New Edition Six).

The entire water catchment area for Highland Spring, extending to 1,270 hectares, is certified organic by the Soil Association. No farming, agricultural spraying, building or habitation is permitted within the 2,000 acres of protected land from which Highland Spring water is drawn. The land has been kept free from pesticides and pollution for more than 20 years, earning Highland Spring its organic land status, and helping to guarantee the purity of the water.

Product

The company offers a comprehensive portfolio of bottled water products, including bottled water for kids, sports caps and bottles ranging in size from 330ml to 1.5 litres – all available as single bottles or multi-packs, as well as a choice of glass bottles or PET plastic for everyday use.

PET bottles made from 25 per cent recycled material were successfully trialled across

Drawn from protected, organic land. Reassuringly pure.

www.highland-spring.com

1979	1993	1998	2001		
Highland Spring Ltd is formed.	Highland Spring displaces Perrier from the number one slot and wins the contract to supply bottled water to British Airways worldwide.	Highland Spring becomes official water supplier to the World Snooker Association.	Highland Spring becomes the first British brand of bottled water to have its land certified organic by the Soil Association.	Gleneagles Natural Mineral Water is acquired and Watermedia established, creating bespoke promotional bottles.	Also in 2001, the brand continues to innovate, pioneering the children's bottled water market.

12.5 million bottles in 2007 as part of Highland Spring's environmental improvements programme. The aim is to increase usage of recycled PET to 50 million bottles in 2008.

Recent Developments
In 2007, Highland Spring launched a sparkling version of its best selling children's brand, Highland Spring for Kids. The product is the first and only sparkling kids' water; available in 330ml bottles, ideal for lunchboxes and designed to fit children's hands easily.

In 2008, Highland Spring announced a record £30 million investment in its Blackford bottling plant – the biggest single investment in the company to date. The £30 million expansion programme will create some 60 jobs and is expected to double production capacity with three new bottling lines by 2011. Phase one is due to start in late 2008 with the first new bottling line operational by the end of 2009.

As part of its work to lessen environmental impact, Highland Spring is the lead participant in the Carbon Action Plan, an international project developing a carbon labelling standard for the global bottled water industry. The project findings will be used to introduce carbon labelling across the Highland Spring range in 2008.

Promotion
The company's first national TV advertising campaign ran in 2006, highlighting that the water is drawn from organic land. An

association with ITV soon followed, seeing Highland Spring become broadcast sponsor of the British Soap Awards, National TV Awards and British Comedy Awards during the same year. In 2008, the brand will again be seen in press and on television, communicating how its catchment area's organic status ensures that Highland Spring water is as pure as it can possibly be.

The company has a successful marketing partnership with VisitScotland, aimed at London commuters, promoting Scotland as a leisure destination and Highland Spring as the purest, freshest bottled water. The campaign leads with heavyweight advertising in London's underground and overground rail networks, and is supported by experiential marketing and PR.

As advocates of a healthy active lifestyle, the company is committed to forging the link between active sport and good hydration. In 2007, Highland Spring became the exclusive drinks sponsor of Britain's number one professional tennis player, Andy Murray, and his brother Jamie Murray, the 2007 Wimbledon mixed doubles champion. Consolidating its role as a significant supporter of British tennis, Highland Spring announced its sponsorship of the British Davis Cup Team in 2007, and is now the official bottled water supplier to the Lawn Tennis Association.

As well as being a major supporter of Glasgow's successful bid to host the 2014 Commonwealth Games, the brand is also

involved in sport at a grassroots level, and is the official water supplier to many high profile rugby and athletics events throughout the year. The support also extends to golf and snooker including sponsorship of a number of the UK's leading players.

Brand Values
Highland Spring is an iconic Scottish brand. The water is drawn from an underground spring water source in the Ochil Hills in Perthshire, Scotland. As guardian of the land, the company goes to great lengths to protect its source, ensuring the water is as pure as it can be.

Highland Spring is committed to protecting the environment and developing its business in a sustainable, eco-friendly way.

www.highland-spring.com

Things you didn't know about Highland Spring

Highland Spring has been ISO 14001 (Environmental Management) accredited since 2001, and in 2003 became the first – and still the only – UK bottled water producer to receive accreditation from the voluntary Eco-Management and Audit Scheme (EMAS).

Pure water from the Ochil Hills has long been held in high regard. In 1488 King James IV of Scotland ordered his coronation ale to be made from Blackford water.

Rainwater takes as long as 15 years to reach the source of Highland Spring deep below the Ochil Hills, having collected the minerals which give the water its unique mineral analysis.

2004
Highland Spring celebrates its 25th anniversary.

2006
The first national TV advertising campaign is rolled out.

2007
Highland Spring is revealed as the exclusive drinks sponsor to British number one tennis star, Andy Murray and his brother, Wimbledon mixed doubles champion Jamie Murray.

2008
Work begins on a £30 million extension to the plant's bottling facilities.

HOVIS®

Hovis is one of Britain's oldest and best-loved brands and has been baking quality bread since 1886. As a result it is now the brand leader in the brown, bread with bits, half and half and crustless sectors. The Hovis brand is worth more than £380 million and is the fifth largest grocery brand in the UK (Source: Nielsen 2008). Hovis prides itself in baking naturally healthy, tasty bread.

Market

The UK pre-packed bread and bakery market is worth £2.4 billion and growing in value at nine per cent year-on-year (Source: IRI March 2008). Bread takes up the bulk of sales with a value of more than £1.6 billion, while other pre-packed bakery items such as rolls, crumpets and wraps take the remaining share (Source: IRI March 2008).

Although white remains the largest sector within the bread market, growth in recent years has been driven by the 'healthier' sectors such as brown and what is commonly referred to as 'bread with bits', which includes Hovis Granary and Hovis Seed Sensations.

Achievements

Hovis has a rich history that began way back in 1886 with a miller by the name of Richard 'Stoney' Smith. Smith rightly believed that the wheatgerm was the most nutritionally rich part of the grain and should be used in the baking process. Until then it had been discarded by millers as it fermented too quickly. Smith found a way to separate the germ from the flour, lightly cook it and then return it to the flour without loosing any of the nutritional content of the wheatgerm. And so the first product in the Hovis portfolio, Hovis Original Wheatgerm, was born.

Hovis has been communicating the nutritional value of its bread since 1892 when it began placing adverts in leading national magazines and newspapers, talking about the health benefits of wheatgerm. In 1924 scientists discovered yet another nutritional benefit of wheatgerm – the remarkable abundance of vitamin B that is essential for keeping the skin, hair, eyes and the liver healthy. Hovis contained six times as much wheatgerm as normal wholemeal bread and this claim was used to further increase Hovis' popularity at the time. Advertising has been a strong part of Hovis' history and the brand was one of the first to advertise on British television in 1956.

Since the wheatgerm discovery Hovis has continued to lead the way in innovation, continuously searching for new ways to bring health benefits into bread. Hovis invented the 'half and half' sector in 2001 with the launch of Hovis Best of Both, a white loaf with the same amount of wheatgerm as wholemeal; it now has annual sales of £113 million. Innovation continued in 2005 with the launch of Hovis Invisible Crust, the world's first bread baked without a crust.

The most recent addition to the range is Hovis Seed Sensations, launched in August 2007. The range is available in two flavours, Hovis Seed Sensations Rich & Roasted and Hovis Seed Sensations Light & Nutty.

Product

The Hovis range includes a number of healthy options including: Hovis Best of Both, Hovis Original Wheatgerm, Hovis Wholemeal, Hovis Granary and Hovis Seed Sensations, which has been a major success for Hovis, tapping into the growing consumer

1886
Richard 'Stoney' Smith discovers wheatgerm flour.

1890
'Hovis' is registered following a national competition to find a brand name and the first Hovis loaves are baked.

1931
'Tea with Hovis' signs appear throughout Britain.

1936
The 'Had your Hovis Today?' campaign begins.

1942
Hovis donates a Spitfire to the RAF, naming it Hominis Vis.

1956
Hovis television commercials start using the slogan 'Don't say brown, say Hovis'.

Hovis AS GOOD FOR YOU TODAY AS ITS ALWAYS BEEN!

trends of health and premium products and gives Hovis a foothold in the growing seeded sector.

Hovis kept with its reputation for innovation and took the category a step further by using the latest 'enrobing' techniques to ensure that the loaves were completely enveloped in seeds in the baking process. Within its first year of launch Hovis Seed Sensations achieved 19 per cent value share of the seeded sector and sales of more than £20 million annualised.

Recent Developments

May 2008 saw the launch of Hovis' softest ever white bread, Hovis Soft White. Independent research by Link shows the recipe is significantly preferred to competitor offerings. Hovis Soft White was launched with bold new packaging which shows the loaf in the shape of a 'tasty looking sandwich'. A substantial outdoor advertising and sampling campaign supported the launch alongside offers within the national press.

September 2008 will see a major landmark for the Hovis brand. The iconic Hovis 'Little Brown Loaf' made so famous back in the early 1900s returns to the Hovis portfolio. The unsliced loaf has the Hovis logo embossed on both sides as the original did. Supported by a major new television and press advertising campaign it is hoped that the loaf will become a firm favourite amongst consumers once again.

Promotion

Hovis quickly became an established household brand after its launch with support from famous advertising campaigns such as the 1956 'Don't say brown, say Hovis'. All advertising featured the now famous image of the Hovis Little Brown Loaf.

Hovis launched one of the most famous adverts of all time in 1973 – the classic 'Boy on the Bike' directed by Ridley Scott and featuring the unforgettable music from Dvorak Symphony No.9. Scott went on to direct a range of epic blockbusters that included Bladerunner (1982) and Gladiator (2000). The advert showed a young boy being rewarded for a hard day's work with a slice of the Hovis Little Brown Loaf. During its launch year it won five major advertising awards and established itself as one of the best-known commercials of all time.

Famous advertising continued in the 1990s with the Harry Hovis cartoon campaign that complemented the daring Big Food packaging. Featuring beans, tomatoes and cucumbers, the designs aimed at showing Hovis' role in providing 'everyday good food for busy modern families'.

A major new television campaign will be launched in September 2008; the aim of which is to become as memorable and as loved as the 'Boy on the Bike' advert.

Brand Values

Millions of people have grown up with the Hovis brand. Today the legacy of Richard 'Stoney' Smith lives on, with Hovis aiming to put the same passion and innovation into the brand to provide healthy, nutritious bread.

www.hovisbakery.co.uk

Things you didn't know about Hovis

The Hovis founder Richard 'Stoney' Smith died in 1980 and is now buried in Highgate Cemetery. His grave is marked by a special headstone in remembrance of his particular contribution to the British diet.

During World War II, Hovis donated a Spitfire to the RAF. It was named Hominis Vis Latin for 'the strength of man'. In its shortened form this is the brand name, Hovis.

In 2000 Hovis' 'Boy on the Bike' ad was voted as one of the nation's favourite advertisements in a poll carried out by The Sunday Times and Channel 4.

1973

The 'Boy on the Bike' TV commercial (directed by Ridley Scott) is first aired.

1991

Hovis begins baking white bread.

2001

Big Food packaging is launched and Hovis is awarded the IPA Effectiveness Award (Silver) and Brand Design Gold Award for packaging and advertising.

2007

The Hovis Seed Sensations line is launched.

Imperial Leather has been in consumers' bathrooms for generations. Today, while we're still all familiar with the original Imperial Leather bar of soap and its little metallicised label, the brand has grown to the extent that, at any given minute, thousands of people all over the world are using a product from Imperial Leather's extensive washing and bathing range.

Market

Imperial Leather is a key player in the UK's personal washing and bathing market. In 2008, this market was worth an estimated £493 million (Source: Nielsen March 2008), up 1.1per cent on 2007. It is forecast that the total soap, shower and bathing category will continue to grow in real terms over the next five years (Source: Mintel November 2006).

With more than one in five UK homes now having two or more bathrooms (Source: GB TGI BMRB 2006/07) and with UK consumers living busier lives (for example, making more visits to the gym) there has been an increase in shower usage occasions. Imperial Leather, with its extensive portfolio of affordably luxurious, feel good, rich lathering products, is well positioned to continue to tap in to this market.

Achievements

Over the last year, one in three people in the UK have purchased at least one Imperial Leather product (Source: TNS) – the equivalent of 16.4 million people.

In 1998, Imperial Leather launched the innovative 'Foamburst' shower product range. It was the first shower gel in a can that dispenses as a gel and transforms into a mass of rich, creamy, lather. This market-leading development has proved to be hugely popular with men, women and children alike.

Imperial Leather is now the leading washing and bathing brand in many key markets across the globe and can be found in countries including the UK, China, Australia, Nigeria, Greece and Indonesia. Over the last year, Imperial Leather has seen 14 per cent growth year-on-year, aided by 16.9 per cent growth in the shower category, seeing it climb to become the number one shower brand in the UK (Source: Nielsen March 2008).

Product

Imperial Leather's product range includes shower gels, Foamburst shower gels, bath foams, hand washes, deodorants and talcum powder, as well as its famous bars of soap.

1768	1938	1940s	1950s-60s	1970s	1998
Russian nobleman Count Orlof challenges perfumers, Bayleys of Bond Street, to create a perfume which embodies the distinctive aroma of the Russian court.	Imperial Leather is brought to the UK by Cussons, introducing the British public to the 'Eau de cologne Imperiale Russe' fragrance.	Manufacturing operations expand rapidly. Marjorie Cussons, the pioneering daughter of the company's founder, is responsible for energizing public interest in the brand.	Expansion of production continues, with the addition of manufacturing sites in Manchester and Nottingham.	Shower Gel is introduced to the product range.	The innovative Foamburst shower gel range is launched, packaged in a rust-free can rather than a bottle.

The range is aimed at the whole family, with products designed to give a trusted, feel good, luxurious washing and bathing experience at an affordable price.

Recent Developments

In 2008 Imperial Leather relaunched its entire range with a contemporary, emotive, disruptive design and livery, further embracing its family orientated positioning.

2008 also saw the launch of Skin Bliss, an ultra mild moisturising shower lotion, targeted specifically at young women looking for an indulgent shower experience offering significantly softer, smoother skin in comparison to the leading shower gel (Source: Skin Investigation Technology December 2007).

This followed on from the successful launch of the brand's Limited Edition range of shower gels and bath foams in 2006 and the release of additional limited editions in 2007, which saw Thai Fusion and Tahitian Retreat bring a tropical flavour to the range. The Limited Edition series will continue in 2008 with the introduction of Hawaiian Spa and Icelandic Spa variants.

Promotion

Imperial Leather was one of the first brands in washing and bathing to recognise the potential and power of advertising.

By 1946, Cussons was spending £100,000 supporting the brand – an enormous sum at the time. Predominantly choosing to advertise in the popular women's magazines of the day, Imperial Leather's advertising campaigns used a series of specially commissioned paintings featuring orchids, tropical fish, miniature gardens and roses. Furthermore, Marjorie Cussons, the marketing-minded daughter of the company's founder, introduced gift sets at key purchasing periods.

During the 1950s, cinema's popularity led Cussons to place commercials on the big screen, in advance of the featured presentation, to convey the brand's everyday luxury credentials.

The brand was also one of the first committed to TV advertising. Imperial Leather's first TV commercial aired in 1959 and featured a mother and daughter using Imperial Leather, creating the link between high quality soap and soft clean skin. It is this investment by Imperial Leather and other similar brands that led to the coining of the phrase 'Soaps' in relation to advertiser-funded TV drama.

The famous Imperial Leather 'Family' campaign was launched in the 1970s, and even today triggers fond memories of the brand amongst the British public. Whether travelling across the Russian Steppes in the Imperial Train, or flying high in their Imperial Leather Spaceship, the family always found time to enjoy a luxurious soak in their decadent mobile bathroom.

More recently, the 'Dancing Duck' commercial for Foamburst shower gel and a series of female fantasy based commercials including footballer Paolo Di Canio and separately, a crew of stripping fire-fighters have resulted in the brand, once again, becoming renowned for its advertising.

The brand's latest campaign celebrates 'the hug', showing people from all walks of life 'getting closer to the ones they love'. The campaign also gives consumers the opportunity to send a personalised e-hug via the internet, with more than a quarter of a million people using the service at Imperial Leather's huggableskin.co.uk website during the campaign launch.

Brand Values

Imperial Leather is a leading quality washing and bathing brand aimed at families. The brand understands the importance of the family bond and believes in developing quality products for everyone at an affordable price.

www.imperialleather.co.uk

Things you didn't know about Imperial Leather

Contrary to many people's belief, the metallicised label featuring the Cussons Imperial Leather logo on each soap bar should face downwards not upwards, to prevent the bar from becoming sodden and waterlogged in the soap dish.

The shape of the Imperial Leather bar has not changed since its inception. Its unique shape was developed to mirror that of saddle soap used by the Russian Imperial household to clean its riding tack.

2000s	**2002**	**2007**	**2008**
Imperial Leather collaborates with The Tussauds Group, sponsoring 'Bubbleworks' at Chessington World of Adventures and 'The Flume' at Alton Towers.	Imperial Leather is a main sponsor of the Manchester Commonwealth Games.	Imperial Leather becomes a major corporate fundraiser for the NCH children's charity.	Manufacturing moves to a new, multi-million pound facility in Agecroft, with significant improvements in efficiency of production and enhanced benefits for the environment.

KicKers®

From its introduction to the UK in the 1970s, Kickers has had an on-going relationship with many of the most vital movements in British youth culture. Originally created in France at the end of the 1960s, Kickers became synonymous with the forward thinking rebels at the epi-centre of the Paris student riots – delighted to have a bold, bright, new kind of footwear.

Market

Kickers operates within the extremely competitive UK footwear market which has a total value of £5.4 billion (Source: TNS Fashion Trak December 2007), split between branded footwear which equates to £2.32 billion and the £3.061 billion own label sector (Source: TNS Fashion Trak December 2007) .

Kickers distribution is split across the channels of multiples, independents, mail order and sports good retail; the brand has more than 400 accounts in the UK and Ireland.

Achievements

As part of the Pentland Group, Kickers strives to approach all aspects of its operations with care and consideration for people and the environment. Kickers is working with its suppliers to ensure the provision of fair wages and working hours, safe and hygienic working conditions, regular employment without discrimination or harsh, inhumane treatment of employees. The Pentland Group has initiated and supported projects to improve the lives of workers in India, Pakistan, Portugal, China and Vietnam. Pentland is a member of the Ethical Trading

Initiative, an alliance of UK-based companies, non-governmental organisations and trade union organisations that promotes and improves the implementation of codes of practice for supply chain working conditions. As a signatory to the United Nations Global Compact, Pentland is also committed to aligning its operations and strategies with 10 universally accepted principles in the areas of human rights, labour, the environment and anti-corruption.

Kickers is committed to progressively reducing the impact that its business has on the natural environment. Its current focus is on making improvements at every stage of the product life cycle and environmental site management at its headquarters in London.

Product

Kickers has a strong sense of heritage which encompasses design and craftsmanship as well as impressive connections with many cutting-edge youth cultures which have surfaced over the past four decades. Of paramount importance to Kickers is a belief in continually pushing this instantly recognisable brand into fresh, new design realms whilst celebrating and building on its heritage.

The Kickers brand has grown from the initial introduction of the Kick Hi boot to the UK in the 1970s, becoming renowned for moccasins in the mid 1990s as well as being a pioneer in the development of the sports casual hybrid shoe that ushered in the noughties. The Kickers range now encompasses men's, women's and kids'

1960s

The Kickers brand is launched in France by Daniel Raufast.

1970s

Kickers is introduced to the UK and Kick Hi boots are seen on the feet of rock royalty such as The Who's Roger Daltrey, Elton John and David Bowie.

1980s

The Football Casuals subculture sees Kickers being worn with Lois cords snipped at the seams, accompanying the pastel shades of Euro sportswear.

At the end of the decade, Kickers are adopted by the Rave Generation.

1990s

The Madchester scene picks up on the boots and they are immortalised on the sleeve artwork of The Farm's 12-inch Stepping Stone/Family of Man.

In the mid 1990s, the Kick Hi boot is adopted by the Brit Pop movement with high profile music mavericks including Jarvis Cocker and Noel Gallagher seen wearing the boots.

footwear. Building on the brand's strong roots in casual footwear, the number of styles available has grown to include trainers, formal shoes, boots and sandals as well as the Kick Hi in a rainbow of colours.

Recent Developments

Kickers has kept its eye on youth culture with the X Project in 2007. Some of the most inspiring, independent UK fashion talents – working in the territories of fashion and jewellery design, styling and illustration – were invited to join forces with Kickers and create their own unique interpretation of the classic Kick Hi boot. Those taking part included Siv Stoldal, Peter Jensen, Griffin, Henry Holland, Charlotte Mann, Husam El Odeh and Simon Foxton, as well as NOKI whose shoe upper was made from recycled leather jackets. The resulting limited edition boots went on sale in autumn 2007, both online and in selected stores.

In 2008, Kickers will focus on collaborations with key musicians and fashion designers who will be asked to represent key movements and periods from the brand's life, connecting with some of the music with which it has been associated over the years.

Promotion

Kickers' 2008 ad campaign, Meet the Kickers, aims to break the advertising stereotype in the footwear sector and build upon the 'feel good' essence of the brand. The campaign brings classics and new styles of footwear to life through the creation of a series of paper-legged characters, which reflect the personality of the individual shoes as well as the Kickers brand.

Beginning with a print campaign in the UK men's lifestyle and music press, as it progresses the emphasis shifts to digital and experience based tactics to engage and entertain the consumer. These activities – based around summer festivals and university campuses as well as online activity through the Kickers

website, blogs and social networking sites such as Facebook – will mirror Kickers' values in their content: fun, light-hearted, irreverent and cheeky. The aim is to leave the consumer with a memorable impression of the brand and prompt a response to encourage a lasting relationship.

Brand Values

For nearly 40 years, Kickers has been immersed in British youth culture, embraced by a diverse range of subcultures. Its iconic status has been built squarely on product innovation. Its distinctive attitude has been defined as being witty, cheeky, unpretentious and always confident.

This is the brand's 'feel good' attitude.

www.kickers.co.uk

Things you didn't know about Kickers

In the late 1960s, having seen the poster for the musical Hair, with kids wearing brightly coloured clothes, denim jeans and no shoes, Daniel Raufast decided he wanted to design and create a pair of shoes that went with denim. He did just that and Kickers was born.

The classic Kickers shoes originally carried a red tab on the left shoe and a green tab on the right shoe, to signify port and starboard navigation lights.

Since the introduction of the Kick Hi boot to the UK, it has sold more than 10 million pairs.

There are more than 60 separate components within the average pair of Kickers shoes.

2000s

The Kick Hi boot is adopted by the UK garage scene; boots are worn by artists such as Ms Dynamite, So Solid Crew and Rodney P.

In addition to this, Kickers are also worn by indie guitar groups such as the Kaiser Chiefs, The Enemy and Arctic Monkeys.

2007

The X Project sees some of the most inspiring, independent UK fashion talent design their own versions of the Kick Hi boot.

2008

Kickers again invites X Project collaborators to come up with their own interpretation of the classic boot. This time designs come from key musicians and fashion designers.

Since its launch in 1937, KIT KAT® has retained its position as the UK's best selling chocolate biscuit bar (Source: ACNielsen). As a key player in the confectionery market, the brand's success is rooted in delivering quality, as well as an ongoing understanding of consumer trends. Both have contributed to shaping its profitable past and with more than one billion KIT KAT® products eaten each year in the UK, a successful future.

Market

The UK confectionery market has experienced considerable growth over the past 20 years and is now worth an estimated £4.5 billion (Source: ACNielsen), equivalent to the combined value of the crisps & snacks, soft drinks and biscuits categories. While the healthy-eating debate has impacted on these rival sectors, the confectionery market has remained solid, continuing to be viewed as an affordable indulgence.

For some time now new product development (NPD) has been firmly centred on brand extension, a successful strategy with consumers who, research suggests, exercise strong brand loyalty. Between 2005 and 2007 the UK confectionery market experienced a growth of four per cent; during the same period KIT KAT® grew at more than twice this rate (Source: ACNielsen), making it the 30th largest grocery brand in the UK with consumer value sales in excess of £150 million (Source: ACNielsen Top 100 Grocery Brand reports).

Achievements

For more than 70 years KIT KAT® has been a firm favourite amongst consumers, ranking today as the UK's best selling biscuit brand (Source: ACNielsen March 2008). The growth of its classic Four Finger product (number three in the UK's top selling chocolate confectionery brands) has out-performed the number one brand in terms of percentage growth (Source: ACNielsen), while KIT KAT® CHUNKY, launched in 1999, has been pivotal in leading the way in brand extensions – rating as the most successful NPD confectionery launch over the last 25 years.

When it comes to changing consumer trends KIT KAT® has proved adaptable. The growth in consumer demand for dark chocolate prompted the launch of the KIT KAT® Four Finger Dark in June 2006, chosen by 12,000 consumers as the UK's most popular new chocolate bar when it was crowned chocolate confectionery Product of the Year in 2007.

Product

Since the 1930s KIT KAT® has been manufactured in York, a tradition that continues to this day. Contrary to its outward appearance of simplicity, KIT KAT® is complex to produce: layers of wafer and praline are coated in milk chocolate before finally being moulded into the brand's signature 'finger' shape.

Since its launch, KIT KAT® has been synonymous with 'breaks', driven not only

1935	1945	1957	1999	2008
Rowntree's Chocolate Crisp launches, changing its name to KIT KAT® Chocolate Crisp in 1937.	Now known simply as KIT KAT®, a dark chocolate recipe is adopted (until 1947) due to a post-war milk shortage; the wrapper also changes to blue.	KIT KAT® makes its first appearance on television.	KIT KAT® CHUNKY is launched.	KIT KAT® SENSES™ is launched.

Have a break. Have a Kit Kat

by the brand's advertising, but also by its intrinsic product attributes; four individual chocolate covered fingers that can be eaten separately – extending the time it takes to eat and, therefore, the length of the consumer's break-time. In 2006, the brand upgraded its packaging on the Four Finger variant to a new foil fresh wrapper, enhancing the product with improved freshness and crispness.

The diverse portfolio of KIT KAT® caters for a range of consumer needs, from the KIT KAT® Two Finger biscuit, a firm family favourite, to KIT KAT® CHUNKY, primarily designed for men on the go. Some of its most recent brand extensions include KIT KAT® Four Finger Dark, KIT KAT® SENSES™ and KIT KAT® CHUNKY Peanut Butter. The brand continues to extend its product offering through flavour variants such as the KIT KAT® Two Finger Cappuccino, aimed at complementing the existing range of milk chocolate, orange, mint and dark chocolate flavours.

Recent Developments
The 2008 launch of KIT KAT® SENSES™ marks the culmination of two years' research and brand development for KIT KAT®. Its aim:

to be a perfectly indulgent break-time snack for women, with each bar containing only 165 calories.

To support the SENSES™ launch, KIT KAT® has invested £9 million into a fully integrated marketing campaign, fronted by Girls Aloud – chosen to epitomise the modern busy lives many women lead and thereby the need for the simple pleasure afforded by an occasional indulgent break.

Promotion
The marketing of KIT KAT® has always been simple and consistent, carving a name for itself over the past 71 years with its memorable strapline: 'Have a Break. Have a KIT KAT®'. The notion of a 'break' has appeared in KIT KAT® advertising since 1939, however its strapline was only introduced in 1959, remaining an essential element of the brand communication ever since.

During the 1940s, KIT KAT® advertising focused on its nutritional benefits and role as a wartime staple. The brand has a history of topical advertising, with seasonal activities often featuring in its campaigns. Its first television commercial aired in 1957, increasing sales by 22 per cent and proving

television to be a powerful new medium for the brand's promotional strategy; its first colour commercial appeared in 1969. Throughout its history KIT KAT® has rolled out a variety of successful advertising campaigns; two of the most popular have been the Panda television commercial from the 1980s and its recent Foil Fresh campaign featuring renowned golfer Colin Montgomerie.

Brand Values
KIT KAT® is a well loved British institution. Since its inception, brand values have centred on quality and simplicity. KIT KAT® champions the 'break', an ethos which has always been, and will continue to be, at the heart of the brand. Over the years KIT KAT® has developed a witty and humorous brand personality, engaging with consumers through its distinctly British sense of humour.

www.kitkat.co.uk

Things you didn't know about KIT KAT®

Thirty-three KIT KAT® products are eaten every second in the UK.

The name KIT KAT® comes from a famous 18th century London Whig literary club called the Kit-Cat Club, which met at the house of Christopher Catling, a well-known pastry cook.

The total weight of all the KIT KAT® products produced each year in the UK is equivalent to 6,000 Indian elephants.

Stacking up a day's production of KIT KAT® products would reach the height of 360 York Minsters.

The LEGO Group was founded in 1932 and today is one of the world's largest toy manufacturers. In 2008 it celebrates the 50th anniversary of the LEGO® brick and the 30th anniversary of the minifigure. The purpose and vision of the LEGO Group is to inspire children to explore and challenge their own creative potential. LEGO products have undergone extensive development over the decades, but the foundation remains the traditional LEGO brick.

Market

Today the LEGO Group is the world's fifth largest toy manufacturer. In 2007 LEGO® UK achieved an unprecedented 24 per cent increase in consumer sales and the largest year-on-year sales growth out of all the top 10 toy manufacturers, despite the economic downturn towards the end of the year (Source: NPD EPOS).

Globally, LEGO pre-tax profit reached £139 million against £126 million in 2006 (conversion from DKK to GBP at exchange rate at year-end 2007).

The LEGO Group has achieved its success by offering a range of quality toys centred around its building systems which has stood the test of time, growing significantly despite the technology boom. LEGO toys inspire fun, creative, engaging and challenging play for children which in turn develops inventive and structured problem solving, curiosity and imagination, interpersonal skills and physical motor skills.

Achievements

With seven LEGO® sets sold each second, it's little surprise that the world's children spend five billion hours a year playing with LEGO toys. Incredibly, over the past 50 years enough LEGO bricks have been manufactured to give each of the world's six billion inhabitants 62 LEGO bricks each.

In recognition of this achievement and its longevity, in 2000 the LEGO brick was awarded double honours – named Toy of the Century by both US Fortune Magazine and the British Association of Toy Retailers.

The LEGO Group has also been awarded the title of the World's Most Respected Company by the Reputation Institute's annual report, which surveyed more than 60,000 consumers in 29 countries.

The LEGO Group is headquartered in Billund, Denmark but has subsidiaries and branches throughout the world and a global workforce of 4,500 people. LEGO products are sold in more than 130 countries.

Product

LEGO® toys are developed and marketed to suit all ages and stages of development from toddlers, schoolchildren and teenagers to young-at-heart adults.

The LEGO Group's core creative team of 120 designers, representing 15 different nationalities, work constantly to develop innovative products that promote creativity and play.

Pre-school products, including LEGO DUPLO, cater for the youngest children, encouraging them through creative play to use their hands and develop their motor skills.

Creative Building sets or buckets contain traditional LEGO bricks and special parts such as windows, wheels, roof tiles and other items made for builders who like to apply their imagination and think creatively.

Play Themes are sets which build up around a story, such as a fire station, the police or a castle. Children can experience enjoyment through the build as well as many hours of play with the finished models. New

1932	**1958**	**1977**	**1978**	**1986**	**1989**
The LEGO Group is founded in Denmark by carpenter and wooden toy maker, Ole Kirk Kristiansen.	The LEGO brick in its present form is launched. The interlocking principle with its tubes makes it unique and offers unlimited building possibilities.	The LEGO TECHNIC brand is introduced, including parts such as gears, beams and gearboxes.	The LEGO minifigure is born. Originally yellow in colour, the figures are generic to capture children's imagination and each minifigure is designed with moveable arms and legs.	The LEGO TECHNIC Computer Control is launched, later paving the way for the first computer-controlled LEGO robots.	The facial expressions on minifigures change, so they can either be 'good' or 'bad'.

themes for 2008 include LEGO CITY Coast Guard and LEGO Agents. Embracing fantasy, BIONICLE continues to grow with the Mistika and Vehicles ranges, and LEGO Technic is brought to life with power functions.

The more advanced software based LEGO MINDSTORMS NXT enables the user to design and build real robots which can be programmed to perform different operations, reacting to the user's voice or controlled via a mobile phone.

The LEGO Factory website gives children the opportunity to build their own virtual models on a computer using LEGO Digital Designer and to have the bricks to build the physical LEGO model sent by post.

Recent Developments

In 2008, the LEGO Group celebrates the 50th anniversary of the LEGO® brick and the 30th anniversary of the minifigure.

Key product developments for the year include a new LEGO Indiana Jones™ range, with play sets representing the most iconic scenes from each of the four movies. Building on the phenomenal success of LEGO Star Wars™, new Clone Wars sets and characters support the new 3D CGI TV series. Another new product bringing a movie to life is LEGO Speed Racer which is based on the futuristic world of Grand Prix jet-powered racing.

Promotion

One of the priorities of the LEGO Group is to have close contact with its consumers throughout the world and it engages in many initiatives to strengthen ties between LEGO® enthusiasts and the company.

In 2008, the LEGO Group is holding a global building competition to find the world's biggest LEGO fan; the competition is open to 6-9 year-olds from 39 countries around the world.

In the UK, the LEGO Group supports the National Autistic Society (NAS). Fundraising activities include a Guinness World Record attempt to build more than 45,000 minifigures in one day, creating an army of Clone Troopers.

The LEGO Club for children in the 6-12 age group has a membership of 2.4 million worldwide, including the US, Canada, Germany, Switzerland and the Netherlands. Through the LEGO Club website, members can share pictures of their favourite building work and draw inspiration for future play. In the UK, 250,000 LEGO Club members receive the LEGO Club magazine five times per year.

In 2007 the main LEGO website had an average of 11,662,740 individual visitors a month – up 43 per cent on 2006 – with each spending an average of 14 minutes at the site.

In addition to these activities, the LEGO Group uses a mix of TV advertising, PR, sponsorship, in-store demonstrators and targeted shows and events to support its brand image and products.

Brand Values

The founder's grandson, Kjeld Kirk Kristiansen, owns the LEGO Group, and has been true to his grandfather's core values while pushing the company forward to achieve worldwide success.

The LEGO® brand is a guarantee of quality and originality and it strives to be the best and most credible company in the toy business.

Children are the basis of the LEGO Group – inquisitive, creative and imaginative – with an innate urge to learn.

It is the LEGO philosophy that 'good play' enriches a child's life – and its subsequent adulthood. With this in mind, the LEGO Group's wide range of products is founded on the same basic philosophy of learning and developing – through play.

www.lego.com

Things you didn't know about LEGO®

The name 'LEGO' is an abbreviation of two Danish words, 'leg godt', meaning 'play well' and also means 'I put together' in Latin.

More than 400 million children and adults will play with LEGO bricks this year.

If you built a column of 40 billion LEGO bricks, it would reach the moon.

There are 915,103,765 different ways of combining six eight-stud bricks of the same colour.

LEGO, the LEGO logo, DUPLO, BIONICLE, MINDSTORMS and the Brick configuration are trademarks of the LEGO Group. ©2008 The LEGO Group. © 2008 Lucasfilm Ltd & TM. All rights reserved. SPEED RACER MOVIE: © Warner Bros. Entertainment Inc. SPEED RACER: TM/MC Speed Racer Enterprises, Inc. (s08)

1998
Software is incorporated into LEGO products, to produce LEGO MINDSTORMS, allowing LEGO robots to be programmed to perform many different operations.

2001
The BIONICLE universe is introduced, marking the first time the LEGO Group develops a complete story from scratch as the basis for a new product range.

2006
LEGO MINDSTORMS NXT is launched – in just half an hour consumers can build and programme a robot that can see, hear, feel, speak and move.

2008
The LEGO brick celebrates its 50th anniversary and the iconic LEGO minifigure celebrates its 30th birthday.

Since production of its signature airy bubbles first began more than 70 years ago, Maltesers has established itself as a firm national favourite with many brand extensions now added to the range. Amongst a nation of chocolate lovers it continues to trade on its unrivalled reputation as 'the lighter way to enjoy chocolate'.

In total consumers spend around £150 million a year on the Maltesers brand.

As part of Mars Snackfood UK, the brand is ultimately part of Mars Incorporated, which employs 39,000 people in more than 65 countries. Its products are now consumed in more than 100 countries, with global annual sales topping US$18 billion, reflecting a growth of 8.5 per cent year-on-year.

Product

Milk chocolate Maltesers come in three main formats – single, box and pouch. The pouch was launched in 2005, in direct response to the growing trend for sharing that continues to drive the bitesize market. All of the products contain the characteristic bubbly centre made famous by the brand and, in line with the strong brand tradition, are still made in the same factory in Slough as they always have been.

The brand also offers a wide range of products to meet the growing diversity of consumer needs; funsize packs, multi-packs and a seasonal selection that includes Easter eggs, stocking fillers, advent calendars and, new for 2008, a box designed especially for

Market

The UK confectionery market is valued at £4.7 billion (Source: IRI Infoscan December 2007) and is currently experiencing a significant period of growth – up 5.2 per cent year-on-year. Within this market the bitesize category is now worth around £464 million and is demonstrating a faster rate of growth than the sector as a whole, currently up 13 per cent year-on-year. Within the lucrative bitesize category Maltesers, which sits alongside brands such as Revels, M&M'S and Aero Bubbles, is valued at £100 million, accounting for over 20 per cent of the market share. The brand is also a major player in the boxed category of the confectionery market, currently worth £700 million (up two per cent year-on-year) of which it accounts for £32 million.

Achievements

After more than 70 years Maltesers is still achieving strong growth and penetration across the UK confectionery market. Despite increased competition within the lighter chocolate category the brand has retained its leading position as the UK's bestselling product across a range of sectors: bitesize, single, pouch and the informal box treat.

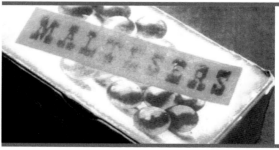

1936

Maltesers are first made in the UK.

1943

The product is temporarily discontinued due to the war and production isn't resumed until 1951.

1959

The first TV advertisement for Maltesers hits the screen, in black and white, advertising 'chocolates with a less fattening centre'.

1985

The larger Maltesers gift box is introduced for the first time.

Christmas. Other product extensions include White Maltesers, Maltesers ice cream, Maltesers hot chocolate and Maltesers frothy cold milk drink.

Recent Developments

Maltesers has always had a strong association with film; many people are familiar with the sound of Maltesers rolling around in the box at the cinema. To build upon this the brand recently launched the Pouch Collector promotion, in collaboration with fellow Mars brands Revels, Minstrels and M&M'S, that enables customers to collect tokens for free cinema tickets.

Summer 2008 sees Maltesers capitalise on its film heritage further with the sponsorship of the new blockbuster film Mamma Mia. The tie-in sees thousands of prize-winning promotional packs in-store and a new television advert from the 'Naughty' campaign showing high-spirited holiday jinx.

Promotion

In terms of product promotion, Maltesers and lightness have always gone hand-in-hand. Since the brand's first television advertisements in the 1960s the product has been used to demonstrate lightness, either in a literal way by playing, rolling or floating real Maltesers across the screen, or in a metaphorical sense through adopting a light-hearted tone of voice.

However, recent years have seen other brands trying to encroach on the lightness territory that has long been associated with Maltesers. This increase in competition has come, not only from the chocolate and confectionery sector but also from other leading categories such as light snacks and cereal bars. In response, Maltesers has given its long-standing 'lightness' positioning a new, updated edge.

Equipped with the fact that Maltesers have less than 190 calories per 37g bag, the brand's ongoing Naughty campaign delivers its message with sharp, contemporary humour, updating the playful brand personality for a modern, savvy and predominantly female audience. This simple strategy offers a modern slant on the lightness positioning of the brand and drives its creative message: 'Maltesers are so light, you'll need new ways to be naughty'.

The new campaign lent itself well to the concept of ITV's popular lunchtime show Loose Women and so the brand became its leading sponsor. The development of some Naughty idents – for example showing a mum brightening up her daily routine by shaking up her husband's can of drink before giving it to him – aims to provide a light-hearted distraction to busy women in the middle of their day, while targeting Maltesers' main audience.

Brand Values

Maltesers has always been associated with a light, playful treat and at its heart is about light-hearted fun and spontaneous, shared moments. The Maltesers target audience is 25-45 year-old women who love the idea of a little treat, whenever the mood takes them – real women who live in the real world. A 'Maltesers girl' should enjoy the little pleasures in life; like the product, she's described as warm and bubbly with a playful sense of humour.

www.maltesers.co.uk

Things you didn't know about Maltesers

It was back in 1936 that Forrest E Mars first came up with the concept of the light and airy bubbles known to this day as Maltesers.

In 2007 more than 10 billion Malteser balls were made in Slough – enough to go around the world over 3.7 times.

A number of top celebrity chefs have admitted to having their own favourite Maltesers recipe.

There are lots of theories as to how the perfect roundness of Maltesers is created, but to date it remains a closely guarded trade secret.

On average, two individual bags of Maltesers are sold every second in the UK.

1993
The brand's renowned ballerina advertisement – 'Chocolate before the performance? No Maltesers' – is launched.

2002
Maltesers ice cream launches with White Maltesers launching the following year.

2006
The 'Naughty' 190 calories campaign is launched.

2007
Maltesers sees its highest rate of sale in over two years, and sponsorship of the daytime television programme, Loose Women, begins.

It's all good.

McCain is Britain's largest chip manufacturer; a family company dedicated to making good food and maintaining high standards. The 'It's all good' philosophy reflects its commitment to using simple, real, natural ingredients across the McCain product portfolio, from classic chips to wedges, roast and gourmet potatoes.

Market

In 2007 the UK potato market was worth £496 million (Source: IRI). Furthermore, in 2007, 241 million packs of chips were sold, with revenues of £327 million, of which McCain's share was 60 per cent. In the potato speciality sector, 143 million packs were sold in 2007, producing revenues of £169 million, of which McCain's share was 30 per cent.

Achievements

2007 was an award-winning year for McCain. Potato Gourmet Mature Cheddar & Wholegrain Mustard Gratin topped the savoury frozen food category at The Grocer's Branded Excellence Awards. Celebrating the best brands in UK grocery today, the awards evaluate products on taste, texture, appearance, packaging, value for money and clarity of labelling.

With three per cent fat, cholesterol free and retaining maximum taste and nutrients by keeping the potato skins on, McCain Rustic Oven Chips became the first chips to be scored 'green' across the board, as measured by the Food Standards Agency (FSA) traffic light labelling system. In January 2008, the chips were voted 'Product of the

Year' in the Home Cooking category in a TNS survey of more than 12,000 consumers.

The 'It's all good' campaign was short-listed for 'Campaign of the Year' at the Marketing Effectiveness Awards, while the TV campaign was also short-listed at the GRAMIA Awards (Grocery Advertising & Marketing Industry Awards).

In 2007 McCain also took steps in a drive to lower its carbon footprint and move operations towards a sustainable future. In October, three 125 metre high wind turbines were installed at the Whittlesey plant – the largest chip factory in the UK – cutting electricity usage by up to 60 per cent; McCain is the first major UK food manufacturer to power a facility of this size using alternative energy.

Product

From classic chips to potato specialities, the brand's product portfolio is built on quality, simplicity and versatility; McCain Crispy Bites, Crispy Slices, Sea Salt & Black Pepper Wedges, Lightly Spiced Wedges and Rosti have all been recommended by Delia

Smith as key ingredients for quick and easy meals (Delia's How to Cheat at Cooking, Edbury Press 2008).

McCain Oven Chips, the brand's hero product, contain five per cent fat and are cholesterol free; simply peeled, washed, chopped and cooked, the preparation process mirrors that of making chips in the home, using just two ingredients, potatoes and sunflower oil.

McCain Beer Battered Ridge Cut Chips make an innovative addition to the frozen chip market, designed to recreate 'pub food' in the home, while McCain Potato Wedges

1957

McCain Foods is established in Florenceville, Canada.

1968

McCain Foods establishes its first UK factory in Scarborough, North Yorkshire – primarily producing frozen chips for the catering market.

1976

A second UK plant is constructed in Whittlesey, Cambridgeshire.

1979

McCain's revolutionary Oven Chips are launched, marking the first of many innovative product developments.

2008

McCain employs approximately 1,800 people in Britain, operating five plants in Scarborough, Whittlesey, Wombourne, Grantham and Hull.

Internationally, McCain employs over 20,000 people and operates more than 55 production facilities across six continents.

Superbrands

offer an alternative accompaniment – a Seasonal Edition is introduced every six months, such as Summer Wedges with a hint of Pesto.

These new additions reflect the key role of product development in the brand's portfolio. In 2007 further launches included Roast Potatoes basted in Goose Fat – the first frozen goose fat roast potato on the market – as well as the launch of the McCain Potato Gourmet range. Products in this range are fully prepared accompaniments, such as Mature Cheddar & Wholegrain Mustard Gratin and Diced Potatoes with Leeks, Onions & Parmesan, offering convenience without compromising on quality or flavour.

In 2007 McCain also conducted an extensive benchmarking survey, which involved a blind taste test with over 400 consumers. The results conclusively voted McCain Home Fries as the best tasting chips, creating an opportunity to reposition and repackage the Home Fries range to reinforce the product quality and communicate the taste appeal to consumers. This is reflected in the strapline 'Chips as chips should be'.

Recent Developments

'It's all good', launched in September 2006, marked a significant marketing and advertising initiative for McCain. The aim was to turn around the business, its corporate culture as well as the public's perception of McCain products. 'It's all good' also seeks to build the brand as being of good quality and a natural healthier option, reminding the consumer that while chips are often vilified by the press, chefs and parents, McCain Oven Chips are made with just two ingredients, potatoes and sunflower oil.

As part of the 'It's all good' ethos, McCain now prepares all its chips in sunflower oil. McCain was one of the first food manufacturers to use both traffic light labelling, as defined by the FSA, and Guideline Daily Amount (GDA) on-pack, receiving industry recognition for its progressive approach to labelling.

In 2007 McCain became the largest frozen food manufacturer to join the Red Tractor Scheme. McCain Oven Chips now carry the Red Tractor logo on-pack, highlighting that the potatoes used are farmed and packed in

the UK to strict standards of food safety and hygiene.

As part of the scheme, McCain has committed to sourcing 100 per cent British potatoes for all its chips, grown by 300 farmers from across Britain, some of whom the company has worked with for three generations.

Promotion

As part of a £20 million advertising and marketing spend for 'It's all good', a TV and radio campaign was created to celebrate 'chips, glorious chips' and their virtues based on the classic musical song 'Food Glorious Food'. So far there have been three TV adverts in this series: 'Sunflower Park' for McCain Oven Chips, 'Chip Factory' for McCain Home Fries (both in 2006) and 'Roof Tops' for the McCain Home Fries reposition in February 2008.

In response to research by the British Heart Foundation, which found that one in three children did not know that chips were made from potatoes, McCain developed The Potato Story. Housed in a redesigned London Routemaster bus, the farmer in his field (top deck) and the cook in her kitchen (lower deck) bring to life the journey from field to fork through an interactive learning experience.

During 2007, The Potato Story visited 73 schools nationwide, teaching in excess of 8,500 pupils about food provenance and the importance of maintaining a healthy balanced diet. The scheme is supported by www.thepotatostory.co.uk; an interactive website offering a series of National Curriculum aligned lesson plans enabling teachers to engage their Key Stage 2 students in the curriculum subjects of lifecycles, plant growth, reproduction and nutrition. The tour continues throughout 2008.

Working with Aardman Animations, McCain created a viral marketing campaign about its

specially selected British potatoes, engaging with consumers to convey the 'It's all good' message. Targeted at 20-35 year-old women, The Potato Parade allows a personalised message to be sent to family and friends. To date, more than 300,000 people have visited www.potatoparade.co.uk.

Brand Values

The McCain brand is built on natural, simple ingredients: the 'It's all good' philosophy. A family company, which aims to take care of its consumers and employees, McCain values are to be open and honest, as demonstrated by its transparent food labelling. A leader in its category, McCain is driven by a passion for real, enjoyable, convenient food.

www.mccain.co.uk

Things you didn't know about McCain

McCain products can be found in almost 70 per cent of the nation's freezers.

One in four UK households regularly buys McCain Oven Chips.

One out of every four British potatoes is made into chips.

The humble potato is an excellent source of carbohydrate, fibre, potassium and vitamin C.

Delia Smith recommends using McCain Crispy Bites, Crispy Slices, Rosti and Wedges in her new cookbook, 'Delia's How to Cheat at Cooking'.

2008 marks the 40th year since McCain was first established in Scarborough.

Microsoft®

Microsoft®, whose software powers more than 90 per cent of all the world's PCs, has been a leader in the personal computing revolution that has transformed the world over the past three decades. During that time, it has created many new products, added new lines of business, and expanded its operations worldwide. Microsoft's corporate mission is to enable people and businesses to realise their full potential through the use of technology.

making global citizenship an integral part of its business, delivering innovative new products, creating opportunity for partners, improving customer satisfaction, putting some of its most significant legal challenges behind it, and improving its internal processes.

Product

Microsoft prides itself on providing software and services that help people communicate, do their work, be entertained, and manage their personal lives. Over Microsoft's lifetime, innovative technology has transformed how people access and share information, changed the way businesses and institutions operate, and made the world smaller by giving computer users instant access to people and resources everywhere.

Microsoft's business continued to grow in 2007, reaching the significant milestone of surpassing US$50 billion in revenue. For the year, revenue reached a total of US$51.12 billion, a 15 per cent increase over fiscal 2006. Indeed, over the past five years profits have doubled.

Market

Microsoft is a worldwide leader in software, services and solutions designed to help people and businesses realise their full potential. It generates revenue by developing, manufacturing, licensing and supporting a wide range of software products for many computing devices. Its software products include: operating systems for servers, PCs and mobile devices; server applications for distributed computing environments; information worker productivity applications; business solutions; and software development tools.

Microsoft also provides consulting and product support services, and trains and certifies system integrators and developers. It sells the Xbox 360 gaming console and games, PC games, and peripherals. Online communication services and information services are delivered through its Windows Live and MSN portals and channels around the world. It also researches and develops advanced technologies for future software products.

Achievements

Microsoft now does business almost everywhere in the world – it has offices in more than 90 countries. Microsoft believes that over the past few years it has laid the foundations for long term growth by

 Windows Mobile®

 Windows Live™

 Windows Vista®

1975	**1982**	**1983**	**1990**	**1995**	**2001**
Microsoft is founded in Seattle by two young men, Paul Allen and Bill Gates, a Harvard college dropout.	Microsoft opens its first international subsidiary in the UK.	Microsoft Community Affairs – one of the first corporate giving programmes in the high-tech industry – is founded.	Microsoft becomes the first personal computer software company to exceed US$1 billion in sales in a single year, with revenues of US$1.18 billion.	Microsoft launches Windows 95 and sells more than one million copies in the four days following its launch.	Microsoft launches Xbox – the most powerful gaming system ever built.

Through its business activities and community support, Microsoft aims to leave a lasting and positive impression on the communities and society in which it works. Years ago, it was convinced that its original vision of 'a PC in every home' could change lives. It remains convinced of the broad and positive power of giving people better technology. It takes corporate responsibilities seriously, and in its interactions with its employees, customers, partners, suppliers and the communities where it works, it aims to reflect its broader awareness and ambitions.

The Microsoft Unlimited Potential programme aims to align Microsoft technologies, partnerships, business and corporate citizenship efforts to bring the benefits of information and communications technology to the five billion people who currently do not have access to it. With Unlimited Potential, Microsoft has set an initial goal of reaching one billion people by 2015. It is partnering with governments, industry partners, non-governmental organisations, educators, and academics to enable new avenues of social and economic empowerment for the underserved populations of the world.

In the UK, Microsoft gives to a range of major charity projects both financially and through the donation of software. Charities including NSPCC, Childnet International, Leonard Cheshire, AbilityNet and Age Concern have all benefited from Microsoft's giving programme.

Recent Developments

Microsoft believes that delivering breakthrough innovation and high-value solutions through its integrated platform is the key to meeting customer needs and to its future growth.

The company continues its long term commitment to innovation and in 2007 invested US$7.12 billion in research and development. 2007 also saw some key product launches, led by the release of Windows Vista®, the newest version of Microsoft's desktop operating system. More than 55 million Windows Vista licenses were sold in its first year.

In April 2008, Windows Mobile 6.1 was introduced.

The newest instalment of Microsoft's software for mobile devices, it was designed to power a new generation of phones, personal digital assistants and media players for people who want to customise devices. Microsoft continues to evolve its product offerings with a new focus on its 'Software-plus-Services' strategy and the development of Microsoft Advertising, an innovative way for advertisers to connect with their target audience through multiple digital touchpoints.

In 2008 Microsoft also launched the futuristic WorldWide Telescope. This web application brings together imagery from the best ground- and space-based observatories across the world to allow people to easily explore the night sky through their computers. The hope is that it will inspire young people to explore astronomy and science, as well as help researchers in their quest to better understand the universe.

Promotion

Microsoft's marketing has come a long way since it kicked off its first television advertising campaign in 1992.

Now no stranger to high-profile launches, Microsoft linked up with MTV Europe to showcase the Xbox 360 game system. Elijah Wood, Scarlett Johansson, The Killers and Snow Patrol hosted a half-hour star-studded European premiere of the new product with performances from The Killers and Snow Patrol airing exclusively on MTV channels across Europe.

Every day, millions of people around the globe rely on their Windows-based devices to manage the growing

amounts of digital information in their lives. While the tools currently used for managing this information are powerful and familiar, Windows Vista aims to cut through the clutter with improved search and management tools.

Brand Values

Microsoft aims to provide people as well as businesses from all walks of life, from all around the world, with the tools to fulfil their potential. It also takes its role as being a good corporate citizen very seriously.

Microsoft also wants to play its part in developing a safer computing environment, to allow people in the UK to benefit from technology advances. It continues to be committed to building software and services that will better protect its customers and the industry. Because there is no one solution, Microsoft's approach to security reaches beyond technology to public awareness. In technology, Microsoft is focused on improving quality, building in greater resiliency, and working with the Government, law enforcement and industry partners to enable them to benefit promptly from developments in this area. In the wider community, it is focused on awareness and education around security and child safety online through campaigns such as Play Smart Play Safe and Get Safe Online, as well as making an active contribution to the public policy debate.

www.microsoft.com

Things you didn't know about Microsoft®

The Windows 95 launch was set for August 24th because it had never rained in Redmond, WA, USA during that week in recorded history. It sold more than one million copies in the four days following its launch.

Bill Gates, Microsoft chairman and Steve Ballmer, chief executive (pictured top left) first met at Harvard University.

Over the past 30 years, Microsoft and its employees have donated more than US$2.5 billion to communities around the world.

2004	**2005**	**2006**	**2008**
Bill Gates delivers Microsoft's vision of digital entertainment anywhere.	Bill Gates is granted an honorary knighthood by Queen Elizabeth II. Now the world's wealthiest man, he is worth an estimated £28 billion.	Microsoft launches its new operating system, Windows Vista, and announces that Bill Gates will transition out of a day-to-day role in the company in July 2008.	Microsoft releases free and enhanced Windows Live services including OneCare Family Safety, a tool to help protect children from online threats, and SkyDrive, an online storage service.

national express

National Express is one of the biggest names in travel and has unprecedented awareness levels throughout the UK. For more than 30 years, National Express, with its red, white and blue coaches, has been synonymous with coach travel. It is now moving in a new direction, uniting all of its UK transport businesses across coach, rail and airport shuttles under a single brand.

Market

National Express Group, a FTSE 250 company, is one of the world's largest international transport groups; more than one billion people use National Express services in North America, the UK and Spain. The business employs around 43,000 people across three continents and operates 16,000 vehicles. In the UK, National Express has a significant share of the surface travel market and operates coaches, buses, rail, tram and airport transfers.

The National Express coach business is Britain's only scheduled national coach network that also offers access to a European coach network of 500 destinations.

The National Express bus operation in the West Midlands makes up the largest single area bus network outside London; it also operates buses in Dundee, London and Surrey as well as running the Midland Metro – the West Midlands' light rail service.

National Express also operates a range of commuter, intercity and rural passenger train services. The portfolio includes two of the most prestigious rail franchises in the country – National Express East Coast and National Express East Anglia, which includes Stansted Express – as well as the London commuter service, c2c.

Achievements

In 2007, National Express Group saw an increase in passenger growth of 11 per cent for bus, coach and rail, with revenues for the period totalling £2.6 billion and a normalised operating profit of £205.6 million. Alongside this success, 2007 also saw National Express

receive a host of industry awards across its businesses.

In trains, National Express East Anglia won the 2007 Green Business Awards' Fleet Management Award for its energy efficiency project, while also claiming customer service awards at both the Rail Innovation Awards and the National Rail Awards. National Express East Coast picked up the National Rail Awards' Innovation of the Year title for its WiFi service, as well as Best Station.

Elsewhere, National Express coach employees were commended for their excellence in the Transport Sector at The

Royal Society for the Prevention of Accidents (RoSPA) Occupational Heath & Safety Awards 2007. At the UK Customer Service Experience Awards, National Express won the business-to-business category, while its bus division received the 2007 Scottish Disability and Business Award for driver training and its contribution to community work in Dundee.

Product

Since the start of 2008, National Express has been rebranding all of its transport businesses in the UK under the master

1974	1988	1992	1995	2000	2003
The National Bus Company adopts a sales and marketing focus and the National Express brand name is introduced.	The de-regulation of the National Bus Company leads to a management buy-out of National Express; a new company, National Express Holdings Ltd, is formed.	National Express is floated on the London Stock Exchange.	The National Express bus operation is launched with the purchase of West Midlands Travel and in 1996 operators in both Dundee and London are acquired.	National Express purchases Prism Rail, which is rebranded as c2c in 2002.	A major rebrand takes place as a multitude of acquired coach businesses come under the National Express umbrella and adopt its identity.

brand, ensuring customers recognise the services as National Express, regardless of the mode of transport they are using. This extends from buses in Coventry, right through to the UK's flagship train route National Express East Coast, which operates between London and Edinburgh.

It is not just the appearance of the brand that is changing, however; new values are being embedded into the business, together with a new customer promise to work together to 'make travel simpler'.

As National Express becomes a more joined-up business with an integrated customer base and brand, it is in a better position to join forces with other powerful brands. New partnerships include combined event and travel tickets with venues such as The O2 arena, Twickenham and Wembley Stadium.

With one brand for all its services, National Express is able to think of the customers' journey from end to end, enabling passengers to relate to the wider range of services, thus leveraging the greater awareness of the brand.

Recent Developments
Customer led innovation and new product development lie at the heart of National Express' brand development, driving it to adopt new technologies to make

travel simpler for the consumer. Recent developments have included train time text alerts for commuters.

A new concept in the UK is 'shared ride' and National Express' Dot2Dot airport shuttle, launched in 2007 between London and Heathrow/Gatwick airports, offers an affordable and luxurious transfer between work or home and the airport. The concept is well established in the US and National Express is spearheading its development within the UK.

Also in 2007, National Express became the Official Travel Provider to Wembley Stadium and the Football Association; operating from 57 locations, coaches are helping to make Wembley Stadium more accessible, encouraging people to leave their car at home.

Promoting the environmental credentials of public transport is at the top of the agenda at National Express. As a founding partner of the Climate Group's 'We're in this Together' campaign, it is committed to delivering a series of community and customer focused initiatives to encourage people to leave the car at home and use public transport.

Promotion
National Express understands that fares and ticket pricing are sometimes over complex and often a barrier to use. Therefore, it has re-engineered the traditional website booking process into one geared around easily identifying the best value fares, rather than solely focusing on train times. This has proved to be very popular and has driven significant growth in the price sensitive leisure market.

National Express coach has also penetrated new markets through the use of yield management. Extremely low cost fares are now exclusively available online, not only promoting greater use of the website, but also stimulating trial amongst those who previously haven't considered coach travel.

Brand Values
The recent rebrand of all services to National Express aims to unify the business and give it a common purpose: to 'improve the quality of life through travel' and to 'make travel simpler'.

The brand strives to put the customer at the heart of everything it does, by offering genuine customer choice, delivering customer led innovations and providing consistently excellent customer service where it matters and is valued most.

www.nationalexpress.com

Things you didn't know about National Express

Coach travel is the most environmentally friendly form of motorised transport with carbon emissions of 0.030kg CO_2/pass.km, compared to a car's emissions of 0.114kg CO_2/pass.km (Source: Based on data from the Edinburgh Centre for Carbon Management, DEFRA and DfT).

Diego Maradonna, Robbie Williams, Gordon Ramsay and Rudd Gullet, amongst others, used National Express coaches as part of the 2006 Unicef celebrity football match, Soccer Aid.

The weekly mileage of National Express West Midlands' bus services is equivalent to circling the world 65 times.

Approximately one third of London commuters travel to work on a National Express train service every day.

ENGLAND
national express
OFFICIAL TRAVEL PARTNER

WEMBLEY STADIUM
national express
OFFICIAL TRAVEL PROVIDER

2004
The 'one' rail franchise, now known as National Express East Anglia, is launched.

2007
National Express becomes a sponsor of The FA Cup, England team and Wembley Stadium.

Also in 2007, National Express launches Dot2Dot, its airport transfer service between Heathrow and Gatwick and central London.

2008
The National Express brand begins to appear on trains, buses and airport shuttles. Journey planning and ticket purchasing can now be conducted across all modes through a central website.

nicorette®

According to the World Health Organisation, smoking is the single most preventable cause of death globally. Many smokers who want to quit find that willpower alone often does not work so need extra help. Nicorette uses Nicotine Replacement Therapy (NRT), through a range of products, to address smokers' individual needs and tailor help to those cutting down gradually or stopping straight away.

Market

There are currently an estimated 1.3 billion smokers worldwide. The health risks of smoking – firmly established in the 1950s – have become more widely publicised in recent years, with bans on smoking in public places now the norm in many European countries. NRT can help smokers by reducing nicotine cravings; it has been shown to double a person's chances of giving up. Nicorette was the first NRT to receive approval in many countries and is now ranked as the number one selling NRT brand in the UK, out-performing its leading competitors Niquitin and Nicotinell, and is the biggest NRT brand in the over the counter (OTC) sector.

Achievements

Through effective product research and development, Nicorette now boasts the widest range of NRT products within the market. Innovation and effective messaging has allowed Nicorette to support many smokers in their efforts to quit smoking.

With year-on-year increases in sales, regular new product launches and successful consumer campaigns, Nicorette has managed to establish itself as a targeted and effective method of smoking cessation. This has been recognised in a number of key ways – by the consumers that have succeeded with the products, the healthcare professionals that have greater information with which to advise patients and through the number of awards that Nicorette has won over the last few years. To name but a

few, the IPA Effectiveness Award for Best Idea, and in 2007, awards for Best OTC Consumer Television Advertising and Best Trade Press Advertising.

Product

Recognising that smokers have different needs forms a fundamental part of Nicorette's brand philosophy, illustrated by

its diverse range of products that include Nicorette Nasal Spray, Nicorette Inhalator, a range of flavoured Nicorette Gums, Microtabs (the only dissolve-under-the-tongue NRT tablets on the market) and the Nicorette Patch. The 16-hour patch mimics patients' smoking patterns by releasing nicotine throughout waking hours to help combat cravings – a first-stop OTC therapy

---

1967
Nicorette gum is invented in Sweden to assist submariners with nicotine withdrawal.

1978
Nicorette gum is sold as a pharmaceutical product to the general public.

1991
The first Nicorette NRT Patch is developed.

1994
Nicorette Nasal Spray is introduced into the market.

1996
The Nicorette Inhalator is developed.

1998
Nicorette Microtab is introduced into the Nicorette family.

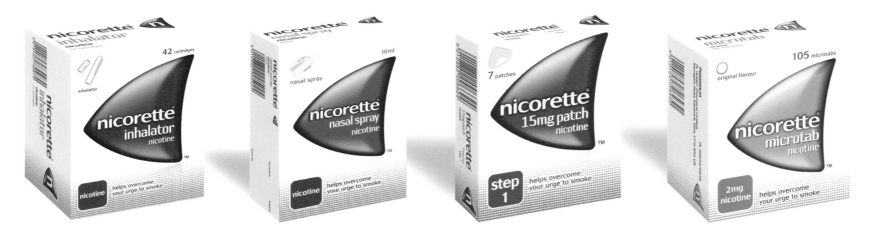

for habitual smokers. The Nicorette Patch is available in three strengths; 15mg (Step 1), 10mg (Step 2) and 5mg (Step 3).

Nicorette Inhalator (sometimes referred to as inhaler) is the only therapy available OTC to address both nicotine addiction and the ritualistic hand-to-mouth action that most smokers tend to miss. As such, it is a product suited to behavioural-dependent smokers.

Recent Developments

Recent brand developments have focused on the introduction of a wider gum range including Nicorette Freshfruit Gum. In consumer trials Freshfruit was rated the best tasting nicotine fruit gum compared to other nicotine fruit gums. Like Nicorette Inhalator and Nicorette Microtab, Nicorette Freshfruit Gum is part of the brand's 'Cut Down Then Stop' approach that can help significantly increase the chances of stopping smoking when cigarette intake is reduced by up to

50 per cent. Recently, there has also been a new coated addition to the Nicorette Gum range; Nicorette Cinnamint Gum.

Understanding that smokers need help with the psychological, as well as the physical, side of quitting is one of Nicorette's unique selling points; ActiveStop, an interactive quit smoking support programme – accessed and monitored via the internet and mobile phones – was developed with this in mind.

Promotion

The makers of Nicorette believe that every smoker is different and therefore one communication channel will not suit all. Devising a range of promotional activities to communicate key strengths of the brand, build trust and promote awareness has allowed Nicorette to become a fast growing NRT franchise globally.

Throughout all promotional campaigns, Nicorette has interspersed education, insight and advice to allow the consumer to make informed and empowered decisions. Traditional above-the-line campaigns have run across TV, press and outdoor including the highly praised 'board' advertising campaign developed specifically for the UK smoking ban which used smokers' personal experiences and insights to demonstrate the achievement felt from cessation. In May 2008, a TV and print campaign ran in parallel with the Inhalator's switch from pharmacy-only to general sales licence, which highlighted the combined physiological and psychological elements of smoking and the unique selling point of the inhalator under the strapline 'Helps satisfy cravings and keeps your hands busy'.

As technology has advanced, Nicorette has been supported by a range of interactive services such as viral mailings, online games and support channels such as ActiveStop. Through this wide array of media channels, Nicorette has been able to educate

consumers on the various forms of NRT available and develop a recognisable and respected dialogue. In addition, it actively works with pharmacists, healthcare professionals and smoking cessation units to provide them with key information to help them support their patients.

Brand Values

Nicorette is positioned as a knowledgeable, empathetic ex-smoker, with a knowing and wry sense of humour. It recognises that every smoker quits in their own way and as a brand offers a range of options to support individual choices.

www.nicorette.co.uk

NICORETTE® is a stop smoking aid. Contains nicotine. Always read the label. Requires willpower.

Things you didn't know about Nicorette

Nicorette was invented in Sweden. It was originally designed for submariners who became distressed and agitated when under water for long periods of time without cigarettes.

Nicorette pioneered the use of NRT for smoking cessation over 25 years ago and now has the widest range of products available to support smokers in their quit attempt.

NRT supplies the body with lower levels of nicotine than cigarettes but enough to relieve cravings and physical withdrawal symptoms.

Most smokers put on weight when they stop smoking, however some NRT products can help quitters to control weight gain during their stop smoking attempt.

Nicotine is not proven to cause cancer. There are more than 4,000 other chemicals in cigarette smoke, many of which are known to cause cancer. The risks of NRT when used to help stop smoking are significantly less than the risks of smoking.

2005
September sees the launch of the 'Cut Down Then Stop' programme.

2006
In December Nicorette ActiveStop is created.

2007
In July, a smoking ban is introduced in England making the whole of the UK 'smoke-free' in public and work places. In October, the minimum legal age to buy cigarettes rises from 16 to 18 in Great Britain.

2008
The Nicorette Inhalator joins the General Sales List in March.

NOKIA

Since launching its first hand-held mobile phone in 1987, Nokia has pushed the boundaries of design and technology to produce cutting-edge, easy-to-use products and services that meet the diverse needs of its customers. As a global leader in mobile communications, the brand's enduring success is not just down to its products but also the way it helps people to 'get close to their passions' – whether it's fashion, music, gaming, navigation, photography or film.

Market

The UK has one of the largest and most advanced mobile phone markets in the world. Within such a competitive arena established manufacturers such as Motorola, Samsung, Sony Ericsson, and most recently Apple, are raising the bar in terms of product innovation and offerings.

In the face of this competition Nokia continues to build on its leading market position, achieving record-breaking device volumes and net sales. By the end of 2007 Nokia market share reached 38 per cent (Source: Nokia 2007 annual information), for the first time, with recorded sales topping 133.5 million units.

A diverse product portfolio, coupled with global manufacturing and effective distribution networks, has enabled Nokia to make the transition into internet services which looks set to enhance the brand's profile and increase its market share further.

Achievements

Nokia has accrued widespread industry and consumer recognition, with recent accolades including the coveted Mobile Choice Awards Manufacturer of the Year in 2007.

Other awards that have endorsed the brand's cutting-edge products include Mobile Choice awards, with the N95 receiving the Reader's Dream Phone award and the Nokia 6110 Navigator named as the Best Sat Nav Solution. In 2007 Nokia also won Pocketlint.co.uk's Best Mobile Phone award and PDA Essentials' Best Smartphone, for the Nokia N95.

Product

Nokia devices have forged a place at the forefront of the telecommunications market through an emphasis on innovation; it was the first brand to offer mobile phones with text messaging features, integrated cameras and access to its own and third-party internet based services.

The brand also leads the way in convergence with its Nseries range of high performance multimedia computers that include the Nokia N95 8GB and N96, and its Eseries devices such as the E90, E61i and E51, offering optimised solutions to business users.

Nokia's recent move into supported services is part of its ongoing evolution that not only provides customers and business users with a range of experiences, but also keeps pace with consumer demands. Brand areas of expertise include music, navigation, video, television, imaging, games, business mobility and, more recently, internet services. With an estimated 60.5 million converged devices sold in 2007 and with 38 million Nseries devices and seven million Eseries devices shipped, Nokia is positioned to connect more people to the internet than any other company.

1987	**1994**	**2000**	**2001**	**2004**	**2005**
The first and original hand-held mobile phone, Nokia Mobira Cityman 900, is launched.	The Nokia 2100 series become the first digital hand portable phones to support data, fax and SMS.	Nokia's first dust, water and shock resistant handset – the Nokia 6250 – is launched.	The first Nokia camera phone – the Nokia 7650 – hits the market.	Nokia introduces its first fashion collection of three handsets.	Nokia brings its first 3G device to market – the Nokia 6630.

Recent Developments

In 2007 Nokia moved into internet services with Ovi, the gateway enabling users to integrate their mobile and online activities. The first services – Nokia Maps, Nokia Music Store and N-Gage – are already live in the UK with additional services planned to follow.

Producing accessible and high quality mobiles remains at the heart of Nokia's business. Its position at the forefront of handset innovation and technology was enhanced in 2007 with the launch of 50 new handsets. Nokia has also been pushing the boundaries of convergence. For example, the Nokia N95 helped to establish the converged multimedia computers category and became the top selling UK handset week-on-week in 2007.

Nokia launched its first UK flagship store in London's Regent Street in February 2008, with further stores in Heathrow's Terminal 5 and Manchester quickly following. All have been designed to set the benchmark in technology retail practice by offering an upscale, high-energy environment to showcase Nokia's portfolio.

In February 2008, Nokia launched Nokia Maps 2.0; sporting a redesigned user interface, enhanced features include improved pedestrian navigation, multimedia city guides and satellite images. This technology was put to the test by Olympic sportsman, James Cracknell in his 2008 world record attempt to travel from London to Morocco by human power alone in aid of Sports Relief. He used the latest Nokia N82 handset with 'Sports Tracker' to navigate the 1,431 miles home, and to keep in touch with family and fans en-route.

2008 also saw the launch of Nokia's N-Gage gaming platform, enabling customers to play high-quality made-for-mobile games directly from handsets. The N-Gage platform has a host of exclusive titles that are among

the most ambitious and graphically rich currently available on the market.

Nokia's reputation for iconic design is evident in its Nokia 8800 Arte and the Nokia 8800 Arte Sapphire handsets. Complementing catwalk trends, both draw upon modern watch-making and jewellery techniques for inspiration. Each distinctive detail has been considered and researched to complement the prestige and quality of the device. The handsets also feature exclusive audio accompaniment by award-winning composer Ryuichi Sakamoto.

Promotion

Nokia's passion for music (which it shares with its customers) is the driving force behind the Nokia Green Room – a 30-minute television music format featuring exclusive live performances from top music acts, with behind-the-scenes footage of artists mingling backstage between performances. The show, which airs on Channel 4's T4 on Sunday afternoons, provides fans with a glimpse into the lives of their favourite acts, thanks to hidden microphones and cameras in the specially created Nokia Green Room. Free and exclusive content from each show is available online at the Nokia Music Store. The Store, launched in November 2007, is also home to a catalogue of more than two million tracks. Exclusive pre-releases from pop royalty, such as Kylie's album 'X', sit alongside tracks from major artists, independent labels and up-and-coming UK acts.

Nokia was one of the first technology brands to work with the fashion industry, sponsoring London Fashion Week from 1999 to 2004, and the Glamour Women of the Year Awards, since 2006. The brand has also worked with leading fashion designers, including Kenzo, Donatella Versace, Cath Kidston and Giambattista Valli, to develop three collections – the Nokia Fashion, the Nokia L'Amour and the Nokia L'Amour II.

Brand Values

Nokia is about connecting people – to the people that matter most and the things they find important. Nokia aims to provide easy-to-use, dependable and secure products – from entry level handsets to sophisticated multimedia computers that utilise cutting-edge technology. The brand has built up a reputation for reliability, becoming one that consumers feel they can trust, with handsets that are easy to navigate and keypads that are comfortable to use.

www.nokia.co.uk

2006

The Nokia N91 – the first mobile device with a hard drive allowing space to store up to 3,000 songs – goes on sale in the UK.

2007

The Nokia N95 is launched. It combines integrated GPS, a five mega pixel camera with Carl Zeiss optics and HSDPA connectivity offering broadband download speeds. An 8GB upgrade soon follows.

Also in 2007, Ovi is launched – a gateway to the brand's new Music Store and Maps services.

2008

N-Gage, Nokia's gaming service, is introduced to the Ovi gateway.

Things you didn't know about Nokia

Nokia is named after the river Nokia in Finland.

When Nokia was founded in 1865, it initially manufactured paper, then card before moving on to rubber.

The world's first transportable phone, the Nokia Mobira Talkman came complete with a 10kg charging box the size of a suitcase.

Ovi – Nokia's new gateway to internet services – means 'door' in Finnish.

OLAY

Olay is one of the world's leading skincare brands, trusted by millions of women around the world for more than 50 years. Its outstanding growth has been driven by its leading-edge science and beauty expertise, combined with its in-depth understanding of women, providing skin care and body care to meet their needs. Over seven million women buy Olay skincare in the UK every year (Source: TNS Past 12 months April 2008).

Market

The UK skincare market was worth more than £1.08 billion in the year to 20th April 2008. Of this, facial care represented 65 per cent of the total, up from 60 per cent the previous year. Olay is one of the leading facial care brands with 35 per cent volume share (Source: IRI Past 12 months April 2008).

Olay has always been an innovative brand with the launch of Total Effects Touch of Sunshine a testament to this. A huge player in anti-ageing, a market that grew by over 90 per cent in the last year, Olay is the number one branded offering in this market with more than a 15 per cent share (Source: IRI).

Achievements

As a brand, Olay has gained a reputation for being a pioneer. In 2000 the rebranding from Ulay to Olay took place and that same year a jewel in the Olay crown was launched in the form of Total Effects, the first 'skincare boutique' for Olay. It was responsible for opening up the 'masstige' category (a combination of the words 'mass' and 'prestige') and quickly became the number one anti-ageing skincare product.

Today, Olay is a worldwide leader in skin care. Every two seconds a bottle of its best selling Regenerist line is sold somewhere in the world. As a brand, Olay has accumulated more than 75 awards including the coveted 'beauty star' award from the Good Housekeeping Institute on both sides of the Atlantic in 2007/08.

Product

Olay's range includes a multitude of products including skin care and body care tailored to meet the needs of every woman's skin. Olay's products are the result of a fusion between leading-edge science and a deep understanding and appreciation of women and their changing needs.

Olay applies its scientific and beauty expertise with the aim of creating skincare

1940s	**1962**	**1991**	**1994**	**2000**	**2003**
Chemist Graham Wulff develops a skin treatment to prevent dehydration of burn wounds on British Royal Air Force pilots. Post-war, he refines the product renaming it Oil of Ulay Beauty Fluid.	Oil of Ulay is introduced into the UK.	Daily U.V. Protectant is introduced nationally (Beauty Fluid and Moisture Replenishing Cream).	Moisturizing Body Wash is introduced nationally.	Ulay is rebranded to Olay and Total Effects anti-ageing moisturiser is launched.	Total Effects becomes the UK's best selling anti-ageing moisturiser and Olay Regenerist, premium anti-ageing moisturiser, is launched.

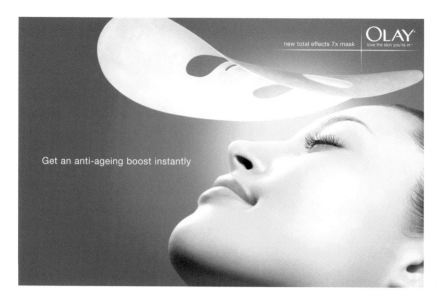

Get an anti-ageing boost instantly

new anti-wrinkle nature fusion OLAY

Natural, younger looking skin in just 3 weeks.

nature fusion

products that are a pleasure to use and enhance women's total beauty, without compromising on continual skin improvement. Its products are backed by world-leading scientific research and data to prove they really work, deliver a noticeable improvement and are pleasant to use.

Recent Developments

Since its launch in the 1950s the brand has grown from its single Oil of Ulay Beauty Fluid product into one of the world's leading ranges of quality skin and body care products. As women's tastes have become more sophisticated and demands more acute, Olay's fusion of cutting-edge science and deep understanding of women's changing needs has enabled the brand to consistently innovate, providing an extensive range of products to fit changing lifestyles.

In 2000, the brand made the move to change its name to just 'Olay' to ensure that it

was clearly communicating the true essence, modernity and breadth of the Olay brand today, on a global scale, whilst retaining the brand's illustrious heritage. The name Olay was chosen as it was felt that it was simple, bold, contemporary and personified beauty.

Olay is renowned as a leading innovator in the anti-ageing skincare category driven by its key product launches, from the introduction of Total Effects to the premium anti-ageing skincare ranges featuring Olay Regenerist in 2003. Since launch, Regenerist has gained iconic status, boasting a following of celebrities, industry experts and women across the UK.

In 2006 the latest family member became Olay Definity, which addresses the two key culprits of ageing – wrinkles and discolouration. Most recently, 2008 saw the launch of Olay Regenerist's first affordable 'Super Cream' – Regenerist Daily 3 Point Treatment Cream which had a waiting list of more than 21,000 customers before it launched on-shelf. Furthermore, it became the fastest selling anti-ageing beauty product on Boots.com in 2008 (Source: Information held by Boots.com).

Promotion

Olay has prided itself on being a leading innovator in its communications approach. Its current integrated communications strategy is designed to inform and inspire women on its extensive range of products tailored to meet their specific needs as well as highlighting its latest innovations.

For the last three years, Olay has focused on building the anti-ageing category and has successfully carved a niche for itself by leveraging credible spokespersons and external endorsements both above- and

below-the-line. When Regenerist was relaunched in the UK in 2006 Olay created its breakthrough commercial innovation – 'The celebrity cream without the celebrity price tag' campaign – leveraging a celebrity beauty journalist which has been reapplied throughout western Europe.

Olay is renowed for creating aspirational in-store promotions specifically designed to inspire women with gifts they most desire. The glittering 'Find A Diamond' on-pack promotion for Christmas 2006 received widespread acclaim and more recently in 2007 it launched its luxury Mother's Day designer shoe competition that was supported through-the-line.

Brand Values

Olay defines itself as a leading skin care brand that is passionate about beauty, inside and out, and combines its scientific and beauty expertise with its unique understanding of women to deliver products that are tailored to meet every woman's wants, needs and aspirations. Olay also aims to celebrate the 'unique beauty within every woman', through its 'Loving the skin you're in' concept.

www.olay.co.uk

Things you didn't know about Olay

In the 1950s, Graham Wulff, a South African chemist, inventor and entrepreneur, set up a small product development laboratory in his own home, and created 'Oil of Ulay'. This was initially a refined version of a topical skin treatment to prevent dehydration of burn wounds on British Royal Air Force pilots during World War II.

Two pots of Regenerist Serum are sold in the UK every minute (Source: P&G data).

More than seven million women buy Olay each year (Source: TNS Past 12 months April 2008).

2004

The launch of Daily Facials Express helps Olay to become the UK's number one cleansing portfolio.

2006

Olay Definity, intensive anti-ageing range, is launched.

2007

Launches include Total Effects Touch of Sunshine moisturiser, Complete Care Every Day Sunshine, Complete Everynight Sunshine, Total Effects Masks, Total Effects First Effects and Clarify Mask.

2008

Regenerist Micro-Dermabrasion and Mini-Peel Kit launch, as does Olay Regenerist's first affordable Super Cream – Daily 3 Point Treatment Cream.

Pret A Manger creates handmade, natural food avoiding the chemicals, additives and preservatives commonly found in much of today's 'prepared' and 'fast' food. It has a reputation for placing importance on continually committing to sourcing and using natural ingredients and its unwillingness to compromise on freshness or quality.

Market

Over the last 10 years the sandwich market has grown substantially. It is currently estimated to be worth around £3.5 billion a year (Source: The British Sandwich Association 2007), making the humble sandwich the UK's most popular fast food.

A primary factor driving growth is the sandwich's reputation as a healthy 'fast food' option. As the public have become increasingly health conscious, market value has increased. The trend for shorter lunches has also impacted with sandwiches offering the ideal convenient, affordable and speedy lunch. Wider availability and choice has strengthened competition but while many have sought to emulate the Pret 'formula', its attention to detail, commitment to natural quality ingredients and unwillingness to compromise keeps it at the forefront of the market.

It was within inner city locations populated by city workers that Pret A Manger first made its debut; today it serves over one million people a week in prime sites across the UK, employing 3,889 staff with an annual turnover of more than £200 million.

Achievements

Pret A Manger's long-standing association with homeless charities is an integral part of the company ethos. A fleet of electric vans deliver more than 12,000 fresh meals to homeless shelters in London each week with other UK-based charities collecting directly at the end of each day. In total, Pret donates over 1.7 million products to UK homeless charities annually, preventing food from ending up in landfills.

Indeed, avoiding landfill wherever possible is a primary brand goal. Pret A Manger believes in reducing energy consumption, so continually challenges its team to adapt habits and business practices to cut usage. Despite costing a little more, all Pret outlets use electricity from 100 per cent 'green' sources – a mixture of wind, wave and hydro-electricity.

Pret A Manger is currently involved in 32 sustainability projects, including paperless banking, thermo mugs (reducing paper usage by some 650,000 cups) and organic waste composting for shop kitchen waste. As a partner of Forum For The Future,

a leading sustainable development charity, the brand recently joined London's Green 500 programme and has been named one of the UK's Top Employers of 2008, scoring highly in both social and sustainability categories.

Product

Since it was established in 1986, Pret A Manger has revolutionised its market, from the outset sticking to its founding principle: to serve freshly prepared, natural food.

Pret operates like a restaurant, with each shop (bar one or two of the smallest) running its own kitchen. 'Sell by' dates are redundant as everything is freshly prepared daily. Food fads are sidelined in favour of ongoing improvements to the existing range. The brand's product focus remains on creating simple, delicious, confident flavours from natural free range source ingredients or organic, where possible.

Attention to detail and flavour are two of the main driving factors behind the brand. The Pret Chocolate Brownie, for example, has

1986

Pret A Manger is founded by entrepreneurs Julian Metcalfe and Sinclair Beecham. Quitting their City jobs, they believe they can provide a better service than many of London's sandwich bars.

1987

Pret A Manger's first shop, on Victoria Street in London, ends its first year of trading by serving more than 7,000 customers a week.

1998

Andrew Rolfe joins Pret as chairman and chief executive and proves crucial in steering the company's expansion.

2001

The McDonald's Corporation buys a minority stake in Pret A Manger, although it has no direct influence over what is sold, or how.

2002

A new stand-alone recruitment centre for the brand opens in Victoria train station.

2005

Pret A Manger takes first place in the Top 50 Foodservice Company awards.

'Just Made'
(and ready to take away)

Preservative free
Picnic
Summer menu 2008

blaah, blaah, blaah

GRAZE AT YOUR PERIL
Go for proper food, three times a day.
(Good for you)

EAT WITH YOUR HEAD

NO FUNNY STUFF
Go for proper, fresh, natural food
(avoid hairy chemicals)

EAT WITH YOUR HEAD

changed 34 times, each change small but significant in terms of flavour improvement. Pret's Fruit & Oat slice is, unusually for today, still stirred by hand. Where mechanical mixers make more commercial sense their tendency to turn mixtures into pulp adversely affects flavour and texture. That Pret favours the more costly and laborious hand mixing method is indicative of the company's commitment to outstanding quality and taste.

The company's mission statement is prominently displayed in all of its shops and everything on the Pret menu – whether it's a special fish sushi, egg and cress sandwich, freshly pressed carrot juice or chocolate brownie – complies with its founding principles of handmade, natural food.

Recent Developments
In 2008 Pret A Manger expanded the concept of seasonality to its shop designs. While it has always emphasised the importance of using fresh, seasonal ingredients it also recognises that in the melee of a busy shop, new product launches can often be overlooked. Updating the look and feel of a shop and its lines in accordance with seasonal changes can make a greater impact on consumers, tying in the changing menu with people's leanings towards using seasonal products in the

home. The concept – still very much a work in progress – kicked off in May with Pret's preservative-free picnic summer menu and will be followed by the all-natural winter menu at the end of September 2008.

Promotion
Pret's unconventional approach to promotional activity keeps direct marketing to a minimum. The absence of a designated press or PR team is a key aspect of its overall cost structure with total communication expenditure budgeted at less than 0.4 per cent of sales, compared to competitors such as McDonald's and Marks & Spencer that run between five and seven per cent. The brand's view is that investing in store staff and quality ingredients is a more effective form of promotion than hiring advertising space.

Commitment to quality ingredients (with no hidden chemicals) lies at the core of Pret A Manger's recent Eat With Your Head campaign, launched in January 2007. Pret's approach to eating well is based around the commonsense principles of eating good, quality, unadulterated food in moderation. The campaign slogan, which appears on all sandwich boxes and packaging, is ingrained in the company ethos, reinforcing

Just for summer **PRET**

MANDARIN & LYCHEE
JUICE

100% natural, freshly squeezed mandarin and lychees

its message that a balanced diet of nutritious, unprocessed food plays a significant role in keeping healthy.

Brand Values
Pret A Manger's success relies on staff pride in their work, a culture that is fostered from within, not from an appointed brand director. This egalitarian hands-on approach filters down from the CEO to shop assistants and emphasises the importance Pret A Manger places on training and retaining good staff. The brand personality is underpinned in its core values: passion for food, enthusiasm, integrity, honesty and belief in its convictions with an uncompromising stance on quality and commitment to innovation.

www.pret.com

Things you didn't know about Pret A Manger

Pret A Manger was the first retailer to move from plastic sandwich boxes to cardboard back in the 1990s; its sandwich 'bio-box' and fully recyclable, biodegradable salad and cheesecake boxes were amongst the first of their kind in the world.

Pret A Manger commissions the Bond Street jeweller Tiffany & Co. to make solid silver stars, which are awarded to staff whenever a customer acknowledges their good service by name.

Pret A Manger's fleet of 19 electric vans saves more than three tonnes of CO_2 emissions a year (compared to diesel vans) and scooped two Green Fleet Awards in 2006.

2007
Eat With Your Head, Pret A Manger's eating well campaign, launches with the slogan rolled out on all sandwich boxes.

2008
Pret celebrates its international expansion with a total of 180 shops now in the UK, New York, Hong Kong and Singapore.

In May 2008, Pret's preservative-free picnic summer menu launches, to be followed by the all-natural winter menu at the end of September.

ROYAL ALBERT HALL

Since 1871, the Royal Albert Hall has had an unrivalled history of associations with some of the world's greatest artists. From contemporary to classic, world-class performances to tomorrow's stars, the Hall's flexibility and diverse programming showcases more than 350 events every year. From global broadcasts to intimate events, the Hall's breathtaking surroundings enhance the experience of the best live performances for well over one million people every year.

Market

The Royal Albert Hall operates in the highly competitive entertainment, leisure and tourism sectors. It is a registered charity and receives no public funding. Its competitors are the other leading UK performing arts and entertainment venues and organisations, many of which receive central or local government funding, and more general competition for a customer's leisure time and pound, especially in the age of digital media and home entertainment.

Achievements

In 2007, the Royal Albert Hall was recognised by the music industry at the 19th Pollstar Concert Industry Awards in America when it won International Theatre of the Year for the fifth year in succession.

The Hall's founding Charter requires it to maintain this iconic Grade I listed building and through it to promote the understanding, appreciation and enjoyment of the Arts and Sciences. The Hall launched an extensive education programme in 2004, providing opportunities to experience and participate in

ENTERTAINING THE WORLD

EVENTS APRIL 08

live performance. This has now enabled more than 100,000 young people from many different backgrounds to explore and engage in the arts, science and the cultural industries.

Key education events during 2007 included Ocean World, a music and dance collaboration featuring over 1,500 children; the Icarus project which, in conjunction with Cirque du Soleil and Rolls-Royce plc, encouraged primary school children to consider the engineering challenges of bringing Varekai™ to the Hall; and the Madam Butterfly Fashion Show which enabled

teenagers to create a fashion event on the set of the production.

The Hall supports other registered charities in their fundraising activities and offers the Hall free of charge to one charity each year. Over the last two years, events held at the Hall have raised £10 million for good causes. Highlights included the concerts in support of the Teenage Cancer Trust, featuring artists such as The Fratellis, Muse and The Who, as well as the Swarovski Fashion Rocks event for the Prince's Trust with Uma Thurman and Samuel L Jackson.

1871	**1909**	**1912**	**1941**	**1963**	**1970**
The Royal Albert Hall is opened by Queen Victoria in March.	A full indoor Marathon is run at the Hall – a total of 524 circuits of the Arena.	The Titanic Band Memorial Concert takes place encompassing 500 performers, with conductors Sir Edward Elgar, Henry Wood, Landon Ronald and Thomas Beecham.	The first BBC Proms season at the Hall takes place.	The Beatles and The Rolling Stones appear on the same bill on 15th September.	Tennis is first played at the Hall.

Product

The Royal Albert Hall hosts live performance by artists from around the world and, with partners, promotes productions of opera, ballet, musicals and organ music. From Verdi, Wagner and Elgar conducting UK premières of their works to performances by Bob Dylan, Jimi Hendrix, Frank Sinatra and The Beatles, the Hall has an unparalleled history of performances by the world's leading artists.

Each year, more than 350 events are held in the Hall's auditorium, including performances of classical music, jazz, folk and world music, circus, rock and pop concerts, ballet and opera, dance, comedy, tennis, film premières, corporate dinners, award ceremonies and occasions of national importance.

Recent Developments

Since its launch in 2005, ignite, the Hall's series of free Friday lunchtime concerts by world music and jazz artists in the Café Consort, has proved extremely popular. Its success resulted in the launch of ignite brunch on Sundays in April 2007 – featuring live jazz and world music with an inclusive brunch menu, which sold to 93 per cent of

capacity in its first year, and brought the total number of ignite performances to over 100.

In 2006 the Hall launched reflect, an engaging free exhibition series. Highlights in 2007 included photographs of celebrities with their children by Scarlet Page and a photography exhibition of cities from around the world taken on a mobile phone, which were displayed both at the Hall and in the virtual world of Second Life.

In 2007 the Hall launched hush, a series of intimate gigs for up and coming artists in its Elgar Room. Sold out since launch, the series has featured bands such as Johnny Flynn and the Sussex Wit as well as Pete and the Pirates. In May 2008, The Albert Sessions, a series of auditorium concerts, were launched with a performance by The Wombats to encourage young artists and support new music.

Promotion

The Royal Albert Hall markets its own programming initiatives and works with its event promoters, assisting them with the ticket sales for their events through the Hall's marketing channels. In 2007, the Hall had more than 1.21 million people through its doors and the average attendance across the year was over 82 per cent, an all time record.

Also in 2007 a new visual language and brand positioning was launched. 'Entertaining the World' is intended to capture the magic of the Hall experience for customers, the wide range of leading artists from around the world that it plays host to and its ambitions to continue to spread the reach of the Hall and its events beyond the building itself through broadcast and new media channels.

The Royal Albert Hall is a brand known around the world through extensive PR

coverage, broadcasts and DVD releases. It also works in partnership with brands to reach new audiences and is interested in exploring new business partnerships. As part of its partnership with iTunes and its support of the Royal Philharmonic Orchestra, it produced the first-ever live classical recording especially for iTunes, which reached number two in its classical charts.

Brand Values

The Hall's brand values are encompassed in the positioning statement – Entertaining the World. It is the Hall's ambition that everyone, young and old, from every nation and culture, should feel welcome at the Hall and able to enjoy the shared experience of live performance by the very best of today's global artists.

Built as part of Prince Albert's vision for a centre for the Arts and Sciences in South Kensington, the Royal Albert Hall is proud of the building and its heritage. It remains true to his founding ambitions to maintain and develop this magical building for future generations and to continue to promote the appreciation of the Arts and Sciences.

www.royalalberthall.com

1996	**2004**	**2006**	**2007**
Work begins on the Royal Albert Hall's eight-year major building development programme and Cirque du Soleil premières Saltimbanco at the Hall.	The official 're-opening' of the Hall by Her Majesty The Queen takes place, celebrating the completion of the Hall's major building development programme.	President Bill Clinton speaks at the Hall about his vision for leadership in the 21st century.	The UK première of Cirque du Soleil's Varekai takes place at the Hall and Swarovski Fashion Rocks is broadcast to more than 40 countries around the world.

Things you didn't know about Royal Albert Hall

There are more than 13,500 letter 'A's in the Royal Albert Hall – featured on the banisters and in the terracotta and stonework throughout the building.

It took six million bricks and 80,000 terracotta bricks to build the Hall, as well as 11,000 gas burners (which lit in 10 seconds) and five miles of steam pipes.

The Hall has hosted many world statesmen including Sir Winston Churchill, President F W de Klerk, Nelson Mandela, His Holiness the Dalai Lama and President Bill Clinton.

ROYAL DOULTON

ENGLAND 1815

Having earned a reputation for excellence, creativity, skilled craftsmanship and distinctiveness of design, Royal Doulton is valued for its sense of heritage and quality. Prized by collectors the world over, Royal Doulton has an international reach extending way beyond its English roots. It has also become known for working with renowned designers.

Market

Withstanding market fragmentation, ceramic giftware has seen considerable growth – gift-giving, home decoration, and investment being the main motivations. Despite the introduction of many alternative forms of gifts, the ceramic form is sought after as offering true qualities of heritage, craftsmanship, and long-lasting value for money.

Royal Doulton is a market leader within the ceramics and chinaware markets, with a large proportion of all English bone china being supplied by Royal Doulton, as well as almost half of the UK's ceramic sculptures.

The key markets worldwide for premium ceramic tableware and giftware are the UK and Europe, North America, Asia Pacific and Australasia. In total the global market is estimated to be worth more than £1.6 billion.

Achievements

Royal Doulton is one of the world's largest manufacturers and distributors in the premium ceramic tableware and giftware market. With 200 years of heritage, Royal Doulton is a thriving global organisation, with around £115 million annual turnover, employing approximately 2,500 people across its production sites and numerous distribution operations worldwide. The company currently operates in more than 80 different markets and has distribution companies in the US, Canada, Australia, and Japan; more than half of all sales are generated outside the UK.

Each of the company's principal brands – Royal Doulton, Minton, and Royal Albert – has a long association of royal patronage, and holds at least one Royal Warrant. They are also trademark registered.

Product

Royal Doulton may be one of the oldest chinaware companies in the world, but it is also one of the most up-to-date; focusing on the customer, understanding its buyers, and creating products that suit individual tastes and needs, it aims to stay ahead of contemporary trends.

When drawing up new product design, Royal Doulton's Design Studio studies the market, analyses consumer research, and

1815	**1875**	**1884**	**1901**	**1930s**	**1960**
John Doulton begins producing practical and decorative stoneware from a small pottery in Lambeth, South London.	John Doulton's son, Henry, relocates the business to Stoke-on-Trent.	Following the introduction of new techniques, production of bone china begins.	King Edward VII permits the company to prefix its name with 'Royal', and the company is awarded the Royal Warrant.	Royal Doulton is involved in the manufacture of figurines and giftware.	A new product, English Translucent China is introduced. Offering the translucent quality of bone china without the expense, this will later become known as Royal Doulton Fine China.

often refers to Royal Doulton's own museum and archives – dating from 1815 to the present day – for inspiration.

Today, Royal Doulton provides a wide selection of domestic tableware manufactured in bone china and fine china. The brand also offers a range of crystal stemware and giftware, as well as character jugs, china flowers, and an array of collectable figurines often known as the Royal Doulton 'pretty ladies'.

The brand has worked with Sir Terence Conran to create the Terence Conran by Royal Doulton collection, which has been inspired by Terence's love of traditional English cooking. This range combines quality materials with an earthy colour palette and simple practical designs, to create timeless products that aim to appeal to a wide range of customers. In addition, the collaboration with celebrated chef Gordon Ramsay saw his Michelin-starred expertise bring a new professionalism to home dining products.

Royal Albert, which traces its origins back to 1896, has also become an internationally recognised brand, offering domestic tableware and gift items. Equally famous, with an illustrious heritage dating back to its inception in 1793 is the Minton range, best known for its most popular pattern Haddon Hall, which is particularly favoured by the Japanese market.

Recent Developments
Known for quality and design, Royal Doulton also has a history of working with renowned designers. Recently, American bridal gown designer Monique Lhuillier has collaborated with Royal Doulton: creating a collection inspired by the luxurious fabrics and

workmanship that are part of her own bridal pieces. Bone china tableware is adorned by delicate patterns reflecting tulle, reptile skins and intricate stitching – all in a warm yet subtle colour palette. Known for dressing some of Hollywood's most glamorous stars, Monique brings sophisticated chic to Royal Doulton.

Inspired by the English country garden, the Royal Albert brand has reached 100 years-old. Royal Albert is marking its 10 decades with a special collection of fine bone china tea ware. Royal Albert 100 Years features 10 designs which have either been taken directly from, or been inspired by past Royal Albert collections. Encapsulating each decade from the 1900s to the 1990s, the 10 sets of teacup, saucer and side plate illustrate significant English and world events through distinctive patterns and designs.

Promotion
Royal Doulton is undergoing an important period of change in its history, implementing a three-brand master strategy as a first step in developing the company's brands. New global merchandising systems, product packaging, an e-commerce website, point of sale and designer endorsement have all been identified as keys to brand development.

The Licensing Division, created in the mid-1990s to propel the three brands into new product sectors, has achieved considerable success, not least with the launch of Bunnykins Clothing and Silverware, as well as its Children's Furniture product range. In the

UK, licensed products include home textiles, jewellery, candles, stationery, child/baby gifts and accessories.

Royal Doulton's promotional and marketing activities have been central to developing and communicating the brand. The introduction of everything from new logos to in-store promotional material and branded fixtures has demanded that the focus of activity be centred on the communication and effective introduction of the recent significant changes.

Brand Values
Royal Doulton is a quintessentially British brand with a strong commitment to craftsmanship and artistic innovation. Excellence and distinctiveness of design are values that it intends to build on in order to take the brand forward.

www.royaldoulton.com

Things you didn't know about Royal Doulton

Royal Doulton ceramics are included in a time capsule inside the base of Cleopatra's Needle on the Thames Embankment in London.

Royal Doulton's largest and most expensive figure takes over 160 hours to hand paint and costs more than £15,000.

Royal Doulton's Royal Albert bone china tableware pattern, 'Old Country Roses', has sold more than 150 million pieces since its introduction in 1962.

Royal Doulton's archives give the business and its designers access to some 10,000 watercolours, which date back to 1815.

1966
The company becomes the first china manufacturer to be awarded the Queen's Award for Technical Achievement, for its contribution to china manufacturing.

1972
Royal Doulton is bought by Pearson and merged with Allied English Potteries – encompassing the Royal Albert and Minton brands.

1993
Royal Doulton separates from Pearson and becomes a publicly quoted company listed on the London Stock Exchange.

2006
Royal Doulton becomes part of the Waterford Wedgwood Group.

Sandals

THE *Luxury Included*™ HOLIDAY

Since opening its first resort in 1981, Sandals Resorts has been at the forefront of the Caribbean all-inclusive travel sector by offering luxury, innovation, and choice. In an industry brimming with new contenders, the combined knowledge and experience of Sandals' management team and resort staff has kept the company at the head of the expanding all-inclusive market by introducing the Luxury Included® holiday experience.

Market

In recent years the concept of luxury travel has steered away from conservative off-the-shelf five star packages towards tailor-made individualism. Luxury, or upscale travel, is now more about what the consumer wants. Indeed, luxury travel could be described as being about making dreams come true.

With travel becoming increasingly associated with personal expression, the luxury holiday market has shown strong growth. It remains people focused and it is people skills, along with an emphasis on personal choice, that Sandals Resorts sees as key in setting it apart from its competitors. Right from the outset, the brand aimed to offer more; where others had inclusive meals and rooms at a set rate, Sandals' prices covered premium drinks, tips and taxes, in addition to all recreational and

water sports activities. Furthermore, while it was common within the market for meals to be served as buffets, Sandals built its reputation on gourmet specialty restaurants and silver service.

Sandals Resorts International (SRI) is now the largest operator of Luxury Included® resorts in the Caribbean. Currently there are 12 Sandals Resorts aimed at 'two people in love' located in Jamaica, Antigua, St. Lucia and The Bahamas and four of its sister chain, Beaches Resorts, catering for couples, families and singles.

Achievements

Both Sandals Resorts and the more family orientated Beaches Resorts continue to accrue industry awards that re-affirm the brand's leading position across the luxury travel market – for the last 14 years the brand

has been voted the World's Best at the World Travel Awards.

The brand has also won a selection of other notable awards recently. These include winning at TripAdvisor's 2008 Travellers' Choice Awards, where Beaches Boscobel Resort & Golf Club was recognised as one of the Top 10 Hotels for Families in the Caribbean and Latin America. In 2007, Travel + Leisure Family Magazine singled out Beaches Turks & Caicos Resort & Spa as the second best overall Caribbean resort. A trio of Sandals Resorts, the Sandals Negril Beach Resort & Spa, the Sandals Dunn's River Villaggio Golf Resort & Spa and Sandals Whitehouse European Village & Spa, made it onto Condé Nast Traveller's Gold List for 2007, an accolade that reinforces the brand's continued dominance within the luxury travel sector.

1981	**1985**	**1988**	**1991**	**1993**
Gordon 'Butch' Stewart buys a dilapidated hotel in Montego Bay, Jamaica. Despite no prior hotel experience he opens Sandals Montego Bay several months later.	Sandals unveils its signature swim-up pool bar, enabling guests to order refreshments without having to leave the swimming pool.	Cuisine becomes sophisticated with gourmet meals prepared by international chefs served 'white-glove' style. Sandals Negril also opens its doors.	Sandals becomes the largest operator of all-inclusive resorts in the Caribbean and opens its first resort in Antigua.	Sandals St. Lucia is launched in April offering guests the opportunity to split their stay between two islands, Sandals Antigua and Sandals St. Lucia.

Product

Sandals prides itself on its top-of-the-range products; from à la carte restaurants, benefiting from the brand's established partnership with California's legendary Beringer Vineyards, to an extensive range of water sports – Sandals Resorts is now one of the largest dive operators in the Caribbean. Its butler service, offered in partnership with the Guild of Professional English Butlers, represents the ultimate in luxury pampering, attending to guests' every need. This includes private in-suite check-in, unpacking and packing as well as any extra special request, such as a moonlit dinner, that individual customers may require.

Sandals was one of the first operators in the Caribbean to offer European style spas. Red Lane® Spas now feature prominently in all of its establishments, with their scenic beachside locations being an enduring signature of the brand.

Recent Developments

Sandals recently introduced the concept of the Luxury Included® holidays through a collection of suites in Jamaica, Antigua, St. Lucia and the Bahamas. The new experience features an extended range of premium services and amenities that include private plunge pools and Jacuzzi baths, as well as a selection of exclusive partnerships with the likes of celebrity designers Preston Bailey and Sylvia Weinstock, the Guild of Professional English Butlers, Beringer Wines and Red Lane® Spa.

Sandals Resorts' new Mediterranean Village at the Sandals Grande Antigua Resort & Spa is

the first all-suite property to offer guests the new Luxury Included® experience and, in doing so, signifies a shift in direction for the company away from the all-inclusive label towards a more contemporary approach.

Promotion

Brand promotion comes in the form of a multi-million pound advertising campaign – that supports the efforts of travel agents and tour operators to market both the Sandals Resorts and Beaches Resorts brands – by using a broad range of mediums. These include: flyers, property-specific brochures, posters, signage, and window displays for travel agents, in addition to the more high profile television and e-commerce activities, consumer and trade advertisements, newspaper advertising and national billboards. Sandals has often been recognised by the strong, vivid and colourful aesthetics that flow through its various media campaigns, however, this visual brand identity is evolving to suit global markets in the ever changing face of luxury world travel. The new brand image is more sophisticated and lifestyle focused, hence able to deliver the Luxury Included® ethos with more success.

Sandals Resorts and Beaches Resorts operate a sophisticated CRM programme which includes a highly attractive loyalty programme named Sandals Select.

In addition, in 2006 exclusive partnerships have been developed with Crayola, defining Beaches Resorts as the first in the Caribbean to offer younger guests Crayola Art Camps. Beaches Resorts is also a sponsor of Sesame

Street®, with an exclusive Caribbean Adventure Programme where children benefit from character activities and weekly shows. Furthermore, Beaches Resorts collaborated with Microsoft® Xbox to create the Xbox 360 Game Garage Video Game Centres.

Brand Values

Sandals is one of the best-known luxury resort brands in the world. It continues to build on its leading position in the Caribbean hotel industry with innovations such as the Luxury Included® concept, making it well positioned to address consumers' growing demand for luxury choices to be included in their package holiday. Throughout its history the company has strived to create the ultimate Sandals experience: luxury, service, and uncompromising quality delivered in picturesque beachside locations.

www.sandals.co.uk

Things you didn't know about Sandals

It took seven months and US$4 million to renovate the first Sandals Resort in Montego Bay to transform it into Sandals' flagship property.

Sandals was the first Caribbean brand to offer Jacuzzi baths, satellite television, swim-up pool bars and to equip every room with a king-size bed.

Chairman Gordon 'Butch' Stewart donated US$1 million worth of holidays to military personnel who served in the Gulf War.

Although best known as a resort for 'two people in love', Sandals Resorts International also offers family holidays with its Beaches Resorts brand.

1994

WeddingMoons™ is launched – a concept combining a holiday wedding with an inclusive honeymoon.

1995

The first Beaches Resort, Beaches Negril – catering for singles, families and 'two people in love' – opens in Jamaica.

1996

Sandals Royal Bahamian Resort & Spa opens, and readers of Condé Nast Traveller name it one of their top 10 spa resorts.

2004

A butler service is introduced to Sandals' top suite categories – an ultimate all-inclusive pampering service.

The world needs ever more energy. As a global energy supplier, Shell has an enormous responsibility as the challenge to meet growing demand responsibly, safely and efficiently, gets tougher. It relies on human intelligence, new ideas, and professional discipline from the people who develop and use the technologies that make the difference.

Market

Shell is a worldwide group of oil, gas, and petrochemicals companies operating in more than 130 countries, with interests in bio-fuels, wind and solar power and hydrogen. It aims to meet global energy demand in economically, environmentally, and socially responsible ways.

Addressing the demand for clean, convenient, and affordable energy head-on, Shell is investing in ways to develop technologies to extract oil and gas previously considered inaccessible, while also developing fuels to meet the needs of the cleaner and more efficient engines of the future, helping them wear less, and travel further.

Achievements

Shell's technical partnerships with Ferrari, Audi and Ducati are a key brand differentiator, highlighting the quality of Shell technology. As part of an extensive R&D programme, motorsport, both four and two-wheel, exposes leading-edge Shell V-Power fuel technologies and Shell Helix motor oils to the scrutiny of consumers and experts alike.

Shell continues to build on a shared passion for performance with Ferrari dating back to the birth of Formula One racing in the 1950s. Since then Shell has fuelled Ferrari Formula One cars to 145 Grand Prix titles, including the 2007 Drivers' and Constructors' Championships. The experience garnered during these years has been passed on to motorists in the form of Shell V-Power, with the proposition that, 'It's not just fuel, it's Ferrari fuel for your car'.

The huge growth in new diesel cars has seen the introduction of Shell V-Power Diesel, a performance diesel fuel designed to help today's generation of diesel cars deliver more power for longer. A component of Shell V-Power Diesel in some markets is Gas to Liquids (GTL) Fuel, which is a synthetic product derived from natural gas with cleaner burning properties, giving both combustion and emissions benefits.

The technical relationship between Shell and Audi Sport continues to flourish, with the Audi R10 fuelled by Shell V-Power Diesel race fuel winning the legendary Le Mans 24-hour race in 2007, for the second year running.

The latest high performance diesel cars also require special lubricants. Shell Helix Ultra Extra is formulated with a low sulphur and phosphorus content to protect the particulate filter, which helps reduce emissions.

Shell's technical partnership, which brought Ducati its first ever MotoGP World Championship in 2007, is also significant in the development of Shell V-Power road fuels and Shell Advance oil products for the motorcycle market.

1833

Shopkeeper Marcus Samuel begins to import shells from the Far East. In the 1890s his relatives begin to export kerosene to the Far East, branding it 'Shell'.

1914-20s

Shell is the main fuel supplier to the wartime British Expeditionary Force and benefits from increased post-war motor car use. Shell Chemicals is also established.

1945-50s

Shell begins a major expansion programme as demand for oil increases massively, and also contributes to the invention of the jet engine.

1960s-80s

The Dutch Groningen and North Sea gas fields are discovered and Shell Chemicals enters a golden period for research. The 1973 oil crisis brings cheap energy to an end.

1990s

Shell grows through acquisitions and begins challenging offshore projects, while moving in to growth areas in the East. Shell's LNG business is also founded.

2005

Royal Dutch and Shell Transport are unified under Royal Dutch Shell plc.

Product
Shell is the global market leader in premium differentiated fuels with products in more than 45 markets. It is also the global leader in branded lubricants, with China the biggest and fastest growing market for Shell Helix.

All automotive fuels and lubricants are not the same and Shell's extensive R&D programmes continually strive to develop new and better fuels and lubricants, to satisfy growing customer requirements for energy efficiency, with improved engine and environmental performance. The overall aim is enhanced mobility. Shell's advanced fuel technologies include developments in deposit control, improved combustion and friction control, for more efficient operation and superior performance. Shell Helix motor oils employ active cleansing technology, designed to prevent dirt building up in the engine, so enabling it to operate to its full potential.

Recent Developments
New corporate brand communications clearly convey what Shell stands for, and what makes it different. They show the creativity and persistence of Shell people, solving problems for customers using all kinds of innovation, but particularly technology.

Promotion
Shell's corporate advertising, media partnerships and associated engagement programme position Shell as a company with a point of view; a company that is positive about energy and rejects complacency; one that listens and responds to the views of key stakeholders on issues that are relevant both to its own business and the energy industry as a whole.

In 2007, Shell engaged directly with more than 1,000 global opinion leaders – such as government and business leaders, NGO officials, academics and the media – at over 30 events across the world, via through-the-line media partnerships. Above-the-line communications focused on providing tangible examples of the way in which Shell is helping to secure a responsible energy future. A new website – www.shell.com/dialogues – features an interactive element which provides an opportunity for consumers to discuss energy issues with major players from Shell and other relevant organisations.

Shell's recruitment communications focus on the attitude of its people, their persistence and their creative problem-solving skills, introducing Shell as an inspirational place to work; an employer that values people who inject fresh thinking into the industry as it tackles some of the world's toughest challenges.

Throughout 2008, a global through-the-line campaign will continue to strengthen Shell's relationship with Ferrari in the eyes of consumers, clearly linking Shell V-Power and Shell Helix with the passion and performance of Ferrari while highlighting the particular benefits for motorists. Furthermore, a global campaign for Shell Helix will communicate its active cleansing technology to support its 'designed to meet challenges' positioning.

There will also be a forecourt promotion for a limited edition range of Ferrari keyrings, enabling consumers to own a 'piece' of Ferrari.

One of Shell's most successful promotions, which to date has seen consumers collect 37 million Ferrari model cars, also continues in 2008, with customers able to collect a set of seven 1:38 scale model Ferraris.

Brand Values
Shell's core values of honesty, integrity, and respect for others have been central to Shell's General Business Principles for 30 years, and remain as important as ever. In the pursuit of a responsible energy future, Shell is positive about the benefits of energy, rejects complacency, and applies creative, persistent problem-solving to the challenges the world currently faces.

www.shell.com

Things you didn't know about Shell

Shell's retail network serves millions of customers every day, from more than 40,000 service stations, in over 90 countries and territories.

Turnbull's of Plymouth was the first Shell garage to be converted to self-service in 1963.

The world's first commercial jet airliner – the de Havilland Comet, built in 1949 – was fuelled and lubricated by Shell.

Shell fuel and lubricants were used for the first successful flight across the English Channel, made by Louis Blériot in 1909.

For more than 60 years Silentnight Beds has been synonymous with providing comfort, support and a relaxing night's sleep to millions of consumers across the UK. Firmly established as the bed industry's largest manufacturer and brand leader, its well-known Hippo and Duck characters, first created to demonstrate the unique 'no roll-together' properties of a Silentnight bed, remain recognisable symbols across the nation.

Market

Consumers are now faced with a wider choice than ever when it comes to choosing a new bed, with products available in all price ranges, from budget to luxury. In 2007 more than five million beds were sold in the UK with a total market value of £1.4 billion. Traditional divan sets continued to make up the largest percentage of sales with 31 per cent of the market (Source: GfK).

The growing trend in the bed market has been towards 'mattress only' sales, which have become increasingly popular, accounting for 24 per cent of sales in 2007 compared to 16 per cent in 2003 (Source: GfK). This has been spurred on by an increase in bedstead sales as a style-led purchase and a growing number of outlets outside of the traditional bed specialists beginning to sell mattresses.

The increasing number of mattresses that are available to be chosen and taken away on the same day has also contributed to this growth. Silentnight Beds has met this demand with its Mattress-Now product, a rolled up mattress that comes packaged in a box for easy same-day transportation.

Achievements

Research shows that Silentnight's consumer awareness levels are at 82 per cent with spontaneous recall 20 per cent higher than its nearest competitor, making it the clear UK brand leader (Source: BMRB 2007).

Since 2003 the brand has delivered continuous innovation to the market. Products such as Chill-OUT™, a bed designed for teenagers, have earned Silentnight the title of Bed of the Year at The Furniture Awards three times in the last five years.

In 2007 Silentnight Beds launched its Book At Bedtime initiative aimed at encouraging reading in young children. Now in its second year, the competition has been endorsed by the Government and is listed on the 2008 National Year of Reading calendar of events.

Product

Silentnight Beds has become synonymous with its signature spring system, Miracoil®. Offering three key benefits – no roll-together, no roll-off and more support for your body in the central PostureZone – these unique features run through every product in the Silentnight range.

Supporting its Miracoil® Spring System, Silentnight uses additional comfort layers, such as Latex and the NASA-inspired Memory Foam, to provide consumers with a feel that best suits them.

| The Unique miracoil Spring System | NO ROLL TOGETHER | NO ROLL OFF | POSTURE ZONE |

1946

Tom and Joan Clarke form Clarke's Mattresses Limited in Skipton, North Yorkshire.

1949

As demand grows, the company relocates to a larger manufacturing site in Barnoldswick.

1951

The company changes its name to Silentnight Limited and is soon producing more than 4,000 divan beds a month.

1961

As production continues to expand at a rapid rate, Silentnight moves to a larger site, which is still in operation today.

In 2007 Silentnight launched the Mirapocket™ Collection, fusing traditional bed production techniques with new technologies. Mirapocket™ is a unique two-layer mattress which combines the support of the Miracoil® Spring System with a layer of hand-crafted mini pocketed springs. In its first year the collection accounted for 10 per cent of Silentnight's total sales.

To capitalise on the increasing trend of 'mattress only' sales, Silentnight Beds launched Mattress-Now in late 2007, a rolled up mattress that can be bought in-store and slept on that night. The mattress offers comfort and convenience, featuring a layer of Memory Foam that responds to the body's contours. More than 15,000 Mattress-Now products were sold in its first six months on sale.

Recent Developments

In January 2008, Silentnight Beds launched its all-new My First Bed™ range for kids, a collection of beds designed with both children and their parents in mind.

The four-bed collection uses Silentnight's bed-making expertise to reassure parents they are purchasing a well-made product that promotes good, health-giving sleep, while at the same time having a structure that not only withstands playtime, but encourages it.

Each mattress features the Miracoil® Spring System that supports young backs as they grow, and has a soft, knitted cover with natural aloe vera to promote a healthy, restful night's sleep. In addition, the headboards feature secret pockets for storing toys.

My First Bed™ is available as a standard child's divan or as a versatile sleepover model, which transforms into two beds.

2008 also sees the launch of Silentnight's baby cot mattress collection, My First Little Bed™, developed in partnership with Rochingham, the UK's leading cot mattress brand.

Promotion

The Silentnight Beds branding was refreshed in 2006 following a significant research programme with British consumers. The results helped Silentnight to update its communications to attract more of the UK's 30-something population, and to map its brand against two key segments of the UK bed market: Premium, those who appreciate their beds; and Functional, those who have a more practical approach to their bed.

Energy and vibrancy were added to all elements of communications but in particular through a heavyweight PR campaign and the Silentnight.co.uk website. As a result, 2006 and 2007 proved to be record years for the brand in both of these areas with more than £2 million worth of PR coverage in each year. Activities such as National Love Your Bed Week, Book At Bedtime, The Bling Bed with Myleene Klass and Big Breakfast in Bed with Jean Christophe Novelli helped to elevate the Silentnight profile.

This coverage increased consumer interest in the brand with almost 500,000 unique users visiting Silentnight.co.uk in 2007.

Brand Values

Silentnight Beds is committed to offering the consumer choice, quality, comfort and support, whilst constantly innovating with an aim of producing the ultimate bed selection. The Silentnight Beds brand is strongly associated with Hippo and Duck, the well-loved characters who add warmth and friendliness to the brand.

www.silentnight.co.uk

Things you didn't know about Silentnight Beds

In its 62 years, Silentnight has manufactured more than 40 million beds; today approximately 1,800 beds are produced each day.

A Silentnight bed is sold every 90 seconds.

Each day, Silentnight delivers 700 beds direct to customers and another 1,300 to retailers across the UK.

To cover all the Silentnight beds sold in the last five years, a duvet twice the size of the City of London would be needed.

1986

The Ultimate Spring System launches – the first new spring system in the UK for more than three decades – and the brand icons, Hippo and Duck, are first introduced.

1990s

The spring system is improved and renamed Miracoil® Spring System.

2001

An animated advert airs, featuring the voices of Clive Rowe and Jane Horrocks reworking Hot Chocolate's 'You Sexy Thing' (I Believe In Miracoils).

2007/08

Silentnight Beds is the UK's largest bed manufacturer – and has been for more than 25 years. Recent product developments include Mirapocket™ and My First Bed™.

Silver Cross®

Silver Cross is passionate about offering parents the highest levels of quality, baby comfort and safety with chic, contemporary design. A British brand with more than 130 years of heritage, Silver Cross now operates distribution channels throughout Asia, the Middle East, North America, Russia and Europe, offering fashionably designed wheeled goods while making its mark in the household with its Home Collection and providing in-car safety through its range of protective car seats.

Market

The UK baby market, which is defined as households with babies and children under the age of four years old, is currently worth an estimated £1 billion.

Already a world leader in the design, development and production of high-quality nursery products, Silver Cross is aiming for an increased share in sales of all wheeled and home goods in both domestic and international markets. Indeed, the particular focus for Silver Cross in 2008/09 is to offer new parents across the globe a truly international selection of quality nursery products.

Achievements

Silver Cross' leading British design and high manufacturing quality has been put through its paces by parents across the country in 2007 and 2008. The brand's Lifestyle range has won 16 high profile parenting magazine awards in just one year, which stands as proof of what parents really think about Silver Cross.

The brand's recent global expansion has come as a result of world wide demand for its products. The growing recognition of the brand across the globe has been aided by the popularity of its products in the UK, while celebrity endorsement has also been a key driver. Celebrity fans include Jennifer Lopez, Nicole Kidman, Charlotte Church, Brook Burke, Steven Gerrard, Frank Lampard,

Kate Hudson, Jessica Alba, Naomi Watts, Maggie Gyllenhaal and Brooke Shields as well as the British Royal Family.

Product

All Silver Cross products are created by in-house designers and product development specialists in the UK, with the aim of making mums' and dads' lives as simple as possible. Along with recent product launches, the Silver Cross brand is famous for its Lifestyle and Heritage Collections.

The highly acclaimed Lifestyle Collection, launched in 2003 with the Classic Sleepover, now encompasses: the best selling 3D Pram System, which is a fully lie-flat luxuriously lined pram, pushchair and travel system in one; an updated Sleepover, which comprises a pram, pushchair and carrycot; and the Linear Freeway – the sleekest, lightest, combination pushchair Silver Cross has ever made. The Collection also includes four car seats: the multi-award winning Ventura Plus; the Explorer Sport, a two-stage car seat that grows with the child; the Explorofix, using a push click ISOFIX installation; and the Navigator, a full adjustable group 2-3 car seat.

1877	1920s-30s	1951	1977	1988
Silver Cross is founded by William Wilson, a prolific inventor of baby carriages who created a reputation for producing the world's finest carriages.	Silver Cross becomes incorporated and is crowned the number one baby carriage for royals, supplying its first baby carriage to George VI and Queen Elizabeth.	Silver Cross launches a new shape; the forefather of the Balmoral, now synonymous with the name 'pram'.	Silver Cross celebrates its centenary by flying customers and buyers around the world in its new centenary aircraft, and by presenting a baby carriage to Princess Anne.	The Wayfarer is launched, later becoming Britain's best-selling pushchair for a decade, selling more than 3,000 a week.

The Heritage Collection includes two traditional coach built prams for newborns. The Silver Cross Balmoral pram has become a global style icon, highly favoured by the Royal Family and A-list celebrities, it sets the highest standard for handmade luxury. In addition to this, the Silver Cross Kensington pram comes from the same line and is defined by a sweeping, curved, hand-painted steel body and highly polished chrome chassis. Kensington is a practical classic with detachable body and wheels, as well as a fully-folding chassis. All coach built prams are handmade to the same high standards employed in the early 19th century. Each comes with an individually numbered plaque and certificate of authenticity, including the craftsman's signature.

The Silver Cross children's heritage toy range includes The Oberon, a carriage-built doll's pram designed as a miniature version of the Balmoral which can now be personalised with a unique plaque on the side of the pram which displays the new owner's name and date of birth alongside a fairy logo or fleur-de-lys design.

Recent Developments

In 2008, Silver Cross continues to drive forward with groundbreaking modern designs. Spearheading this activity is the new Fizz, an ultra-lightweight stroller weighing 4.5kg. It is the only stroller in its class that is reclinable and incorporates some of the sleek designs of the stylish Dazzle. Silver Cross has also pledged to donate £5 of every Fizz sold in 2008 to The Meningitis Trust, a charity close to the hearts of a number of people at Silver Cross.

Two new travel cots join the Silver Cross Home Collection, launched in 2007. The Dream Sleeper and the ultra-compact and lightweight Easy Sleeper require minimal effort to put up and down and offer a cosy and luxurious environment.

Silver Cross' unique Microban® antibacterial protection is still exclusively used within the Sovereign highchair, Boost, a toddler's booster seat and the Spa, a combined bathing and changing station.

These innovative new products are a long way from the traditional image the brand used to conjure up. While still proud of its heritage, Silver Cross also strives to provide top quality wheeled and home goods designed with the 21st century parent in mind.

Promotion

Silver Cross has always invested heavily in marketing and 2008 has seen a large rise in this investment, with consumer advertising in lifestyle and parenting titles, a presence at trade and consumer events, point of sale promotions and online promotions. The brand's new website was launched in

November 2007, aimed at building valued online relationships. The new 'Your Silver Cross' club section encourages parents to join in and share their parenting experiences online.

Silver Cross' marketing communicates in a straightforward, frank and honest way about its products. Indeed, its strongest marketing communication tool has always been word-of-mouth. From trendsetters in the film and music world to everyday British mums, the brand is endorsed by those who have first-hand experience of Silver Cross products.

Brand Values

Silver Cross is one of the UK's most loved and established brands. In 2008, over 130 years after its launch, Silver Cross still stands for elegance, fashion and cutting-edge British design. It strives to be known worldwide for its experience and passion in producing stylish and innovative products that deliver genuine value for money while making the lives of modern parents easier.

www.silvercross.co.uk

2002
Entrepreneur and businessman Alan Halsall purchases Silver Cross and relaunches the famous Balmoral.

2006
Silver Cross goes global, forging partnerships with distributors in Europe, America, Canada and Japan.

2007
Silver Cross launches its Home Collection and the combination stroller, Dazzle.

2008
Silver Cross launches its lightweight new stroller, Fizz, with £5 for every Fizz sold being donated to The Meningitis Trust.

Things you didn't know about Silver Cross

Founded in 1877, Silver Cross is the oldest nursery brand in the world.

More than 1,000 individual hand operations are required to make a Balmoral pram.

Silver Cross prams have been used by royalty for nearly 100 years.

Silver Cross sells prams in more than 30 countries worldwide.

SONY®

Sony is a global manufacturer of audio, video, communications and information technology products for consumers and professionals. With its music, pictures, game and online businesses, the company is uniquely positioned to be one of the world's leading digital entertainment brands, offering a portfolio of multimedia content. The brand that first made music with the WALKMAN® and redefined home entertainment with Trinitron® TV is leading customers into the new world of high definition.

Market

Sony holds the number one brand position in the AV/IT* sector of the UK electronics market with a value share of 14.1 per cent (Source GfK year ending March 2008).

Within this market the HD1080 LCD TV market is worth £515 million in the UK; Sony has a 31.2 per cent value share (Source: GfK year ending March 2008). Furthermore the HD1080 Camcorder market was worth more than £29.6 million for the year ending March 2008, with Sony taking a leading value share of 62.1 per cent (Source: GfK year ending March 2008). The Blu-ray Disc™ player market was worth more than £11.6 million for the same period with Sony having a leading value share of 50.1 per cent (Source: GfK year ending March 2008).

Achievements

The product that launched Sony as a consumer brand was the WALKMAN®. Released in 1979, it quickly became synonymous with the brand name. Initially described as a 'small stereo headphone cassette player', the WALKMAN® introduced the concept of mobile entertainment, selling 1.5 million in its first two years. In

2008 Sony unveiled the WALKMAN® Wirefree, an MP3 player that does more than just play tracks. As portable multimedia is an essential part of modern life, the new WALKMAN® is an all-round entertainment device. Capable of managing music collections, video downloads and photo slideshows, it comes complete with wireless bluetooth headphones to enhance today's digital lifestyles.

Over the past two years, Sony has been a driving force in the introduction of flatscreen televisions and Sony's BRAVIA

range of LCD Televisions is now a leading brand in its own right. The introduction of High Definition has relvolutionised the home entertainment experience and earlier this year Blu-ray Disc™ technology became the undisputed global industry standard. More than two and a half million discs have been sold so far in Europe and with an ever-growing catalogue from Sony Pictures Home Entertainment.

Product

2008 sees Sony continuing to pioneer the HD revolution with a broad range of innovative products, including HD1080 BRAVIA™ televisions, Blu-ray Disc™ players and recorders, HD Handycam® camcorders, Cyber-shot cameras with HD output, advanced VAIO notebooks with Blu-ray Disc™ drives and PLAYSTATION® 3.

Containing numerous features and delivering exhilarating HD 1080p picture

1946	**1950**	**1968**	**1979**	**1990**	**1995**
Tokyo Tsushin Kogyo K.K. – later to become Sony Corporation – is established with start-up capital of 190,000 yen (equivalent to about £900).	Japan's first magnetic tape recorder, the 'G-Type', launches.	Sony launches the Trinitron colour TV.	The first personal headphone stereo – the 'WALKMAN®' – is launched.	An HD-ready, widescreen, 36-inch television for home-use is launched.	Sony launches the Digital Handycam, the first consumer-use digital video camcorder.

quality, BRAVIA™ televisions are at the heart of the High Definition experience. Designed to make a home cinema experience even more accessible, the latest models have features such as BRAVIA Theatre Sync for one touch control of a home cinema setup and multiple HDMI interfaces. A device such as a Cyber-shot Digital Still Camera or a Digital SLR camera from the Sony Alpha range can be connected to a BRAVIA™ television to create photo slideshows and home videos in High Definition.

The latest Blu-ray Disc™ players aim to transport consumers into a 'high octane world of entertainment'. Current models output the superior quality of HD 1080p pictures via HDMI and preserve the intensity of original cinema films with 24p True Cinema technology. Sound quality is also intensified with Dolby® Digital Plus Surround Sound and Dolby® TrueHD decoding.

Recent Developments

In terms of product development, 2008 is proving to be a prolific year for Sony. New product launches reinforce the brand's prominence in the electronics sector. For instance, the Handycam® HDR-TG3E is the smallest, slimmest, lightest camcorder ever to feature 1920x1080 Full HD recording with 5.1ch

surround sound (among 1920x1080 Full HD Camcorders, as of April 2008 – Source: Sony Research). Small enough to carry at all times it is designed for active modern lifestyles with a titanium body and scratch-resistant hard coating.

The VAIO TP2 Home Entertainment Centre provides HD entertainment in any room with an integrated Blu-ray Disc™ Combo drive and HDMI connectivity. Digital TV can be watched, paused and recorded, as well as on demand entertainment accessed using its 500GB hard drive. Music can also be downloaded and photos and movies viewed on the big screen.

Promotion

Sony not only offers a wide array of consumer electronic products but content to bring the experience to life, whether that be a blockbuster movie from Sony Pictures or a High Definition game for PlayStation. Sony is committed to promoting 'Sony United' to consumers now and in the future to ensure that consumers receive the best possible experience from Sony.

Following the award-winning BRAVIA trilogy of adverts – 'Balls', 'Paint' and 'Play-Doh' – Sony has set out to captivate the advertising world once again with a new commercial designed to showcase the capabilities of its award-winning range of digital imaging products – including the latest models from its Handycam, Cyber-shot and Alpha ranges. The advert, entitled 'Foam City', involved the Downtown area of Miami city being transformed into a foam-filled wonderland, with streets full of foam and bubbles.

Sony recently became the new sponsor of ITV's Formula One coverage. The 18-race championship fits well with Sony, representing best-in-class technology and entertainment. Showcasing the HD range of products in an engaging and entertaining way, the ad campaign includes seven different scenarios 'Testing HD to The Limit'. Just as Formula One teams test their automotive equipment to the absolute limit, Sony tests its High Definition products in a myriad of challenging settings to ensure that they deliver the ultimate viewing experience.

Brand Values

Sony aims to be a practical visionary, predicting which products and technologies are necessary for day-to-day life and then applying them to enhance everyday living. As a company it aims to provide a dynamic working environment and open-minded corporate culture that fosters creativity and innovation, evident in its product portfolio.

www.sony.co.uk

2000	**2003**	**2007**	**2008**
Sony launches the first 'CLIE' personal entertainment organiser.	The first 'QUALIA' products are launched.	Sony introduces a full line of Blu-ray Disc™ products to the European Market.	Sony launches the world's smallest (and lightest) High Definition 1080 Handycam®.

Things you didn't know about Sony

The first-ever Sony product was a rice cooker.

The company name 'Sony' was created by combining two words: 'sonus', the Latin root of the words 'sound' and 'sonic'; and 'sonny', meaning little son, depicting a small group of young people with the energy and passion for unlimited creation.

*AV/IT equals CE, DSC, Notebooks + Desktops (Notebooks + Desktops retail market only)

Specsavers®

Specsavers is the largest privately owned opticians in the world and the market leader in the UK (Source: Mintel February 2008). Furthermore, one in three people who wear glasses in the UK buy them from Specsavers (Source: Mintel). Run by husband and wife founders Doug and Dame Mary Perkins, Specsavers is also a success abroad, where it has more than 1,000 stores in Europe, and a rapidly expanding group of 100 in Australia.

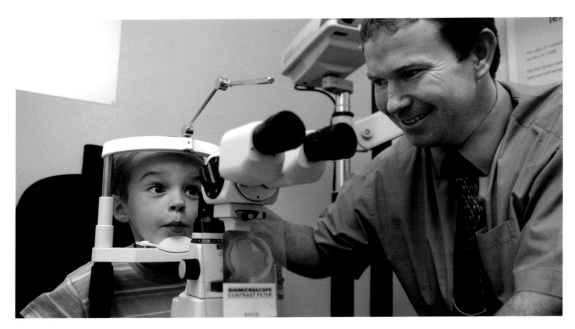

which were through the NHS. A further 257,000 eye examinations were conducted in Republic of Ireland stores and 14,000 in the Channel Islands, where there is no NHS.

Much of Specsavers' success can be attributed to its joint venture concept. Stores are owned and run by more than 1,600 optician joint venture or franchise partners, while a full range of support services, from accounting to marketing, are provided by a team of professionals, freeing the optician to do what he does best – provide the highest quality customer service.

Achieving exacting standards in a high volume business requires state-of-the-art operations, so Specsavers has invested heavily in new systems and equipment to ensure that its supply chain partners attain world-class standards.

Market
The current UK market for eyecare products and services is estimated at more than £2.6 billion, with less than 49 per cent still being provided by small independent opticians. Specsavers currently has a 35 per cent share of all transactions within the opticians' market (Source: GfK) – three times that of its nearest competitors Dollond & Aitchison and Vision Express (Source: Mintel February 2008).

While the demand for glasses has flattened out with sales barely ahead of inflation (Source: Mintel), Specsavers continues to expand, celebrating record like-for-like increases in 2007 and record sales of nearly £18 million in one week.

Expansion in Europe, where Specsavers is one of the few British retail success stories, continues to be brisk with the acquisition of a large chain in Finland and further stores opening in Spain.

Achievements
Specsavers turnover reached a record £1.02 million in 2007/08 across all markets. In the UK, more than £5 million was invested in upgrading and expanding stores. A further £4 million was invested in 25 new optical stores, creating 300 new jobs. Specsavers now employs nearly 17,000 people throughout the business.

The optical company performed 5.5 million eye tests in the UK in 2007, 66 per cent of

Product
Specsavers has maintained the Perkins' philosophy of providing affordable, fashionable eyecare for everyone. The company keeps its prices low but does not stint on quality, investing in new technology and continuing to scour the world for fashionable frames to suit all ages.

Specsavers offers its customers more than 2,000 styles to choose from, including designer brand names, such as Jasper Conran, Tommy Hilfiger, FCUK, French Connection, Red or Dead, Missoni, Quiksilver, Roxy and Bench as well as its own best-selling range of Osiris glasses.

All Specsavers glasses include Pentax lenses as standard and pricing is kept as

1984	**1997**	**2002**	**2004**	**2007**	**2008**
Specsavers Optical Group is founded by Doug and Mary Perkins, who open the first Specsavers Opticians in Guernsey, Bristol, Bath, Plymouth and Swansea.	The first overseas Specsavers Opticians opens in Haarlem, Holland. Two years later, its flagship branch in London's Tottenham Court Road opens.	Specsavers expands into hearing, acquiring the Midlands based Hearcare chain.	Specsavers celebrates 20 years of business and record profits, with expansions into Sweden, Norway and Denmark as well as the opening of the 500th store in the UK.	The retailer establishes a new product supply chain in Australia, and expands into Finland. Co-founder Mary Perkins is made a Dame of the British Empire.	Specsavers opens 150 stores in Australia and is named the Most Trusted Brand of Opticians, for the seventh year in a row, in the Reader's Digest European survey.

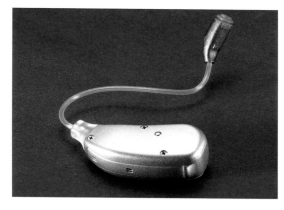

FREE
REACTIONS
WITH COMPLETE GLASSES FROM £75 RANGE OR ABOVE

Specsavers

WIN
A YEAR'S
SUPPLY OF
CONTACT
LENSES

Cannot be used with any other offer. See leaflet for details.

Specsavers

simple and clear as possible so that there are no hidden extras, proving that high quality and low price can go hand in hand. Specsavers also offers a store voucher for employers, meaning companies can now offer their staff more affordable eyecare.

The largest retail provider of home delivery contact lenses in Europe, Specsavers was one of the first optical retailers to introduce a direct debit scheme for contact lens wearers. Its own-brand easyvision lenses include daily disposables, monthly disposables and continuous wear lenses, which can be worn for up to 30 days and nights without removal.

Recent Developments
Specsavers is bringing its core offers to its rapidly expanding hearing service, which is now doing for hearing what the retailer has already achieved in optics – dramatically reducing prices and waiting times and making audiology services more accessible for everyone. Specsavers is already the largest retail dispenser of digital hearing aids in the UK and will offer a hearing service from more than 400 locations by the end of 2008.

The future continues to look bright for Specsavers' core optical business: a new store opens somewhere in the UK or Europe every week and turnover has already exceeded the £1 billion target set for the end of 2008.

Specsavers has also broadened its online offer by launching the sale of glasses. Customers are able to order from a wide range of frames and have the benefit of having them professionally fitted in-store.

Promotion
Specsavers' marketing has helped revolutionise the optical market with its 2 For 1 promotion and Clear Price policy that other opticians have struggled to replicate.

Indeed, Specsavers has been the largest advertiser in the optician sector for many years, with a total gross spend of more than £25 million per annum to promote its special offers and build its brand.

The company's 'Should've gone to Specsavers' campaign was the first to win Retail Week's Marketing Campaign of the Year award two years running and the phrase has been adopted by the nation. Its sponsorship of football and rugby referees has also attracted much support as it reflects a sense of humour appreciated by consumers.

Specsavers also runs an annual Spectacle Wearer of the Year competition to find the UK's sexiest specs wearers and the nation's favourite specs-wearing celebrities.

The company also respects its duty of care to inform people when their next eye examination is due, which is done through more than 400,000 letters to customers each week.

To keep customers informed, Specsavers' in-store magazine, View, is published three times a year and is available free of charge.

Brand Values
Specsavers is still very much a family run business with family values to match and over the past few years the company has donated more than £1 million to various charities. Recipients include Guide Dogs, Deafness Research UK, Fight for Sight and Vision Aid Overseas, for whom stores collect and recycle unwanted glasses to send to the developing world.

Every two years the company also nominates a national eyecare charity to support – its current relationship is with Diabetes UK for whom it has already raised £180,000 to fund vital research and raised awareness of diabetic retinopathy.

www.specsavers.com

Things you didn't know about Specsavers

Specsavers carried out more than 5.5 million eye examinations in 2007 in the UK – more than a quarter of all the sight tests carried out in Britain (Source: Mintel).

During 2007, 17 million Pentax branded lenses and 8.5 million frames were sold.

Specsavers sells a pair of glasses every three seconds.

If all the glasses ever sold by Specsavers were laid end to end they would wrap around the world more than three times.

Stanley's vision is to be the world's number one branded tool and tool storage supplier and to develop its high-growth security systems business. Stanley has expanded into diverse territories including the Far East and Eastern Europe. The Stanley brand name is known around the world as a reliable guarantee of quality and value. The brand is the leader in the hand tools market with a 25 per cent market share in the UK (Source: BRG 2007).

Market

Stanley is a worldwide manufacturer and marketer of tools, hardware and speciality hardware products for home improvement, consumer, industrial and professional use. The company still bears not only founder Frederick T Stanley's name but also the spirit and passion which drove him to success where others have failed.

Achievements

Stanley has recently won a number of awards. In 2007, its FatMax XL FuBar won a coveted new product innovation award at Interbuild, the annual exhibition for the building industry, which attracts tradesmen, contractors, installers, clients, architects and specifiers. In addition, Stanley was voted Hand Tools Supplier of the Year by Contract Floors magazine.

Stanley has also received several accolades and awards for its innovative and unique approach to marketing, including a National Construction Marketing Award for its launch of FatMax XL and a New York Festival Award for Best Copywriting for the company's 2007 collection of press ads.

Stanley supports an array of local and global causes and pledges to continue its legacy of charitable responsibility. Every year, Stanley and its employees partner to support thousands of worthwhile organisations across the globe.

Product

As a world leader in the design, development and delivery of tools, Stanley aims to bring to market the strongest and most innovative tools available. With thousands of products on the market and hundreds introduced each year, Stanley develops the tools people require to get a job done. Since 1857, Stanley has produced some of the most iconic tools ever made. Among these are the Powerlock tape rule, the famous Stanley knife and FatMax anti-vibe hammers.

1902	**1926**	**1937**	**1966**
Stanley makes its first exports.	Stanley's first overseas location is established in Germany.	Stanley enters the UK market via the acquisition of J A Chapman.	Stanley is first listed on the NYSE.

More recently, Stanley introduced its most ingenious tool range to date, FatMax XL. This responds to the needs of professional users and the demands of today's construction methods and materials. As a result, these are not only the toughest, most durable hand tools available on the market but they have also turned some traditional thinking on its head. For example, the FatMax XL screwdriver becomes a Demolition Driver, the FatMax XL tape reaches new levels of strength and stand out, whilst a new type of hand tool, the Functional Utility Bar – or FuBar for short – creates a unique tool category of its own.

This investment in new product development will continue throughout 2008, with the introduction of new products in all major hand tool categories.

Stanley also manufactures big tools for big jobs such as industrial hand tools, professional and industrial mechanics' tools, electronic diagnostic tools, pneumatic fastening tools and fasteners, hydraulic tools, shearers, breakers and crushers. Recognised as a leader in industrial tools, Stanley's products are used to build everything from cars and trucks to roofs and floors.

Recent Developments
In 2006, Stanley acquired Facom and Britool from Fimalac for 410 million euros. The aim was to bring together two leading European suppliers of tools with complementary brands and products. Facom and Britool have strengthened Stanley's offerings of high-end industrial and automotive tools.

Promotion
Not one to rest on its laurels, Stanley is continuing to invest in strengthening both its product range and the Stanley brand throughout 2008. Particular emphasis will be placed on supporting the professional user and promoting the FatMax XL range. With these aims in mind, Stanley took its new products to building sites across the UK in 2007 with the Judgement Day tour. This gave construction professionals the chance to road-test the new products in a number of extreme challenges.

Stanley's fully integrated media campaign will continue to utilise a new, harder hitting look and tone for the brand and will include advertising within key trade, national and consumer media titles. A continuous programme of PR activity throughout the year will also be supported with ambient promotional activity, which will include on-site demonstrations and major trade shows across the country. 2008 will also see the introduction of Stanley's new Creative Media Award competition, which will be awarded to the media partner that formulates the best campaign for promoting Stanley's professional brand of hand tools, FatMax and FatMax XL.

Brand Values
Stanley tools are designed and built for the professional and those who think like professionals.

Innovation has always been important to Stanley ever since the company was founded over 160 years ago. Furthermore, the brand has gained a reputation for excellence and so continually tests, designs and improves its products to ensure quality and maximum function.

This is summed up in the brand's strapline: Stanley – make something great.

www.stanleyworks.co.uk

Things you didn't know about Stanley

Each of Stanley's Wheeled Toolboxes is tested for 25km before being put into production.

Stanley Air Tools are used to build nearly every car and truck made in North America.

Millions of people pass through Stanley Automatic Doors every day.

Stanley Hardware is used in some of the most famous buildings in world, including Buckingham Palace, Windsor Castle and the Empire State Building.

1980
Stanley acquires MAC Tools, Proto and Bostitch.

1990
Stanley acquires Goldblatt and ZAG Industries.

2000
Stanley acquires Blick and CST Berger.

2006
Stanley acquires Facom and Britool.

Stannah
The Stairlift People

Since 1975 Stannah Stairlifts has built up an enviable reputation for delivering quality, design and innovation. Yet throughout the brand's ambitious expansion – it now employs 644 people worldwide – the UK-based, family-run enterprise has remained committed to providing a tailored service; from the conventional to the curved (and even outdoors), Stannah stairlifts can be customised to suit the style of any home.

Market

Increased life expectancy and lower birth rates have produced an ageing population. Over the next 30 years, the population aged 65 years and over is set to rise from 9.7 million to 17 million; an increase of 76 per cent. The predicted increase is even more dramatic for older age groups; the number of people aged 85 years and over is likely to rise by 2.3 million, an increase of 184 per cent (Source: A National Strategy for Housing in an Ageing Society, Department of Health/Department for Work and Pensions).

The number of stairlift users within this new demographic has been steadily rising, alongside increased Government funding of the Disabled Facilities Grant (DFG) – from £57 million in 1997 to £126 million in 2007. The DFG provides funding to people with disability and mobility needs for home improvements, such as stairlifts. By 2010 the DFG budget will reach £166 million, an increase of 31 per cent from 2007/08 (Source: DH/DWP).

Within this highly competitive market Stannah leads the way for safety, quality of service and product design. Although UK-

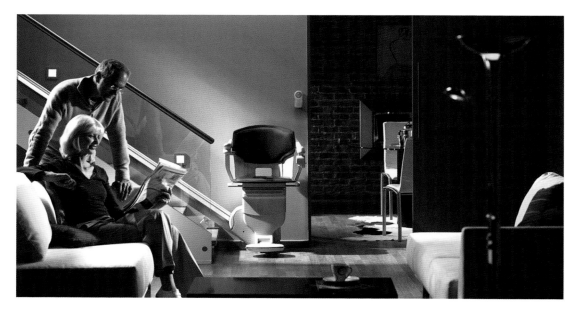

based – more than 500 stairlifts are produced every week at its factory in Andover – the brand operates globally across over 40 countries including the US, France, Holland, Italy and Germany. That 'Stannah Stairlift' has become a phrase in its own right is testament to the dominance of the brand in this burgeoning market. Stannah is not only a household name within its industry, but also more crucially, amongst consumers.

Almost 40 years of experience has furnished Stannah Stairlifts with an unrivalled range of affordable, top quality products. In addition to the company's global reputation for the use of technology in stairlift design, its range is also highly rated for the choice of fit, simple installation, ease-of-use, reliability and, most importantly, safety.

Achievements

Stannah Stairlifts is the first (and to date only) company within the stairlift market to accrue independent certification for its health and safety systems. The OHSAS 18001 standard – awarded to the brand in 2007 – is an industry accreditation established by a number of the world's leading national standards bodies, certification bodies and specialist consultancies. Achieving the standard reinforces Stannah's belief in an occupational health and safety management system that promotes consistency in risk assessment, reduces the potential for accidents and improves overall performance.

Being awarded key certifications such as the OHSAS 18001 demonstrates the brand's commitment to its ethical code and core

1860s	1975	1993/94	2003	2005	2008
Joseph Stannah starts manufacturing hoists and cranes in London, introducing hand-powered lifts soon afterwards.	Stannah produces its first stairlift and begins exporting the range in 1979.	Stannah opens subsidiaries in the US and Holland and produces its 100,000th stairlift. The division also wins its second Queen's Award for Export Achievement.	Stannah Stairlifts wins awards from the Department of Trade and Industry for the best UK manufacturing and engineering factory, and opens a subsidiary in Slovakia.	Stannah Stairlifts' new Solus chair wins the Golden Trophy Award for design. The division also purchases its distributor in Ireland and sells its 300,000th stairlift.	Stannah Stairlifts is awarded Superbrand status.

values, that place an emphasis on protecting employees, visitors and the public, as well as sharing knowledge and best practice.

A further notable achievement is Stannah's prestigious 10-year contract with Essex County Council, which makes it the chosen supplier for all stairlifts provided by the Council. When choosing the brand over other bidders, the Council commended Stannah for its innovation, design and manufacturing capabilities. It also praised Stannah's sustainable practices by way of the facilities, processes and procedures it already has in place for recycling stairlifts.

In addition, Stannah's international successes have also been recognised over the years, receiving the prestigious Queen's Award for Export Achievement three times since 1987. Today, Stannah continues to be market leader in more than 40 countries.

Product

Stannah's recent work with renowned international designers, SeymourPowell, has culminated in two new groundbreaking stairlift chairs: the Stannah Solus and Sofia. The design and quality of these chairs has been credited with elevating the global image of stairlifts, by presenting them as acceptable designer items of furniture for the home.

The design brief was to produce a choice of stairlifts, contemporary in design while being both intuitive and easy to use for elderly people. Both products feature a unique 'one-step folding system' – folding the seat, armrests and footrest away in

one simple operation – as well as a seat belt and clear controls.

Designed using contemporary materials, repositioning the product as a stylish home adaptation, Solus and Sofia are available in a range of fabrics including a leather option – a first for any stairlift.

Stannah Stairlifts has always offered a swivel option for the top of the stairs; a unique feature of both new models is the two-way automatic swivel that allows the seat to swivel at the bottom of the stairs as well. Enabling the user to get on and off the stairlift, without having to stand on the footrest, is particularly beneficial for narrow hallways where space may be limited; in accordance with Stannah's exemplary safety record, the downward swivel only functions when the stairlift is at the bottom of the stairs.

The enhanced features of the Stannah Solus and Sofia chairs are available on Stannah's complete range of stairlifts for both straight and curved stairs. This continued attention to product design detail, practicality and safety ensures that Stannah retains its prime position as the leading brand in the stairlift market.

Recent Developments

In January 2007, Stannah launched the 'Think Again Fund' in response to research that revealed many of the UK's over 50s would pursue lifetime ambitions if they had the resources to do so. Money from the fund is allocated to one applicant each month (anyone over 50 living in the UK can apply) to help them achieve their lifelong dream. The aim of the scheme is to challenge the negative perception many still have of older people.

Promotion

With 33.3 per cent of over 55s now shopping online for household white goods it makes sense for Stannah, advocates of the ageing population, to offer a web-based shopping facility. The launch of the Stannah eShop reinforces the brand's commitment to increasing accessibility to services and products for its mobility restricted customer base. The Stannah eShop not only improves

accessibility but also offers customers a 10 per cent discount on straight stairlifts.

All brand promotional activity is web-linked, where appropriate, to involve as many customers as possible and increase access to the brand by making it as simple and far-reaching as possible.

Brand Values

Stannah aims to be a caring brand that champions the older generation and those with mobility difficulties worldwide. Its family-led, almost 'paternalistic' ethos engenders loyalty in its experienced staff – which Stannah views as important when promoting a good working environment. Stannah remains committed to producing consistently high quality, reliable and well-designed stairlifts that enable its customers to maintain mobility and independence by remaining in their own homes for longer.

www.stannahstairlifts.co.uk

Things you didn't know about Stannah Stairlifts

All Stannah products are supplied with full guarantees – including access to locally based service engineers, seven days a week, 365 days a year – and are fitted by specialist installers to the stairs, not the wall.

Stannah provides solutions for all stair types, including curved, narrow and outdoor stairways.

The Stannah Think Again Fund allowed 86-year-old RAF veteran Derrick Davenport to carry out his life long dream of parachuting – jumping from a plane in tandem.

British actress Susan Hampshire OBE featured in a Stannah-produced fitness video, designed to help its customers improve their ease of movement and loosen stiff joints.

Starbucks is the leading retailer, roaster and brand of speciality coffee, with more than 15,000 retail locations around the world. The company is committed to offering the highest quality coffee and the 'Starbucks Experience', while operating in ways that produce social, environmental and economic benefits for the communities in which it does business. Starbucks entered the UK market in 1998 and now employs more than 8,500 'partners' in more than 600 wholly owned stores.

Market

Throughout 2006 the branded coffee chain market continued to expand rapidly in the UK, with more than 3,000 outlets and an estimated £1.3 billion turnover. The market has been growing at more than 15 per cent for the past eight years and is expected to almost double in size over the next 10 years, to an estimated 6,000 outlets. In the next decade turnover is expected to reach £2.5 billion.

Starbucks is recognised as the UK's favourite coffee chain, with 27 per cent of UK coffee shop visitors rating Starbucks as their preferred brand (Source: Allegra Strategies, Café7).

Achievements

Starbucks is very proud to have been named one of the FT's Best Places to Work in 2008 for the third consecutive year. Starbucks believes that investing in the development of its partners contributes to the success of the business, evidenced by the six consecutive years of high single digit growth in comparative sales in the UK.

Starbucks has always been committed to purchasing high-quality coffee in a socially responsible manner and has adopted a model called Coffee and Farmer Equity (C.A.F.E.) Practices. C.A.F.E. Practices is based on six principles that include: paying premium prices to help farmers make profits; purchasing conservation, certified, organic and Fair Trade Certified™ coffees; and investing in social development projects in coffee-producing countries. In fiscal 2007, 65 per cent of Starbucks coffee was purchased through C.A.F.E. Practices.

In 2007 Starbucks was again awarded a Business in the Community Big Tick for excellence in CSR. Starbucks works closely with the National Literacy Trust on two programmes aimed at improving literacy levels in young people. All Books for Children (ABC) is a programme that introduces pre-school children to their local library, with the chance to choose free books to take home and keep. ABC has reached 8,495 pre-school children and their families, who have chosen more than 25,485 free books.

The annual Starbucks Bookdrive was born out of the success of ABC and is designed to drive involvement of Starbucks customers and partners in collecting books for children. The Starbucks Christmas Bookdrive collected

a record 221,414 books in 2007. Since its launch in 2002, over 420,000 books have been collected in Starbucks stores and distributed to primary schools, nurseries and hospitals identified by the NLT.

Product

Starbucks purchases and roasts high-quality whole bean coffees and sells them along with fresh, rich-brewed, Italian style espresso beverages, a variety of pastries and confections, and coffee-related accessories and equipment – primarily through its company-operated retail stores. In addition to sales through its company-operated retail stores, Starbucks sells whole bean and ground coffees through selected UK supermarkets.

1971	1982	1987	1991	1998	2000
Starbucks is founded in Seattle by three friends who met at the University of San Francisco in the 1960s.	The first store is a success and catches the attention of Howard Schultz, who joins the company.	With the backing of local investors Schultz purchases Starbucks.	'Bean Stock' is introduced – a stock option scheme for all employees to make them 'partners'.	Starbucks enters the UK market through the acquisition of 60 stores from Seattle Coffee Company.	The now-annual Starbucks Christmas Bookdrive is launched with the National Literacy Trust. In the same year, Starbucks forms an alliance with Transfair USA and begins to sell Fair Trade Certified™ coffees in-store.

Recent Developments

Starbucks has had a long-standing relationship with NGO Conservation International and has recently entered into a new five-year partnership with them to address climate change. The programme will begin with two launch sites in Sumatra, Indonesia, and Chiapas, Mexico and will focus on supporting farmers, workers and their communities to help ensure their coffee is responsibly grown and ethically traded, while contributing to the search for global climate solutions.

Starbucks also has a long-standing relationship with CARE International. In 2007 the two organisations agreed to work more closely together over the next three years to improve economic and educational prospects for more than 6,000 people in a coffee growing region of West Hararghe, Ethiopia. The programme will provide farmers and their families with better food, safe drinking water and greater income, as well as enabling communities to work together to invest in their businesses and plan for the future.

2008 has also seen the launch of mystarbucksidea.com, Starbucks' first online community that takes the Starbucks Experience outside the store and enables customers to play a role in shaping the company's future.

Starbucks is continually innovating in order to improve the Starbucks Experience for its customers. Recent initiatives include an agreement to acquire The Coffee Brewing Equipment Company, making Starbucks the exclusive provider of the Clover brewing system, which is regarded as the gold standard in brewing equipment. In addition, a new espresso machine will be rolled out globally over the next 12 months. The Mastrena™ grinds every shot to order and offers many other features that result in superior espresso shots.

Starbucks aims to maintain an innovative beverage and food offering that is constantly evolving. Recent popular introductions include Starbucks' premium Signature Hot Chocolate, Crème Brule Latte and limited availability Black Apron Exclusives coffees. Under the Black Apron programme, Starbucks has recently introduced to the UK its first ever wholebean coffee from Rwanda – Rwanda Blue Bourbon.

Promotion

Storytelling is part of Starbucks' culture and, as part of a non-traditional marketing model, the success of the company's communication strategy is rooted in its partners' passion for and involvement in the company's innovative product and experience. The company has established seasonal favourites in the UK and Ireland, including Gingerbread Latte and Frappuccino™ Iced Blended Coffee and will introduce further choices later in 2008.

Starbucks has been at the forefront of innovating the coffee house experience in the UK over the last 10 years and coined the phrase the 'third place' – a restful environment between home and work in which to relax, take time for yourself and enjoy a freshly brewed cup of high quality coffee. Partnerships with a leading mobile network and national quality newspaper have further enhanced the experience.

Brand Values

Starbucks was created and is run on what has been described as 'a new way of doing business'. Its mission is to establish itself as the premier purveyor of the finest coffee in the world, while maintaining its uncompromising principles as it grows. While applying the highest standards of excellence to the purchasing, roasting and fresh delivery of its coffee and recognising that profitability is essential to its future success, Starbucks aims to make a positive contribution to the global and local communities in which it works, through working with a number of trade partners with expertise in areas such as social development, employability and literacy.

www.starbucks.co.uk

Things you didn't know about Starbucks

Starbucks is one of the largest purchasers, roasters and distributors of Fair Trade Certified™ coffee worldwide, offering Fair Trade Certified™ coffee in 28 countries.

Starbucks offers 87,000 different ways of preparing a cup of coffee – choosing exactly how you want your coffee prepared is known as 'customisation'.

The baristas wearing black aprons, rather than the famous green, are 'Coffee Masters'.

Starbucks only buys from the top 10 per cent of Arabica beans grown between 900 and 1,500 metres altitude.

2003
The Starbucks Coffee Master Programme is launched.

2006
Starbucks is awarded a Business in the Community Big Tick for excellence in CSR – for the second consecutive year.

2007
Starbucks is named by the FT as one of the 10 Best Places to Work in the UK.

2008
Starbucks reaches its 10th year of operation in the UK.

Tate & Lyle Cane Sugar has been produced at Tate & Lyle's UK-based refinery since 1878. The company first became famous as a pioneer of the sugar cube. More recently Tate & Lyle has announced its intention to switch all of its retail cane sugars range to Fairtrade, the largest wholesale transfer to an ethical scheme by any major UK food or drink brand; an ongoing commitment to sustainable development and progressive thinking from one of the world's leading sugar suppliers.

Market

The UK retail sugar market is worth £320 million, of which Tate & Lyle Cane Sugar has a 21 per cent brand share (Source: Nielsen MAT 2007). According to a recent survey by Millward Brown, Tate & Lyle is the best-known sugar brand amongst consumers, with 98 per cent spontaneous awareness.

Its Thames-based Silvertown refinery, the only cane sugar refinery in the UK, is one of the largest cane sugar refineries in the world – processing more than one million tonnes annually at up to 160 tonnes per hour.

Achievements

In November 2007 Tate & Lyle announced that while its cane sugar carbon footprint was low – 0.43 tonnes per tonne of sugar – it aimed to reduce it further by constructing a biomass boiler at its Thames refinery site. Post 2009 – and with the boiler working at full capacity – the carbon footprint of cane

sugar produced at the refinery will decrease to 0.32 tonnes per tonne of sugar.

The biomass project demonstrates the brand's ongoing commitment to sustainable production; raw cane sugar milling is virtually carbon neutral and shipping the sugar utilises one of the most energy efficient modes of transport, producing low levels of CO_2 emissions per tonne shipped.

The company's commitment to sustainability includes investing time and resources into projects that directly address local needs. This long term focus on community involvement has been recognised by a host of industry awards that include the Food and Drink Federation 2006 Gold Award, for education support programmes, and Silver Award in the 2007 Workplace Community category, for its employee health and well-being programmes.

The recent commitment to Fairtrade was born out of Tate & Lyle's historical long term trading relationships with sugar cane growing countries in the Caribbean and Pacific regions and Africa. Tate & Lyle recognises its responsibility as a significant contributor to many of the local economies and it was a natural progression for the company to help Belize to gain Fairtrade certification and to make a commitment to switch all of its retail cane sugar to Fairtrade by the end of 2009.

Product

The Tate & Lyle Cane Sugar range offers a variety of sugars to suit all occasions: from granulated, demerara, cubes, crystals, light

cane and fruit sugar, for adding to drinks and food, to sugars for baking such as caster, three types of icing sugar, light and dark soft brown and special jam-making varieties. The packaging, which is being updated to reflect the brand's new Fairtrade status, helps consumers to navigate the range with bright colours differentiating the products.

At the core of the brand's quality is cane sugar which differentiates Tate & Lyle Cane Sugar from its beet-based competitors in

1859
Henry Tate becomes a partner in John Wright & Co. Sugar Refiners.

1869
Tate gains overall control of the company and renames it Henry Tate & Sons (later to become Tate & Lyle).

1878
A second sugar refinery is opened, on the banks of the River Thames in Silvertown.

1897
Tate donates his collection of British 19th century art to the public and provides funding for a building to house it – his name was subsequently given to the Tate Gallery.

the market. When it comes to cooking, cane sugar, grown in sunny climates, is acknowledged to be superior to beet and 94 per cent of shoppers agree, saying they prefer cane sugar to beet (Source: Tate & Lyle consumer survey 2007).

Recent Developments

Tate & Lyle's recent focus has been on two consumer concerns: healthy choices and sustainability. In 2004 the brand launched two new product lines in response to increased demand for healthy sugar alternatives: Tate & Lyle Fruit Sugar, with a low Glycaemic Index that releases energy into the body slowly and Tate & Lyle Light Cane, with 33 per cent fewer calories than conventional sugar.

In regard to ethical production, in February 2008 the company announced its intention to move its retail cane sugars range to Fairtrade, marking the largest wholesale switch to an ethical scheme by any major UK food or drink brand. In the first year it is anticipated that the changeover will create a return of at least £2 million in Fairtrade premiums for 6,000 cane farmers in Belize. The first product licensed to carry the Fairtrade mark will be Tate & Lyle Granulated Cane Sugar, sourced from Belize; the brand's first accredited grower-partner from whom it has purchased sugar for more than 35 years.

Promotion

Research suggests that a popular image evoked by Tate & Lyle is that of childhood family baking sessions, particularly from consumers who place a high value on quality and authenticity. The brand's marketing campaigns focus on this British lifestyle association through recipe-led promotions. Seasonal periods for baking and preserving, such as the marmalade and jam making seasons and Christmas and Easter see increased brand activity. Online promotion includes emails to subscribers to the brand's website that convey a mixture of seasonal news, recipe ideas and offers. New product lines, such as Light Cane and Fairtrade, have seen sustained launch campaigns that incorporate press advertisements, posters, radio and sample tastings, in addition to the more conventional PR promotional packages.

Brand Values

Tate & Lyle Cane Sugar's upbeat philosophy aims to encourage consumers to 'taste and smile'. This aims to reflect Tate & Lyle's ethos: to enhance the taste of food and drink through its range of cane sugars, and celebrate the good times whether it's a relaxing cuppa, baking with the children or a full-on celebration, while reaching out to new and existing customers through quality innovation.

www.tasteandsmile.co.uk

Things you didn't know about Tate & Lyle Cane Sugar

Sugar arrived in England around 1100, yet it remained a rare delicacy for several hundred years.

In the 1500s a 100-ton shipload of sugar was worth about £1 million at today's prices.

In 1875 the sugar cube was introduced to the UK by Henry Tate; prior to this sugar was distributed in conical loaves, which the grocer had to break up.

Vessels delivering raw cane sugar to Tate & Lyle are the largest cargo ships to berth in London.

1921

Descendents of Henry Tate and Abraham Lyle form Tate & Lyle. It's said that, despite operating refineries located less than one mile apart in East London, Henry and Abraham never met.

1932

Tate & Lyle becomes a founder member of the FT 30 Index, and is one of the few still in business today.

2008

Tate & Lyle is the only cane sugar refiner in the UK, and the largest in Europe. The refinery's annual output exceeds one million tonnes per annum.

Also in 2008, Tate & Lyle commits to turn its entire retail cane sugars range Fairtrade.

TED BAKER
LONDON

What started out as a fairly modest men's shirt specialist in Glasgow 20 years ago has developed into a leading designer fashion brand. Its unconventional approach, quirky sense of fun and, above all, commitment to quality and detail has helped Ted Baker to establish a loyal and expanding worldwide following.

Market

Ted Baker operates globally across a number of highly competitive fashion markets although its primary focus is clothing. In the UK clothing retail sales are predicted to grow to £30.4 billion in 2008, an increase of 26 per cent since 2002, and by 2012 are expected to account for some 12.6 per cent market share of all retail sales (Source: National Statistics Office/Mintel September 2007).

Fuelled by a desire for constant new trends, in recent years, the value clothing sector has seen huge growth – presenting a challenge to more premium brands such as Ted Baker. It is predicted however, that there will be a move away from disposable fashion with a new kind of consumer emerging who equates value to quality and design rather than price. These shoppers still want to be seen as style conscious and fashionable, without being slaves to fashion. This trend will see consumers, often concerned about the green and ethical issues surrounding the production of cheap clothing, choosing to buy less items, but of a higher, more durable quality. For the retailer, differentiation will be key, offering consumers a wider brand proposition and a more comprehensive range of services to capture their imagination.

Achievements

2008 marks an important year for Ted Baker; not only does the company celebrate 20 years as a brand and 10 operating as a PLC but it also sees the 10th anniversary of the launch of its inaugural New York store – the first of the brand's stores to open in the US. 2008 is also a defining year for the brand's

underwear and fragrance collections by reaffirming their longevity within such a highly competitive sector.

Ted Baker has 62 stores located across the globe as well as more than 90 concessions in the UK selling its clothing collections and range of accessories, which spans shoes and jewellery to mobile phones and fragrances. Further to which, plans are underway for new store openings.

Product

Ted Baker creates distinctive collections with a particular emphasis on design, detail, product quality and value. There are four

main launches each year, in spring, summer, autumn and at Christmas. Ted also has season changeover transitional collections and fresh product stories launching weekly throughout each season.

The menswear collection offers both everyday wear items such as shirts, jersey, knitwear, denim and outerwear alongside its Phormal range (formalwear with a fashion edge) – which features product from the mainline, Endurance suiting line and the luxury limited edition Global collection. The latter being an innovative combination of leading-edge technology and traditional tailoring techniques. The latest addition to

1987	**1988**	**1990**	**1997**	**1998**	**1999**
The idea for a global brand comes to Ted Baker – a eureka moment while out fishing.	The first Ted Baker store opens in Glasgow, quickly followed by stores in Manchester (King Street) and Nottingham (Exchange Arcade).	Ted Baker's first London store starts trading in Covent Garden.	With its first continental franchise in Zurich, the brand branches further into Europe and in the same year becomes a public company.	The first standalone Ted Baker store opens on American soil in New York, and its first website is launched.	Ted Baker's largest store to date opens in Bluewater Shopping Centre. The Endurance range of suits is launched as well as a new fragrance, Woman.

the Phormal collection, 'Pashion', offers the ultimate in sharp suiting and has been designed to inject passion back into formalwear.

The womenswear collection at Ted Baker was launched in 1995, and has changed emphasis dramatically over the last few years. While the focus remains on the design, quality and attention to detail synonymous with the brand, there has been a conscious move towards developing more sophisticated, on-trend silhouettes, prints and colours to remain relevant yet distinctive in an increasingly competitive industry.

Dresses remain an integral part of the collection with styles, fabrics and shapes aimed at accommodating wide-ranging tastes and preferences. While sophisticated knitwear, jersey, outerwear, denim and tailoring in high quality natural fabrics complete the offer.

The brand prides itself on delivering superior quality for less – 'twice the product for the half the price'. This maxim is carried through to its burgeoning accessories and footwear collections for men and women. These ranges are designed to complement the clothing collections, incorporating the same directional colours, patterns, textures, trims and prints.

Recent Developments

One of the key areas of brand development in recent years has been store expansion. Recent store launches have ranged from as far a field as Taiwan, which saw its first opening in 2007, to Belfast and Cambridge,

much closer to home, where two new stores have been opened in 2008. Additional openings are also in the pipeline.

A further new venture for the brand has been the launch of its latest store concept, Ted Baker & Friends. This collaboration between Ted Baker, King of Shaves Pro, The Carphone Warehouse, Cushion The Impact and Street Shine, aims to provide an engaging shopping experience for busy City types in Cheapside, in the heart of the City of London.

Promotion

Ted Baker has prided itself on building up a global reputation without the help of conventional advertising. As one of the pioneers of experiential marketing, the brand's irreverent sense of fun is used to connect and engage with consumers and engender customer loyalty.

The first Ted Baker store, offering a shirt laundry service to customers, established the approach that brand communications remain focused on to this day: forging a personal relationship with the customer. This core principle of establishing a direct and engaging connection with customers has been at the forefront of the brand's communication strategy since the beginning and is firmly entrenched in the Ted Baker ethos.

Communications synergise closely with the product, store environment, and service delivery to create an integrated brand and customer experience. Humorous and off the wall, Ted Baker's communications are never ordinary; irreverent window displays, unusual

store events and quirky messages, games, gifts and giveaways are designed to surprise and delight the customer – adding value to their experience each time they visit a store. Brand communications are aimed at creating and retaining customer loyalty and endeavour to deliver a healthy return on investment.

Brand Values

The brand's values lie in the uncompromising quality of its products coupled with attention to detail and an innate sense of fun – evident throughout its ongoing in-store communications with customers. It is this irreverent humour and quirkiness, long associated with the brand, that makes it stand out as a global leader rather than follower of fashion.

www.tedbaker.com

Things you didn't know about Ted Baker

Ted's first store in Glasgow offered a complimentary laundry service to its customers.

While sharing a common feel, each Ted Baker store is bespoke, designed with its own distinctive personality.

Ted Baker's Regent Street Store has a revolving front room on its first floor.

Ted Baker sponsors Team Bath, the Bath University Football Team who, in the 2002/03 season, were the first university side to reach the first round of The FA Cup since 1881.

Ted Baker celebrated the opening of its first Australian store, in Melbourne, with a village fête complete with morris dancers.

2003

Ted Baker's luxury collection, Global, launches alongside its own limited edition fragrance of the same name.

2006

Ted becomes the official suit supplier to Australia's Socceroos for the football World Cup and launches its first ever Cool Camping collection.

2007

New stores open, from Dubai and Malaysia, to Miami and Melbourne. The Pashion and Livewire Endurance suits hit the market, as do a jewellery line and mobile phones.

2008

Ted Baker celebrates its 20th year by opening its first US outlet store and more UK stores. A new collaborative store concept, Ted Baker & Friends, also launches.

Born in the early days of the Texas oil boom, Texaco has grown from a small, dynamic enterprise into one of the world's major petroleum companies. The Texaco brand has been an active force in UK society, fuelling industry and the economy, keeping people on the move and participating in a range of community and environmental projects for more than 80 years.

Market

The market is in a mature state and presents a challenging environment to major oil companies and independent operators alike.

Change has been driven by a combination of high fuel taxes, low margins, aggressive hypermarket expansion and a subsequent fall in the total number of service stations in the UK to the lowest level since 1912. This contraction has focused primarily on company-owned and operated service stations with the remaining dealer network being noticeably improved through the addition of impressive non-fuel concepts. The market is now characterised by sophisticated shop formats, as well as alliances between traditional oil companies and convenience store operators. A strong brand and reputation for quality fuel has proved key and the Texaco-branded network now accounts for an increasing share of total UK service stations.

Chevron, under the Texaco brand, markets its fuel through around 1,100 service stations in the UK – the largest branded network of independently owned service stations in the country.

Achievements

In 1975, the Tartan field was discovered east of Shetland and the first oil came ashore in 1981, making it one of the UK's earliest producing oil fields.

Texaco has been well known for more than 50 years for its children's road safety awareness initiatives, including the 'Children should be seen and not hurt' campaign in the early 1990s. In 2006, new road safety messages for children were provided in a series of booklets, available at Texaco service stations, featuring a cartoon character called Hector. The campaign proved to be

1901	**1903**	**1911**	**1916**	**1964**	**1970s**
The forerunner of Texaco, the Texas Fuel Company is established in the US. Its first international shipment of one million barrels of crude oil a year is made to the UK the following year.	The first Texaco Company refinery starts operations in Port Arthur Works, Texas, and processes 318,364 barrels of oil in its first year.	Texaco opens its first service station on a street corner in Brooklyn, New York – the beginnings of a rapidly growing retail network.	Texaco Petroleum Products Company arrives in the UK.	Her Majesty, the Queen Mother opens the company's Pembroke Refinery.	Texaco-sponsored Emerson Fittipaldi becomes Formula One World Champion in 1972, clinching his second world title in 1974. James Hunt, also sponsored by Texaco, wins the 1977 championship.

successful with both children and their parents. In response, a new Hector safety campaign was launched in 2007 with animated DVDs designed by the creators of Wallace and Grommit, Aardman Studios – available free with a fuel purchase at Texaco service stations. The superior animation and clear messages were recognised when the campaign won the title of New Media: Best Commissioned Animation, at the 2008 British Animation Awards (BAA) and a Gold Award at the 2008 Institute of Sales Promotion (ISP) Awards for Art Direction and Copywriting.

Many local charities across the UK receive support each year from Chevron, the owner of the Texaco brand. However, the firm has been supporting the children's charity NCH for more than 15 years and recently the amount raised by staff and customers, to help vulnerable young people, reached more than £1 million.

Product
The Texaco brand is best known by consumers for its quality fuels and Havoline branded oils and lubricant products. Chevron however also supplies fuels and lubricants to major airlines and shipping customers as well as products and services for industrial and commercial use.

Recent Developments
The last few years have seen a significant increase in emphasis on both energy security and climate change awareness. Chevron acknowledges that biofuels have a role to play in reducing CO_2 emissions and is committed to working with governments, engine manufacturers and consumers to reduce these. Chevron believes in encouraging the debate on meeting the world's future energy needs and to support this, launched the online forum www.willyoujoinus.com to encourage comment. Chevron is also committed to making its own operations more energy efficient and is investing US$2.5 billion between 2007 and 2009 in alternative and renewable fuels. In the UK, it has also invested in its business to be able to offer biofuels and sulphur-free fuels to its customers.

James Hunt
1976 McLAREN M23

72

Fire Chief

Oil Delivery Pick-up

Take home a Texaco Old Timer

Only
£3.49

when you spend £10 or more here (fuel or instore)

Convertible Pace Car

Tow Truck

Trust your car to the

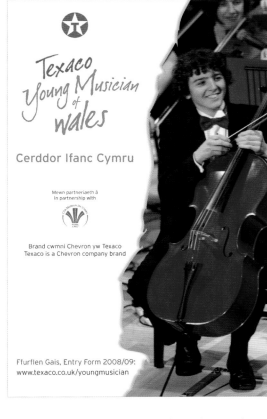

Texaco Young Musician of wales

Cerddor Ifanc Cymru

Mewn partneriaeth â
In partnership with

Brand cwmni Chevron yw Texaco
Texaco is a Chevron company brand

Ffurflen Gais, Entry Form 2008/09:
www.texaco.co.uk/youngmusician

Promotion
In 1990, a 1940s model Texaco service station was built in Universal Studios in Orlando, Florida. The motion picture company used this authentic recreation of a Texaco station for 1940s-era films and to provide present-day motorists with a nostalgic experience while they purchased Texaco fuel. It was the popularity of this experiential brand work and the consumer's love of a bygone age that lead to the creation of the Old Timers model car promotions during 2008.

The Texaco brand has been rewarding loyal customers for more than 30 years through a range of innovative loyalty schemes. In 2008, its programme was relaunched as Star Rewards, with a dedicated website – www.starrewards.co.uk. This scheme enables customers to be rewarded with shopping and fuel vouchers with every pound they spend in a Texaco service station.

A core group of Texaco customers are families and the company has been encouraging motorists to help their children become more aware of road safety with the help of the award-winning cartoon character, Hector.

With the company's refinery in Pembroke, fuel terminal in Cardiff and an extensive network of service stations across Wales, Texaco wanted to give something back to the Welsh community. In 1989 the Texaco Young Musician of Wales competition was launched to recognise classical talent across the country. Since then, the competition has grown steadily and 2009 will see the finals taking place in Cardiff's St David's Hall with the Cardiff Philharmonic Orchestra and Côr Meibion De Cymru, the South Wales male voice choir.

Brand Values
The Texaco Star was designed to be a beacon on the road for motorists – an enduring symbol portraying a sense of performance, quality and trust for the Texaco brand.

Texaco aims to be a strong, reliable, trustworthy, iconic, knowledgeable and experienced Americana brand, known for enduring performance and established trust amongst customers who love their cars.

www.texaco.co.uk

Things you didn't know about Texaco

Although the Texaco Petroleum Products Company was trading under the Texaco brand in 1916, following a merger in 1947, the service stations were rebranded to the Regent Oil name. This remained until they were returned to the Texaco brand in 1967.

In 1977, Texaco ran a series of TV advertisements with Formula One champion James Hunt and Morecambe & Wise, which were voted the most memorable advertisements of that year.

1984
Texaco sponsors the Texaco Trophy One-Day Cricket International series.

1989
The inaugural Texaco Young Musician of Wales competition takes place.

2005
ChevronTexaco Corporation is created from the merger of Chevron Corporation and Texaco Inc. It becomes Chevron Corporation in 2007 – one of the largest corporations in the world.

2008
Texaco becomes the largest branded network of independently owned service stations in the UK and Texaco's loyalty card scheme relaunches as Star Rewards.

The Daily Telegraph

The Daily Telegraph, established in 1855, is the UK's best-selling quality newspaper, with an audited circulation of 881,071 (Source: ABC, average daily circulation February 2008). In its broadsheet format, the newspaper offers home and international news coverage, a stand-alone business section, which is highly respected in the City, and a compact daily sport section.

Market

The UK's quality daily newspaper market comprises The Daily Telegraph, The Times, the Guardian and The Independent which together account for 2.1 million copies per day (Source: ABC Monday-Saturday average February 2008). The Daily Telegraph is the market leader with a 42 per cent share, approximately 248,000 copies ahead of The Times.

Achievements

At the 2008 British Press Awards, The Daily Telegraph's Matt Pritchett was named Cartoonist of the Year, taking his tally of honours – which includes an MBE – to 13 during his 20 years with the newspaper. Charles Spencer, The Daily Telegraph's theatre critic, was awarded Critic of the Year. In October 2007 The Daily Telegraph was named Best Consumer Online Publisher at the Association of Online Publishers' awards and in March 2007 it was awarded Best Newspaper Sport Coverage at the Sports Industry Awards.

Product

The Daily Telegraph is known for its line-up of distinguished journalists and columnists, who lend the paper its distinctive voice and personality. Delivering lively and challenging comment on the issues of the day, The Daily Telegraph boasts such unique contributors as Craig Brown, Con Coughlin, Andrew Pierce and Simon Heffer. The Sport team includes football writer Henry Winter, as well as numerous sporting luminaries such as Alan Hansen, Brian Moore, Zara Phillips and James Cracknell. The Daily Telegraph Business section is famous for its accurate, bold and insightful coverage, provided by an award-winning team of journalists including the business editor-at-large, Jeff Randall.

Fashion director, Hilary Alexander, is a stalwart of the world's catwalk front rows. She brings her flair and experience to the fashion pages not only in the newspaper and online, but now in her own Telegraph TV programme, Hilary & Co, where she talks to top designers and takes viewers behind the scenes of the fashion industry.

The Daily Telegraph has been home to the Matt cartoon – the creation of the award-winning cartoonist Matt Pritchett – since 1988 and one of the most popular features of the Business section is the Alex cartoon, which comments on the wheeling and dealing of the business world. In December 2007 Alex was brought to life on stage in London's West End in the form of Alex the Play.

September 2006 saw a design revamp of The Daily Telegraph on Saturday, introducing a new technology section, Digital Life. The redesign also involved other sections including Motoring, which features James May's column and advice from Honest John; Weekend, featuring Graham Norton and Ruby Wax's outspoken advice column; and the award-winning Telegraph Magazine.

August 2007 marked the passing of one of The Daily Telegraph's most esteemed contributors, the columnist and former editor,

1855
The first Daily Telegraph & Courier is published, having been founded as a vehicle for its proprietor, Colonel Sleigh, to wage a vendetta against the Duke of Cambridge and his conduct in the Crimea War.

1897
A young Winston Churchill reports from the North West Frontier for the Telegraph.

1987
The Telegraph moves from Fleet Street to the Isle of Dogs then moves to Canary Wharf five years later.

1994
The Electronic Telegraph becomes the first British newspaper to launch on the internet.

2006
The Telegraph Group rebrands to become Telegraph Media Group and moves from Canary Wharf into state-of-the-art offices in Victoria, central London.

2007
The Telegraph launches Telegraph TV.

W.F. Deedes, who first joined The Daily Telegraph in 1937.

Recent Developments

In 2006, Telegraph Media Group embarked on a momentous shift in the way it published news. Where previously stories were broken in the newspaper and subsequently posted online, stories are now reported as they happen and published across several platforms. In order to provide the state-of-the-art newsroom required for this new approach, the Telegraph moved to new offices in central London. It now occupies one of the biggest open office spaces in Europe, accommodating the new 'hub and spoke' editorial system.

This move also reflects the Telegraph's commitment to offering its customers quality news content when – and how – they want it. Since launching its daily podcast in November 2005 – the first UK quality newspaper to do so – the Telegraph has constantly innovated in bringing new features to its audience in the digital environment. Recent advances include a portfolio of widgets and online applications that allow users to place Telegraph content within their own social network profiles and homepages, such as Facebook and iGoogle.

Launched in September 2007, Telegraph TV has taken The Daily Telegraph's journalists from pages to programmes. There are now 12 shows produced exclusively for Telegraph.co.uk. These include the travel show, Real Trips; the daily Business Bullet; and Lloyd Grossman and Xanthe Clay's cookery show, 10 Minutes to Table. A recent highlight on the sporting front was Carling's Round, Will Carling's Six Nations chat show.

As Telegraph.co.uk continues to bring new audiences to the Telegraph portfolio, so a

'Would you also photograph my suitcase, so I have something to remember it by?'

constant programme of product development is helping to build distinct communities of interest on the website. These now range from a crossword community, to communities centred on dating and genealogy. The MyTelegraph online blogging community also invites users of Telegraph.co.uk to create their own blogs, post their views and contribute to a varied array of online discussions.

Promotion

April 2008 saw the launch of Thatcher – a series of eight DVDs charting the political and personal life of the former Prime Minister. This series was produced exclusively for The Daily Telegraph and features rare archive footage and recent interviews from leading political figures such as Sir Bernard Ingham, Lord Howe and Lord Kinnock.

The Daily Telegraph creates dedicated events for its customers, ranging from an exclusive performance of The Sound of Music to nationwide shopping evenings held in collaboration with major brands, including Jaeger and Fenwick.

The Daily Telegraph is the official media partner to the Orange BAFTA awards, a partnership highlight of the year. Other events in which the Telegraph has been involved include the RHS Chelsea Flower Show, the CLA Game Fair, the Bath Children's Literature Festival and the Ways with Words Literary Festival.

The Daily Telegraph is the official newspaper of the England cricket team, thanks to its partnership with the ECB. Each year thousands of readers and online users compete to manage the best team of the season in Telegraph Fantasy Football. Fantasy Football fans can also fill the off-season void with Fantasy Cricket. In addition, The Daily Telegraph supports a grassroots Junior Golf programme, attracting more than 41,000 entrants in 1,000 regional competitions.

In September 2007, The Daily Telegraph launched an integrated marketing campaign to support its editorial coverage of the Rugby World Cup in France featuring Telegraph experts Brian Moore, Keith Wood and Will Greenwood. The activity included giant inflatable billboards outside grounds; posters at Premiership clubs; a partnership with the radio station talkSPORT; press advertising;

and dedicated online match reports, videos, blogs and competitions.

The Telegraph's coverage of Alistair Darling's first Budget speech as Chancellor of the Exchequer included exclusive interviews on Telegraph TV with industry experts and the most recent Conservative Chancellor, Kenneth Clarke. Telegraph.co.uk ran up-to-the-minute news and instant reaction, helping readers to understand what the Budget really meant for them, with expert analysis and Budget calculators to bring it all to life. Budget Day was followed up with an eight-page broadsheet Budget special featuring in-depth commentary and insight from Jeff Randall, Roger Bootle, Edmund Conway and Ian Cowie.

To support the Telegraph's Budget coverage, thousands of 'Budget Box' flyers were distributed at mainline and underground stations in London's business districts during that morning, followed by a four-page Budget special, featuring news and analysis for commuters travelling home in the evening. An extensive online advertising campaign, targeting business and political websites, helped raise awareness of the Telegraph's online coverage throughout the day.

Brand Values

The Daily Telegraph brand values are defined as: accuracy, honesty, integrity, quality and heritage.

www.telegraph.co.uk

Things you didn't know about The Daily Telegraph

In 1925 The Daily Telegraph became the first British newspaper to publish a daily crossword.

In 1887 the Telegraph hosted a party in Hyde Park for 30,000 school children to celebrate Queen Victoria's Golden Jubilee, which was attended by Her Majesty.

In 1899 a Telegraph Appeal for the Widows and Orphans Fund raised an astonishing £255,275.

Thomas Cook

Thomas Cook first took Britons away from home in 1841, invented the first-ever overseas package holiday in 1845 and now takes more than six million people on a Thomas Cook holiday every year. Thomas Cook is one of the two largest travel groups in the UK with 19,000 employees, 800 high street stores, Thomas Cook Airlines, a TV channel, leading websites and a growing financial services and foreign exchange offering.

Market
The travel industry is rapidly changing. The companies who 'create' the holiday – tour operators – have expanded into selling directly to customers, becoming retailers; retailers have expanded into tour operations; and shopping online came from nowhere and now accounts for a quarter of all travel bookings.

2007 saw one of the biggest changes in the travel industry for many years with the four main companies – Thomas Cook, MyTravel, Thomson and First Choice – merging into two: Thomas Cook and TUI.

During 2007, a record 71 million people in the UK took an overseas trip. Nineteen million of these were package holidays – an increase of almost one per cent on 2006, and, contrary to popular belief, the package holiday is as popular now as it was in the mid-1990s (Source: International Passenger Survey (ONS) April 2008).

The travel industry is notoriously affected by many factors, from weather conditions and sporting events to terrorism and consumer debt. Thomas Cook, however, consistently outperforms the market during these difficult times and remains the most trusted travel brand in this country, if not the world (Source: Conquest Research February 2008).

Achievements
Thomas Cook and MyTravel offically merged on 19th June 2007, leading to significant changes for not only the company but for the international travel industry as a whole. As a result, in December 2007 Thomas Cook Group was offically promoted into the top 100 listed companies on the London Stock Exchange, securing a much-coveted place in the FTSE 100.

Other key accolades include being voted the Travel Agency of the Year, Best Tour Operator in the Caribbean and Best Tour Operator to Eastern Mediterranean at the British Travel Awards, Best Short Haul Operator at the Triton Travel Group Conference Awards and even Best Credit Card Design at the UK Credit Card Awards.

The company takes its role as a responsible business very seriously. Thomas Cook raises money for Travel Foundation – the charity that establishes sustainable tourism projects around the world – contributing £500,000 per year to the organisation.

In 2004 Thomas Cook selected the Variety Club Children's Charity as its corporate cause, based on a vote across all company employees. The company pledged to raise £2 million to build a state-of-the-art critical care unit at the Variety Club Children's Hospital based within King's College Hospital. In May 2008 The Thomas Cook Children's Critical Care Centre opened, housing intensive care and high dependency units – made possible through customer donations and fundraising efforts from both teams and individuals, company-wide.

More recently, Thomas Cook has put its weight behind campaigning for an extra bank holiday for the UK. This has resulted in over 500,000 signatures to a petition that was handed in to 10 Downing Street in March 2008.

1841	1855	1872/73	1874	1892	1939
Thomas Cook's first excursion, a rail journey from Leicester to a temperance meeting in Loughborough, takes place.	Thomas Cook's first continental tour takes place. Thomas takes two parties from Harwich to Antwerp, then on to Brussels, Cologne, Frankfurt, Heidelberg, Strasbourg and Paris.	Thomas Cook guides the first around-the-world tour and is away from home for 222 days, covering more than 25,000 miles.	Cook's Circular Note, the first travellers' cheque, is launched in New York.	Thomas Cook dies, aged 83.	Holidays by air on chartered aircraft are included in the summer brochure for the first time.

Product

Thomas Cook is home to a porfolio of brands catering for all areas of the evolving travel market. From its leading mainstream brands such as Thomas Cook, Airtours, Panorama and Sunset, to Direct Holidays – the UK's number one brand for holidays sold direct to the consumer – to specialist brands such as Thomas Cook Signature, CruiseThomasCook, Cresta, Neilson, and Club 18-30. In 2008 Thomas Cook added Hotels4u.com and Elegant Resorts to its expanding portfolio.

As the company who created the package holiday, Thomas Cook has in recent years focused heavily on taking package holidays to the next level. Far from a 'one size fits all' approach, Thomas Cook has reinvigorated its product ranges over the last few years to offer everything from budget short breaks to five star luxury holidays of a lifetime.

Thomas Cook Airlines now has a fleet of 42 aircraft and recently increased the seat pitch on its long-haul aircraft to 33 inches – more than either Virgin or British Airways.

Recent Developments

A key growth area for Thomas Cook has been travel-related financial services. Thomas Cook has always had a strong presence in foreign exchange, with its founder inventing the 'circular note' in 1874 – the forerunner to the travellers' cheque. Every Thomas Cook store offers a travel money bureau, stocked with all the leading currencies, travellers' cheques and pre-loadable cards. Thomas Cook also operates 17 Foreign Exchange Bureaux at Manchester Airport and Heathrow Terminal 5.

The Thomas Cook Credit Card carries a number of features, from no fees on Thomas Cook holidays and no overseas charges, to interest-free periods on travel transactions and cashback via Thomas Cook Travel Pounds. Thomas Cook was also the first travel company to become Financial Services Authority (FSA) regulated.

With over 1.3 million passengers in the UK opting to holiday at sea every year, cruising has become one of the fastest growing holiday choices (a further 11 per cent growth last year) and CruiseThomasCook is the biggest selling cruise retailer in the UK.

The company's sports division, Thomas Cook Sport, is the largest UK provider of team and supporter travel. In 2007 Thomas Cook Sport carried 25,000 sports fans to various sporting events worldwide.

Sports packages to major sporting events around the world encompass football matches, motorsports, rugby, golf, boxing, tennis and horseracing.

Promotion

Thomas Cook actively markets holidays, cruises, independent travel, foreign exchange and financial services with its 'four ways to book' communication – driving customers to stores, sales centres, online and to Thomas Cook TV, its own television channel. TV, press, radio, outdoor and point-of-sale merchandising are used, alongside a significant direct marketing programme to communicate with new and existing customers.

On and offline media are planned together to provide greatest reach and to give customers a choice of information gathering and booking channels.

Campaigns for core holiday products are based around the key sales periods of post-Christmas and summer, with the key message 'Our world revolves around you', focusing every campaign around customer benefits. Increasingly, activity takes place throughout the year, particularly in the growth areas of independent travel and financial services, which are less seasonally-driven.

Thomas Cook also works with partners such as McDonald's, Heinz, Disney, American Express and a range of tourist boards, airlines, hotel groups and press and magazine titles to create innovative and topical promotions capturing consumers' imaginations.

Brand Values

Thomas Cook believes that its biggest differentiator is its people, and the 'Spirit of Thomas Cook'. Employees are encouraged to work for the brand with pride, and make it their personal mission to deliver the best possible service.

Thomas Cook is one of the oldest and most respected names in the travel business. The newly formed Thomas Cook Group will continue to build on this heritage, maintaining its position as a well trusted brand and ensuring that it remains at the forefront of development within the travel industry.

www.thomascook.com

Things you didn't know about Thomas Cook

Thomas Cook & Son transported the British Army relief force sent to rescue General Gordon from Khartoum in 1884.

Thomas Cook was the first UK company to introduce online holiday booking, in 1997.

Thomas Cook is the official travel partner for Chelsea, Liverpool, Manchester City, Arsenal, Celtic, West Ham, Tottenham and Rangers football clubs.

November 2008 will mark Mr Thomas Cook's 200th anniversary.

2003

Thomas Cook rebrands its airline to Thomas Cook and launches a tour operating brand under the same name.

2007

Thomas Cook officially merges with MyTravel to form Thomas Cook Group plc. Also in 2007, Thomas Cook UK & Ireland becomes a FTSE 100 company listed on the London Stock Exchange for the first time in the company's history.

2008

The Thomas Cook Children's Critical Care Centre officially opens at King's College Hospital, London, thanks to the £2 million raised by Thomas Cook staff and customers.

TONI&GUY™

TONI&GUY has long been renowned as a pioneer and innovator within the hair industry, changing the face of the British high street and providing the link between high fashion and hairdressing. The Mascolo family's franchise model has maintained the company's high education and creative standards, protected the brand and made successes of thousands of TONI&GUY hairdressing entrepreneurs worldwide and is widely regarded as the number one global hairdressing brand.

Market

In the 45 years since the birth of TONI&GUY, hairdressing has become a sophisticated industry worth billions, spawning some of the most influential and creative artists in the beauty and fashion sector. From individual salons to global chains, competition is fierce with both men and women now seeking quality as well as service from their hairdresser.

Achievements

TONI&GUY has helped to change the face of the hairdressing industry on an international scale, dominating the UK high street, with 230 salons and 64 essensuals salons as well as 175 salons in 41 countries worldwide, with an annual turnover of more than £185 million.

TONI&GUY has an unsurpassed worldwide brand presence model with a strong education network, currently operating 27 teaching academies globally – three in the UK and 24 internationally. An average of 100,000 hairdressers are trained each year, with more than 5,500 employees in the UK and a further 3,500 worldwide. This philosophy of motivation and inspiration is seen as fundamental to the brand's success.

TONI&GUY has won in excess of 47 British Hairdressing regional and UK awards including Best Artistic Team a record 11 times and British Hairdresser of the Year three times. Co-founder and chief executive Toni Mascolo is a former winner of London Entrepreneur of the Year, while his daughter, global creative director Sacha Mascolo-Tarbuck, was the youngest ever winner of Newcomer of the Year at just 19, has won London Hairdresser of the Year and been nominated for both Avant Garde and British Hairdresser of the Year. In 2007 Sacha was nominated for the Hair Magazine Awards Hairdresser of the Year, Creative Head's 'Most Wanted' Look of the Year as well as winning the title of Fashion Focused Image of the Year from the Fellowship of British Hairdressers.

TONI&GUY haircare products have won numerous awards from magazines including FHM, Hair Magazine and Grazia. In addition, the company was the first ever winner of Hair Magazine's Readers' Choice Award for Best UK Salon Group in 2006.

From the TONI&GUY electrical range, the Pro Control Dryer won the coveted title of Best Appliance at the Pure Beauty Awards in November 2007.

Product

TONI&GUY salons aim to offer a consistent level of service, guaranteed quality and affordable hairdressing throughout the world with simple but well-designed salons offering high levels of customer care, exceptional cutting and innovative colour. All the techniques practiced by hairdressers are taught by highly trained and experienced educators in 27 academies around the world.

1963	**1982**	**1990**	**1997**	**2001**	**2002**
TONI&GUY is launched from a single unit in Clapham, south London by Toni Mascolo and his brother Guy.	The TONI&GUY Academy launches.	TONI&GUY's first international salon opens in Tokyo, Japan.	Toni's eldest son Christian co-launches sister-brand essensuals with his sister Sacha.	The TONI&GUY signature haircare range is launched.	Toni and Pauline Mascolo launch the TONI&GUY Charitable Foundation, which is currently raising money for a TONI&GUY ward at King's College children's hospital.

Within the salons, clients can watch TONI&GUY.TV, read TONI&GUY Magazine and take away samples of luxury brands, as well as get their hair cut and coloured.

In addition to the salon experience, TONI&GUY offers four ranges of haircare products: label.m, TONI&GUY, Model.Me and a range of electrical styling tools.

Recent Developments

In February 2007, the TONI&GUY signature range of products was relaunched with a 45-piece colour-coded haircare system. The aim was to make navigation easier between products and specific benefits clearer.

In May 2007, TONI&GUY launched the Model.Me haircare range developed in partnership with leading fashion and music personalities Erin O'Connor, Helena Christensen and Jamelia. This collection of 15 products marked the first ever haircare range not just endorsed by leading personalities, but also developed as a collaboration between them and a hairdressing brand.

Model.Me has already been recognised through various awards, including Best use of Press at the Beauty Magazine Awards 2007 and a Silver accolade for Best Haircare Launch at the Pure Beauty Awards 2007, as well as more recent endorsements by Company and Cosmopolitan magazines.

2008 will see the launch of both TONI&GUY.TV and Magazine across all territories enhancing the client experience in every TONI&GUY salon and Academy.

Promotion

As a brand, TONI&GUY juggles the need for consistency, the desire to be fashionable and the reassurance of solid service values with the excitement of the avant-garde, supported by its philosophy of continual education.

TONI&GUY.TV launched in 2003, to enhance clients' in-salon experience. Containing up-to-the-minute content, from music and fashion to travel and interviews with the TONI&GUY artistic team, it adds an extra dimension to

a client visit that can last anything from 45 minutes to two hours. With more than 90,000 viewers per week in the UK it has also become an outlet for associated, appropriate brands to communicate to this sought-after audience.

TONI&GUY Magazine was also launched in 2003 to echo and communicate the brand's heritage and philosophy, focusing on key trends in fashion, the arts, beauty, grooming and travel. Distributed in salons across Europe and globally as far afield as Australasia, the magazine promotes an inspirational and yet accessible face of the company to customers, employees and franchisees alike. In November 2004 it was recognised with the Association of Publishing Agencies' (APA) Launch of the Year award.

TONI&GUY's sampling initiative has seen it form mutually beneficial relationships with other carefully selected partners, while giving clients free samples of products and adding to their in-salon experience.

TONI&GUY remains committed to its involvement in, and vision to link the fashion industry with hairdressing through its sponsorship of London Fashion Week and London Fashion Weekend, which began in September 2004. Having completed eight successful seasons, the TONI&GUY session team works on almost 40 shows a year in the UK alone, supporting key British design talent including both Gareth Pugh and Giles Deacon. This commitment to support the fashion industry is highlighted by the company's collaboration with numerous fashion photographers, in-house

annual awards ceremony and promotion and development of staff via external competitions such as the British Hairdressing Awards.

Brand Values

TONI&GUY's reputation has been built on the foundations of education, fashion focus, and friendly, professional service. TONI&GUY aims to encompass the importance of local individually tailored, customer-led service, promoting an authoritative, cohesive and – most importantly – inspiring voice.

TONI&GUY is one of the most powerful hairdressing brands in the world, offering some of best education and guaranteeing superlative cutting and innovative colour. It aims to be über-cool but friendly and welcoming and to provide the ultimate link between fashion and hair being pioneering, passionate and inspirational.

www.toniandguy.com

Things you didn't know about TONI&GUY

TONI&GUY co-founder and chief executive Toni Mascolo still cuts hair once a week, alternating between London's Sloane Square and Mayfair salons.

In 2007 the TONI&GUY International Artistic Team made more than 70 overseas visits, educating and performing in shows and seminars to over 100,000 hairdressers globally.

TONI&GUY has published 32 collection books and 28 video/DVD educational collections and now produces one each year – bought by more than 20,000 hairdressers each year.

TONI&GUY educates more hairdressers than any other company in the world.

2003

Sacha's husband James Tarbuck launches TONI&GUY's own TV channel – TONI&GUY.TV – and TONI&GUY Magazine is launched.

2005

The professional haircare range, label.m launches, growing to include more than 45 products, distributed in over 47 countries internationally.

2007

The Model.Me haircare range and TONI&GUY's electrical line are launched.

2008

The company currently comprises two global, franchised hair salon groups – 294 in the UK and 197 international.

★ wagamama

In 1992 the first wagamama restaurant opened in London's Bloomsbury. With little marketing the restaurant soon developed a reputation for its delicious noodles. wagamama has since grown into a cult casual-dining phenomenon, with restaurants on major high streets across the UK and all over the world. wagamama's philosophy has remained unchanged: 'to combine fresh and nutritious food in an elegant yet simple setting with helpful, friendly service and value for money.'

Market

wagamama is the most popular chain of pan-Asian inspired noodle restaurants in the UK (Source: Zagat). Its competitors are extremely diverse ranging from lunchtime cafés to fast food establishments to formal restaurants. It has the advantage of appealing to a wide range of people – business professionals, backpackers, families, students and ladies who lunch, to name but a few.

In the 16 years since wagamama was founded, 90 restaurants have opened – firstly in the UK, then Europe, the Pacific Rim, the Middle East and the US. No matter which location, wagamama remains committed to ensuring customers receive the same wagamama experience wherever they are.

Achievements

wagamama has received many awards since its launch, reflecting the enduring appeal of the brand. Recent accolades include Best Company at the Retailers' Retailer of the Year Awards 2008, and for the third year running it was voted 'most popular London restaurant' for 2008 by Zagat.

wagamama is also one of the first restaurant brands to be awarded CoolBrand and Superbrand status simultaneously.

Product

The wagamama concept is modelled on Japan's ramen shops, which have been popular ever since their introduction in the 1940s.

wagamama sets itself apart by using canteen style seating, with long benches that are frequently tightly packed with diners. In addition, all orders are entered on an electronic handheld PC by the servers and instantly transmitted to the kitchen to speed up the ordering process.

Key to wagamama's menu is ramen (thread noodles), served in soups with toppings or griddle-cooked (teppan-fried) meat. This offers a perfect fast food – a nutritionally complete meal in a bowl. Other signature dishes include stir fried noodles and rice based options as well as salads and desserts. These can be accompanied by freshly squeezed juices and a wide selection of other beverages. For the hungry, a variety of side dishes are available including meat and vegetable dumplings, skewered chicken, deep-fried prawns as well as raw salads.

wagamama also offers a children's menu, high chairs, kids chopsticks and noodle doodle activity sheets to cater to families.

1992	1995	1998	2000	2001	2003
wagamama opens its first restaurant in London's Bloomsbury.	As a result of its growing success, wagamama opens the doors to its second restaurant, on Lexington Street in London's Soho.	The first international franchise is opened in Dublin.	The first out of London restaurant is opened in Manchester and the second international franchise is launched in Amsterdam.	wagamama moves into Leicester Square followed a year later by the first Australian restaurant in Sydney.	As wagamama expands in the UK, the 20th restaurant is opened in Canary Wharf.

For real wagamama addicts, a range of merchandise is available in restaurants and online including ramen bowls, t-shirts and wagamama's award-winning cookbooks, written by acclaimed food writer Hugo Arnold.

wagamama also offers an eat-out service where customers can ring in an order and collect it.

Recent Developments

wagamama opened its first UK airport site at Heathrow Terminal 5, in spring 2008, where for the first time ever wagamama UK introduced a breakfast menu to meet the needs of early morning airport travellers. The breakfast menu is diverse, with everything from pan-Asian breakfast dishes to traditional European dishes with a wagamama twist. Breakfast is exclusive to the airport location with the possibility of offering the menu at additional sites in the future.

wagamama opened its second US restaurant in Harvard Square, Massachusetts in the summer of 2007, and plans to open further US restaurants at unconfirmed locations as of autumn 2008.

Promotion

wagamama's most effective form of promotion has always been the wagamama experience itself. Word-of-mouth recommendations are largely responsible for much of the brand's growth.

In addition, wagamama utilises the full marketing mix. It raises awareness of the brand and what wagamama is all about through national/local press. Outdoor advertising is used to direct customers to its restaurants and targeted media ensures that the right type of audience is being reached.

New media is used to a great extent, with the brand's fresh, vibrant website changing almost daily to communicate its latest offers, promotions and menu changes. Customers are encouraged to become online members so that alerts can be sent to them via email with news and rewards for their loyalty. wagamama also uses viral campaigns to engage its customers with the brand.

Partnerships have been developed with other brands with similar audiences such as Time Out, STA Travel, Handbag.com and Rough Guides, to reach other membership bases through joint promotions.

The wagamama message is also communicated in the restaurants themselves.

All staff are trained to exude the brand's essence, and the design and ambience of the restaurants supports this too.

Brand Values

wagamama's moto is Positive Eating + Positive Living. Its aim is for everyone who comes into contact with the brand to have a positive experience. This encompasses its food, people and restaurants. It works hard to be in tune with its customers' needs and aims to run its restaurants to the highest standards with energy, attitude and enthusiasm.

The wagamama brand stands for individuality with fresh and nutritious Asian inspired food served in a simple, well designed, quality environment. The brand aims to employ knowledgeable, helpful, friendly staff who love their jobs and can be themselves at work.

It also strives to offer value for money as well as 'experience for money', always questioning and challenging itself to be better at what the brand does.

www.wagamama.com

Things you didn't know about wagamama

wagamama's top five selling dishes are Chicken Katsu Curry, Yaki Soba, Cha Han, Chicken Chilli Men and Chicken Ramen.

Each week 13,063 Yaki Sobas are served.

Every day 1,500 portions of edamame are eaten.

Twelve tonnes of noodles are served by wagamama each week.

No MSG is added to wagamama's food.

Local school children are regularly invited on educational visits to wagamama restaurants.

2004

wagamama opens in Dubai and the first award-winning cookbook – 'the wagamama cookbook' – is launched.

2006

The 38th UK restaurant opens in London Victoria's Cardinal Place. The second cookbook – 'ways with noodles' – is launched, as well as a range of sauces.

2007

The first US restaurant opens in Faneuil Hall, Boston. A restaurant also opens in Cyprus in the autumn and six further restaurants open in the UK.

2008

wagamama serves its first breakfast in the UK, at Heathrow Terminal 5, and the first restaurants in Egypt and Switzerland open in spring.

WEDGWOOD

In 2009, Wedgwood will celebrate a milestone in its rich history. For 250 years its fine ceramics and gifts have graced the tables of palaces, parliaments, leading hotels and homes the world over. Its unique English heritage is being marked in its anniversary year with a series of global celebrations bringing together modern classics and fashion accessories with the best of its international design, quality, and craftsmanship.

Market

Wedgwood remains a market leader in luxury lifestyle within the ceramics industry. Part of the Waterford Wedgwood Group, it distributes to more than 90 countries worldwide providing premier fine bone china, earthenware and its unique Jasper stoneware, together with a range of silver and crystal accessories, textiles, gourmet foods, specialist teas and bespoke prestige items influenced by the company's unparalleled archive records.

Its key markets are the UK, North America, Western Europe and Japan, with a rapidly expanding operation both in China and Russia and a thriving corporate, sporting, hospitality and governmental portfolio.

Achievements

Wedgwood has two and a half centuries' experience of supplying giftware and stylish tabletop products to the luxury sector of the market. With its superlative standards of craftsmanship, quality, record of innovation and bespoke timeless design, it maintains a leading position in all of its key markets.

With a multi-million pound turnover during 2007, it employs more than 1,000 people in its sales and marketing divisions worldwide with the aim of providing superb customer service and retail excellence.

Holders of the Royal Warrant from Her Majesty Queen Elizabeth II, Wedgwood includes among its past customers the White House, the Kremlin, the House of Lords and numerous other governments and Royal Houses.

Such is its popularity and heritage, this classic English brand attracts almost 100,000 visitors a year to its multi-million pound visitor centre in Staffordshire where people can immerse themselves in the history of the company, while seeing for themselves exactly how products are crafted during factory tours.

A new £10 million museum also opens in 2008 at the company's Greenfield headquarters on the rural outskirts of Stoke-on-Trent. The museum, built by the independent Wedgwood Museum Trust, will house thousands of priceless artefacts from the last 250 years of the company's history; approximately 6,000 Wedgwood pottery artefacts, 75,000 manuscripts and 680 pattern books, as well as the results of 10,000 trials conducted by the young Josiah to develop 'new' ceramics, such as the now world-famous Jasper. The museum will also house a host of other exhibits, from the portraits of Josiah and his wife Sarah by Sir Joshua Reynolds and paintings by George Stubbs, through to a fire engine used at Wedgwood's original Etruria Works.

1759	1773	1774	1789	1902	1940
The Wedgwood Company is founded by Josiah Wedgwood.	Empress Catherine the Great of Russia commissions a 952-piece dinner service, known as the Frog Service, for her imperial palace. It is now a Russian national treasure.	After thousands of experiments Josiah Wedgwood perfects the world famous Jasper ceramic.	Wedgwood successfully reproduces in Jasper the iconic Portland Vase – a copy of the ancient Barberini Vase is now housed in the British Museum.	President Theodore Roosevelt orders a 1,282-piece fine bone china banqueting service for the White House.	The Wedgwood factory moves from Etruria in Stoke-on-Trent to a new 300 acre greenfield estate at Barlaston. The factory remains the company's international HQ.

Product

Wedgwood's product range has grown significantly in recent years. Beyond its designer tableware, it encompasses a nursery collection, cutlery, crystal glassware, linens and jewellery as well as a collection of gifts providing a diverse portfolio of lifestyle items such as clocks, photo frames and table accessories.

Throughout its history Wedgwood has pioneered innovation in the ceramics industry. The founder, Josiah Wedgwood, was given the title of Potter to Her Majesty in the 1760s after he developed cream coloured earthenware and provided a service for Queen Charlotte, wife of King George III. After thousands of experiments he also developed the now iconic Jasper, along with a Black Basalt body. Innovation continued with the development of the pyrometer – the first time the temperature in kilns could be accurately measured. But it is not just technical innovation that Wedgwood is famous for – design is also central to the brand.

Wedgwood blends its own design expertise with that of international designers to provide a constant flow of contemporary classics. In recent years, fashion designers Martha Stewart, Vera Wang, Jasper Conran and interior designers Barbara Barry and Kelly Hoppen have each in their own way partnered with Wedgwood to create fashionably relevant products for the modern consumer.

Recent Developments

Innovation plays a key role in the development of Wedgwood's product. Wedgwood has experimented with clays from as far away as Australia, China and the Cherokee (Ayoree) Lands in America to find the perfect recipe for its diverse portfolio. Most modern clays however continue to be drawn from high quality deposits in Devon and Cornwall.

Recently, contemporary colours including delicate taupe, light turquoise and romantic chocolate have been created for the company's iconic Jasper ware, as well as a unique lead free lustre glaze to add further glamour and sophistication to its armoury of products.

Even though Wedgwood products may look delicate, independent compression tests show Wedgwood fine bone china to be among the strongest ceramics in the world, with an average of 17,597 pounds per square inch needed to break it.

Promotion

The company's marketing dates back to its early days, with the introduction of the first money back guarantees in the early 1770s, predating John Wanamaker, who is normally given credit for this concept, by nearly a century.

The speed of innovation still keeps apace. The company is forging sales opportunities by establishing new distribution channels and agreements with key retail partners throughout the world, developing the width and scope of its appeal while maintaining its classic modern brand heritage.

It is also contemporising its product portfolio to ensure continued relevance to today's discerning customers.

Astute in its self promotion, the company targets its key knowledgeable audience through top magazines and newspapers, with

the majority of its promotion through careful product placement in films, television programmes and magazines.

In addition, Wedgwood sponsors premier fashion events and sporting competitions such as the World Golf Championships, the World Sailing Championships, horse racing, tennis and selected charitable events.

Brand Values

Wedgwood has a reputation for timeless luxury developed through its high standards of authenticity, quality, heritage, innovation, design, craftsmanship and customer service.

www.wedgwood.com

Things you didn't know about Wedgwood

Josiah Wedgwood was the grandfather of Charles Darwin, the controversial naturalist who wrote the famous 'The Origin of Species.'

Approximately 165,000 separate ceramic items are produced each week at the company's manufacturing headquarters at Barlaston, Stoke-on-Trent.

By 1763, Wedgwood had already begun to crack the all important American market, with records showing goods being despatched to Boston, Philidelphia and New York on a regular basis.

Josiah Wedgwood was one of the first industrialists to provide new housing for his employees and their families. The homes were erected in a specially built village adjacent to his Etruria factory in Stoke-on-Trent in 1769.

1953

A 1,200-piece Wedgwood Persephone dinner service is chosen as the tableware for Her Majesty the Queen's coronation banquet.

1986

Wedgwood merges with Irish crystal producer Waterford to form the luxury Waterford Wedgwood Group.

1994

The Russian Government orders a 47,000-piece fine bone china service, believed to be the largest banqueting service ever produced, manufactured for use in St George's Hall in the Kremlin.

2009

Wedgwood will mark its 250th anniversary with global celebrations.

SENSING THE DIFFERENCE

Whirlpool's emphasis on innovation has made it one of Europe's leading household appliance brands. The strategic investments it continues to make in design, manufacturing and the community lie at the heart of its commitment to maintaining customer loyalty and retaining its prominent position within such a competitive industry.

Market

Whirlpool is a leading producer of major home appliances in North America and Latin America with a significant presence in markets throughout India, China and Europe, where it is outpacing industry growth.

Indeed, Whirlpool Europe's net sales for 2007 increased by 12.1 per cent to a record US$3.8 billion. These strong results were driven by gains in market share and new product introductions leading to a widened mix of products on offer, particularly with the expansion of its built-in appliance range.

Achievements

With 14,000 employees, a sales presence in more than 30 European countries and manufacturing sites in seven, Whirlpool Europe is a wholly owned subsidiary of Whirlpool Corporation, the world's leading manufacturer and marketer of major home appliances. Whirlpool Corporation has annual sales of more than US$18 billion, 73,000 employees and more than 70 manufacturing and technology research centres strategically positioned globally. The company markets Whirlpool, Maytag, KitchenAid, Jenn-Air,

Amana, Brastemp, Bauknecht and a host of other major brand names to consumers around the world.

Whirlpool's structured design and creativity led to it being named one of the world's 100 most innovative companies by Business Week magazine and to be listed in the Ocean Tomo 300 Patent Index, the first equity index based on the value of corporate intellectual property.

In April 2008, Whirlpool gained 'Honorary Mention' (second place) in four different categories at the ninth Annual Process Excellence Summit in London. The awards were for Best Project Contributing to Innovation, Best Fast Track Project, Best Process Improvement in Manufacturing Project and Best Design for its 6 Sigma Project.

Product

Space-conscious kitchen appliances that seamlessly integrate function with design aesthetics have become the industry benchmark. Whirlpool, which manufactures and markets a full range of home appliances, consistently produces innovative technological solutions to better meet consumers' evolving needs.

The brand's range of built-in products plays a vital role in its growth strategy. The built-in segment is a growth area in which Whirlpool continues to allocate significant resources. Characterised by elegant ergonomic design and high-quality materials, Whirlpool's range of built-in products demonstrates the company's spatial thinking, a defining brand characteristic. The range offers style combined with intelligent functionality and

1911	1919	1989	2006	2007	2008
Upton Machine Corporation is founded in St Joseph, Michigan, to produce electric motor-driven wringer washers. In 1929 it merges with the Nineteen Hundred Washer Co.	Gottlob Bauknecht starts a small electric workshop in Taillfingen, Germany, eventually establishing his first factory in 1933. Philips acquires the Bauknecht business in 1982.	Whirlpool Corporation and Philips form a European joint venture, of which Whirlpool Corporation becomes the sole owner in 1991.	In March Whirlpool completes the acquisition of Maytag.	Whirlpool launches the Essence and Gallery built-in collections across Europe.	GreenKitchen, a prototype for a sustainable integrated kitchen and an industry first, is launched. It is scheduled to enter the marketplace in 2010.

customised features such as text-assisted displays and its patented 6th Sense technology designed to sense, adapt and control.

Whirlpool's Essence and Premium ranges of built-in products offer high-specification, anti-fingerprint stainless steel ovens, wine cellars, coffee machines, extractor fans and under-counter cooling drawers – all made to fit precisely into kitchen units and designed to free up time and space in the kitchen.

The side-by-side Espresso fridge freezer – with integrated coffee maker and water and ice dispenser – is an example of the type of product that has helped Whirlpool to become a market leader in designing multi-functional appliances that meet ever-changing consumer needs.

Recent Developments

Whirlpool's commitment to innovation and design enables it to challenge convention through taking risks and developing solutions that break through boundaries. It recently unveiled GreenKitchen, its prototype for a sustainable integrated kitchen and an industry first. GreenKitchen – scheduled to enter the marketplace in 2010 – has been designed in response to increasing consumer demand for more eco friendly products as a key part of the brand's environmental strategy. The concept is to deliver ecological benefits – through adapting, recycling and reducing – that are achieved with a range of integrated appliances optimising the use of heat and water and increasing energy efficiency by up to 70 per cent. With green living at the forefront of today's consumers' minds, GreenKitchen focuses on four distinct areas to achieve energy savings: products; eco-system; behaviour; and a concept called co-generation whereby domestic electricity is generated via systems that produce both hot water and electricity at the same time.

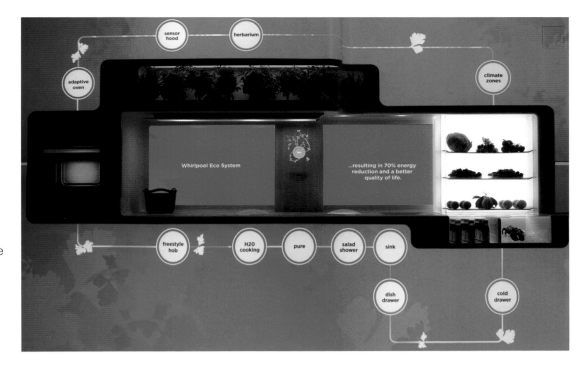

In 2008 Whirlpool once again set an industry precedent by becoming the first European manufacturer to produce a dishwasher with an integrated steam function. The advanced kitchen appliance range, 6th Sense Steam Range, combines 6th Sense technology with steam and includes a Steam Assisted Oven, the AquaSteam Washing Machine and a microwave with steam cooking feature. These products aim to save energy and money by offering consumers improved performance with reduced cooking and washing times.

Promotion

Whirlpool's award-winning consumer campaign, which has been running for nearly 10 years, is unique within the kitchen appliance market. Based on a 'goddess' theme it spans print and online. The latest advertisements feature a goddess wearing a dress by cutting-edge Italian designer Antonio Berardi.

Whirlpool pursues its business objectives while helping to improve the lives of people in the communities in which it operates. The most important corporate social responsibility project supported by Whirlpool is its partnership with Habitat for Humanity, which is committed to providing simple, decent, affordable houses for families in need, in more than a hundred countries. Whirlpool has supported this global, non-profit organisation in many ways for a number of years; not only providing products, to date more than 3,500 employees have volunteered to help physically build new homes.

In 2001, the charity recognised Whirlpool Corporation for its commitment as the largest corporate donor to the project; since the beginning of the programme, Whirlpool has supported Habitat for Humanity with an investment of more than US$25 million and donated 62,000 appliances.

Three years later, Whirlpool announced the extension of its collaboration with Habitat for

Humanity in Europe, creating a three-way partnership whereby tennis players Nadia Petrova and Agnes Szavay represent the Whirlpool-sponsored Women's Tennis Association (WTA) as official ambassadors for Habitat for Humanity in Europe.

In 2005, Whirlpool launched a series of initiatives including 'Aces for homes', the Whirlpool 'Love Food' cookbook and the Whirlpool 'Players Painting' to raise further funds and awareness of the work done by Habitat for Humanity.

Brand Values

Whirlpool strives to make intelligent appliances that make people's lives more efficient and pleasurable. The brand is about relentless inquiry and innovation, to produce industry-leading design and technological solutions to better meet consumers' needs. New design trends, technological advances, evolutions in society and changes in domestic behaviour have all played a part in the development of its groundbreaking designs.

www.whirlpool.co.uk

Things you didn't know about Whirlpool

A refrigerator in the GreenKitchen range is designed to save up to 46 per cent more energy, compared to regular models, thanks to new insulation materials, variable capacity compressors and more efficient heat-exchangers.

Whirlpool operates three of Europe's seven largest factories.

Whirlpool products can be found in more than 200 million households worldwide.

Whirlpool has been a specialist in home appliances for 97 years.

Yellow Pages has been putting buyers in touch with sellers since it was first published in Brighton in 1966 and is currently used around one billion times each year. In 2007, more than 28 million Yellow Pages directories were delivered to homes and businesses, helping to make it the UK's most used printed classified directory (Source: Saville Rossiter-Base 2006/07).

The award-winning directory enquiries service from Yellow Pages

Market
Yell is one of the biggest players in the £6 billion UK classified advertising market (Source: The Advertising Association 2007). This highly competitive market consists of a range of media, including the classified elements of national and regional newspapers, consumer and business/professional magazines, printed directories and the internet.

Achievements
As the biggest directory publisher in the UK, Yell takes its environmental responsibilities very seriously and is committed to sustainable development. Yell works closely with local authorities who have responsibility for waste collection and 99 per cent offer some sort of directory recycling opportunity. The directories are made from 52 per cent recycled fibre, sourced from sustainably managed forests in Finland.

In April 2007, Yell won a second Queen's Award for Enterprise, recognising it as a benchmark for sustainable development. Special mention was given to the Yellow Woods Challenge, Yell's flagship environmental campaign for schools, which is run in partnership with the Woodland Trust and local authorities across the UK.

In 2007, the campaign reached a key milestone of involving more than two million schoolchildren, recycling more than two million directories in the five years since it launched. It is based on a simple concept: pupils recycle old Yellow Pages directories and compete against other local schools while learning about the environment through curriculum-linked activities.

Another successful Yellow Pages schools' programme is Mini Pots of Care. Run in partnership with Marie Curie Cancer Care, this fundraising initiative saw 281,000 youngsters aged between 3-11 getting involved in growing their own daffodil, while raising £400,000 to support the work of Marie Curie Nurses in 2007. Overall, Yellow Pages has helped the charity raise more than £21 million since 1999.

In 2007, Yellow Pages 118 24 7 beat its rivals to become a top five UK brand for customer satisfaction, in an annual consumer survey across key business sectors. The service came fourth in an analysis of consumer perceptions of more than 35 organisations, as part of market research agency FDS International's annual CompariSat benchmarking study.

1966	**1973**	**1979**	**1993**	**1996**	**2001**
Yell's first Yellow Pages directory appears in Brighton.	Yellow Pages is rolled out across the UK.	Yellow Pages becomes a registered trademark.	Talking Pages is launched.	Yell.co.uk is launched; in 2000 it is replaced by Yell.com.	Full colour advertising is launched nationally in Yellow Pages. In addition, Yellow Pages Insurance Guide is launched.

Product

Published by Yell, Yellow Pages lists around two million businesses across the UK and forms part of a family of information services which includes Yell.com, Yellow Pages 118 24 7 and Business Pages.

Yellow Pages is the UK's most used printed classified advertising directory and it is used by 84 per cent of UK adults (Source: Saville Rossiter-Base 2006/07).

In 2007, 104 editions of the directory were printed across the UK, each offering an effective and simple service to enable consumers to find the business they want. In fact, nearly seven out of every 10 'look-ups' result in a business being contacted and more than half (57 per cent) of contacts result in a purchase (Source: Saville Rossiter-Base 2006/07). This high level of usage means that for many small businesses, the Yellow Pages directory represents a significant source of sales leads.

Yell.com is Yellow Pages' online service, which offers more than two million business listings in the UK. It can be accessed via the website and on web-enabled mobile phones, with both a JAVA™ application and browse (WAP) services.

Yell.com provides useful features such as zoom-enabled maps, driving and walking directions and a personal Yell.com address book to keep a record of regularly used businesses.

118 24 7 offers a classified business directory service over the phone. Its UK-based call centres also offer consumers added-value information, including advertisers' opening hours, store locations, promotions, delivery and payment information.

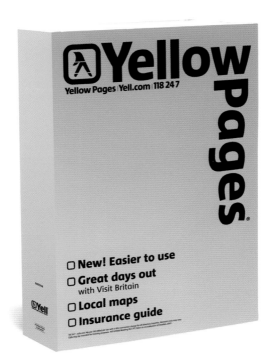

Recent Developments

Yell is constantly looking at new and innovative ways to meet the growing and changing needs of consumers. Yellow Pages has recently undergone a series of enhancements, marking the start of a programme of initiatives designed to help make the directory even more user friendly, with new local information, updated classifications and easier ways to search.

Yellow Pages teamed up with Visit Britain, the organisation responsible for promoting Britain as a world-class tourist destination, to create six pages of 'Great Days Out' information, detailing attractions and events close to home or up to two hours away for directories issued throughout 2008. All 14 London directories will include six pages of specialist 'Discover London' information, provided by Visit London, and 16 pages of travel guide content, supplied by Transport for London, covering everything from information on the congestion charge to local bus maps and cycle routes.

Yell.com revealed a new homepage in November 2007, including features such as a 'tag cloud' of the most frequently searched terms. This page provides users with a clear, simple way to find the business or service they require. The mapping of local businesses has also been updated: Yell.com is the first site in the UK to enable users to display local businesses and services on a map, with 360-degree 'bird's-eye' views for selected locations. Yell.com also enables users to layer multiple business and service types onto the same map.

Promotion

Yell has sponsored network film on Channel 4, including films across E4, More4, Film4 and Movie Rush online. This activity was complemented in the early part of 2007 with a strong TV, radio, digital and poster presence.

In the latter part of the year and early 2008 the campaigns moved on to highlight the family link between 118 24 7, Yell.com and Yellow Pages. Yellow Pages directories were used to build giant representations of 'Yell.com' and '118 24 7' and were seen across outdoor, radio and digital display ads. This culminated in March 2008 with one of the biggest outdoor campaigns in the UK, using around a quarter of large format sites available. As part of this campaign, Yell also became a launch partner for a new innovative digital poster format in key locations across central London.

Brand Values

Yell believes that flourishing, diverse enterprise, both large and small, enhances communities and all of our lives.

www.yell.com

Things you didn't know about Yellow Pages

New classification headings in 2007 include Civil Ceremonies & Partnerships, Copywriters and Pilates.

Yellow Pages can be recycled into animal bedding, stuffing for jiffy bags, egg boxes, newsprint and cardboard.

Yell.com has discovered that the day most likely for people to search for a new job is 5th January, while the most popular day for organising a party is 8th August (Source: Yell.com analysis of trends in searches 2006/07).

In 2007, Yellow Pages appeared 72 times on The Apprentice, had 130 sightings on EastEnders and was on screen for 1,058 seconds in Emmerdale.

2003

The Yellow Pages 118 24 7 directory enquiry service is launched.

2006

118 24 7 wins five awards at the International Directory Assistance Awards – including Best UK 118 Service for the third year running.

Also in 2006, the Transport for London travel guide is launched across London Yellow Pages directories.

2007

Yell.com mobile is launched.

Brands to watch

On the pages that follow you will find brands that the Expert Council 2008/09 has rated as:

"Brands that have, through exceptional marketing and communication strategies, positioned themselves as significant challengers to established rivals. These brands are expected to grow market share and have the potential to develop into Superbrands of the future. They are either new or rejuvenated brands, whose reputation and brand strength make them an emerging force in the market. These brands have been tipped as the 'ones to watch'."

Dave

the home of witty banter

On 15th October 2007, UKTV G2 rebranded to Dave and entered the confusing and complex world of the TV marketplace. The channel immediately struck a chord. Its creative and distinctive personality won over a whole new, mostly male, audience who were looking for programming offering witty banter, akin to a night in the pub with friends.

Brand Overview

Dave was born out of UKTV's objective to increase the number of 16-44 year-old men watching the network. At the time, UKTV G2 was a minor player comprised almost entirely of repeats with little resource to buy new shows. It had virtually no awareness – compounded by the fact many people watching its programmes didn't realise that they were watching them on UKTV G2. The available marketing budget only gave three per cent share of voice compared to the terrestrial channels.

In defining what it was about the programming that current viewers liked, the phrase 'The Home of Witty Banter' was coined. This provided a clear point of difference and was the springboard for a category-breaking name, stand-out identity and communications.

The rebrand of UKTV G2 to Dave has seen the channel grow three-fold which is testament to the power of a strong brand,

as the only key difference between UKTV G2 and Dave was the name and the marketing. Indeed, the channel has seen a 47 per cent share increase and a 68 per cent volume increase, which is solely attributable to the rebrand. Dave's incremental growth is forecast to contribute £25 million ad-sales revenue in 2008.

Since launch, Dave has grown from the 29th biggest channel in multi-channel (MC) homes to the 10th biggest and is the joint largest MC channel amongst men.

Marketing and Communication

The key marketing challenge for Dave was how to create stand-out in a highly competitive market and present the channel's programming, which included Top Gear, Mock the Week and Never Mind the Buzzcocks, in a way that was interesting and compelling for the target audience.

Research found that the channel's content satisfied the male need of 'having a laugh with other men' at a time when they couldn't physically be with their friends. It was also found that the channel was seen as a 'place' to spend quality time with very funny men – a key factor in the naming of the channel. 'Dave' fitted with the channel being seen as a friend and the idea that everyone has a mate called Dave. It is also a name with comedy credentials, befitting the humorous content – Baddiel, Gorman, Radio 1's Comedy Dave to name but a few funny Daves.

The basis of the promotional strategy was to create on an on-screen presentation (OSP) package. The creative invention drew on the audience insight that treated the channel as a 'place' to 'spend time with witty men'. So, rather than present Dave as a person, it could be represented as a location.

A world was created to resemble Peter's Friends meets Royal Tennenbaums via Life Aquatic, subverting expectation through

highly visual communication. The idents depicted a weekend in 'The World of Dave', engaging viewers with unusual situations and stories, the setting for which was a rich visual ephemera with oil paintings, gilt frames and stuffed giraffes. The overall OSP uses these to build a sense of place.

Thus, the world of Dave was born – defined as a compelling, adventurous and ever evolving brand with the feel of a gentlemen's club where (as in its programming) quirky, unexpected things happen. The off air poster and press advertising reflects this stately world, featuring stills of the programmes in gilt frames on flock wallpaper.

www.dave-tv.co.uk

Future Plans

To continue to act innovatively and creatively so that Dave remains one of the most talked about TV channels.

To extend the brand into a non-linear arena.

To become known for creating high quality commissioned programmes.

FitnessFirst

Health and fitness now take a prominent place in the hearts and minds of many. People of all ages are seeking out places to exercise in pursuit of the feel good factor, whether they want to lose weight, tone up, improve their health or simply shake off the stresses of the day. Fitness First has grown in strength in recent years to meet these needs.

Brand Overview

From its first club in Bournemouth in 1993, Fitness First has grown to become the largest health club group in the world and is synonymous with fitness expertise. More than 1.5 million people worldwide attend one of Fitness First's 550 clubs. In the UK alone there are 171 Fitness First clubs with more than 450,000 members – making it the clear market leader.

The vision of Mike Balfour, who identified a gap in the market for a health and fitness club with good facilities, strong service and value for money, Fitness First launched to offer affordable fitness for everybody in the UK.

This ethos has seen Fitness First take a leading position in the world of health and fitness. Using its size and experience, it focuses on channelling expertise back to its members with innovative fitness classes, top of the range equipment and fully trained personal trainers, gym and fitness instructors.

Fitness First has grown on a virtually uninterrupted basis since its inception. Three years and six clubs after the first club opened its doors, Fitness First was the first health and fitness club to float on the Alternative Investment Market. This proved to be a turning point for the brand and provided the funds to roll out the chain of fitness clubs across the UK. Growth was rapid, with seven new clubs in 1997 and nearly double that number in the following year.

In 1998 Fitness First was the first UK health club operator to enter continental Europe and in 2000 the business expanded further into Asia and Australia. By 2002 there were 49 clubs in the UK alone, employing 3,000 full and part time staff looking after more than 100,000 members.

In 2003 Fitness First was taken into private ownership, and in 2005 the company was acquired by BC Partners, a private equity group and officially recognised as the largest health club group in the world.

Today, Fitness First continues to build on this success with growth in the UK and beyond, with the latest clubs opening in India.

The brand is evolving, with a specific focus on individual customer care and community involvement, as well as a commitment to forming long term partnerships to benefit the health of the nation as a whole, for example with the British Heart Foundation and BUPA.

Marketing and Communication

Despite its success in the UK, Fitness First has never run TV advertising. From the start, marketing activity focused on the club and has proved to be successful in communicating with new and existing members.

The club network runs core campaigns, which include signage, posters, leaflets and incentive-driven direct mail, all refreshed bi-monthly. The use of real club members and staff in communications was first

introduced in 2005 and has been a feature ever since. Regular optional themes are also available throughout the year and used depending on a club's demographic.

Partnerships with key consumer media focus on incentive-driven promotions, and strategic PR raises brand awareness, helping to drive membership on a national scale.

All of Fitness First's marketing and communication places the emphasis on value, fitness and the accessibility, ease of use and quality of the product – split into two target markets, male and female.

www.fitnessfirst.co.uk

Get yourself a
BEACH BUM

JOIN THE NATION'S FAVOURITE
from only
£19.95
per month*

Call in today
Hurry offer ends soon

Terms and conditions apply. Please ask in club for more information.

FitnessFirst

Future Plans

To utilise marketing to further grow the brand globally, communicating Fitness First's value for money and expertise.

To aim towards opening 40 new clubs each year, across the 21 countries of operation, with India a key new market.

To continue to build its reputation as the place where members are highly likely to achieve their health and fitness goals.

To continue to develop ties with local communities in which the brand operates through programmes such as Adopt a School.

To roll out the 'New You Achievement Awards' programme across the world. First developed in the UK, it is a unique member recognition programme for people who have transformed their lives through their relationship with Fitness First.

MORE TH>N®

It's not by accident that MORE TH>N has as its corporate strapline 'We do more'; the brand has come a long way since its launch in 2001. MORE TH>N aims to bring a fresh approach to the rapidly changing and fiercely competitive direct insurance market. It has shown dramatic growth year-on-year and continues to make significant inroads in the sector, delivering impressive results.

Brand Overview

MORE TH>N's parent company, RSA Group, has been a major global insurer for nearly 300 years. Though well-respected and trusted, consumers thought RSA to be a little too conservative and traditional to achieve stand out in the overcrowded direct insurance marketplace.

Enter MORE TH>N with its distinctive bright green colour palette and its brand positioning so prominently represented in its name. It swiftly achieved the awareness it needed and is now one of the UK's largest direct insurers.

At its heart, the MORE TH>N brand is about 'doing more' and going the extra mile for its customers.

MORE TH>N's product development ethos is centred on the customer. Identifying key segments and insights into their needs and aspirations, it strives to provide innovative solutions, packaged, delivered and communicated in a simple and consistent way, demystifying the often complex world of insurance.

Its product range is broad including car, home, pet, travel, breakdown and life insurance. In addition, it offers business insurance direct to small businesses.

Recent developments which reflect the brand's 'doing more' maxim include: car insurance tailored for women, featuring benefits such as priority breakdown assistance, handbag and shopping cover and a guaranteed courtesy car within two hours of an accident; Green Wheels insurance, offering individual reports on the environmental impact of the customer's driving styles and advice on how to reduce this; and DriveTime, a product using GPS technology to reward young drivers with a discount if they don't drive during the most dangerous hours – between 11pm and 6am.

Targeted customer research has revealed that many consumers found dealing with call centres one of the most frustrating aspects of their day-to-day lives. Long waiting times, slow callbacks and being passed from pillar to post were cited as just a few of the problems. To counter such issues, MORE TH>N launched its Personal Customer Manager service. All MORE TH>N customers are offered their own single point of contact within the company to deal with all their insurance needs. This is a first in the UK market.

Marketing and Communication

MORE TH>N launched in 2001 with a heavyweight advertising campaign featuring brand icon Lucky the dog and the strapline 'Don't accept less than MORE TH>N'. While the brand personality has evolved over time, the recent 'More Is…' creative execution is still firmly entrenched in the brand promise of 'We do more'.

Currently a media mix of brand TV, direct response TV and radio is used to heighten general brand awareness and engagement, while national press drives stand out.

Extensive direct marketing activity – including direct mail, door drops, email and outbound telemarketing activity – is key to driving sales.

PR is also a major driver of brand awareness. MORE TH>N swiftly built a high profile in the media, particularly with financial journalists. Key highlights include being the only insurer invited to take part in a major climate change initiative sponsored by Tony Blair in 2007 – an award-winning campaign to highlight the problem of underinsurance amongst homeowners – and lobbying of the Government for additional spending on flood defences.

Overall integration of the 'More Is…' creative execution between above- and below-the-line communications also achieves greater brand awareness and leverages both the brand and sales performance.

www.morethan.com

MORE IS…
> rewarding your loyalty

FREE home contents cover up to £75,000 when you buy buildings insurance

MORE TH>N®
WE DO MORE

Future Plans

To continue to grow the business and deliver on the brand promise – 'We do more'.

To increase customer loyalty in a traditionally difficult sector by offering products and services tailored to key customer segment needs.

To lead the development of the growing small business direct market.

ST.TROPEZ
THE ULTIMATE TAN

St.Tropez has achieved cult status in tanning and was ahead of its time when it entered the market 10 years ago. Professionally led since the outset, it has a strong in-salon heritage. The choice for celebrities, beauty professionals and trendsetters alike, the brand defined the sunless tanning market. Now, with the raised awareness of sun damage, self-tanning is even more important.

Brand Overview
When St.Tropez launched with its in-salon Original Lotion Treatment the tanning category was non-existent. For many years, it remained a niche category with few brands. However, since the arrival of gradual tanning, it is becoming more prominent as a category with many high profile beauty brands launching tanning products. Furthermore, it is now attracting a cult following online among tanning addicts.

St.Tropez operates from professional salons and every year trains more than 20,000 therapists. Its spray tan equipment is the most advanced in the world and is market-leading in terms of safety. Pioneering new techniques is key to the brand. For example, the 'Double Dipping and Contouring' concept is now a cult trend. This treatment involves a total body exfoliation which is followed by an application of St.Tropez Original Tan and then, the next day, by a spray tan to deepen the first application.

Continual development of product formulation is also of great importance. All St.Tropez self-tan products are uniquely formulated to ensure that the tan does not turn orange. Products also include DHA (dihydroxyacetone) which is a natural active ingredient derived from sugar beet plants. This doesn't build up on the skin, so the self-tan fades in the same way as a natural tan would. Its Bronzing Mousse has become a hero product within the industry and the Everyday product has become its gradual tanning heroine.

St.Tropez also offers a range of more than 20 award-winning retail products, available from high street stores as well as salons. Recent additions to the range include Tan Intensifier and Rapide Face, which incorporates DHA rapid that produces a tan in just two hours.

Marketing and Communication
St.Tropez marketing has become synonymous with the use of the iconic image of a woman in a white swimsuit. This instantly recognisable image has been used since the brand launched over 10 years ago but has recently been updated to include a male alongside the female model, photographed by leading fashion and beauty photographer Solve Sunsbo. This new look was unveiled in the brand's first ever piece of consumer advertising in the June 2008 issue of UK Vogue. St.Tropez will now continue to advertise in targeted women's and men's magazines as well as trade press.

Prior to this, the brand has been PR driven, and is the celebrities' choice. Indeed, the brand has an international team of three dedicated Tanning Specialists who work with A-list performers, TV shows, film and fashion shows to keep them tanned with St.Tropez.

Sponsorship is also key to St.Tropez's marketing strategy. In 2008, the brand was involved with London Fashion Week and sponsored London Fashion Weekend. It also sponsored the BRIT Awards and had a tanning suite backstage. Further to this,

St.Tropez is the official sponsor of the British Surf Association and is collaborating with Quiksilver for a summer event at Newquay during Bank Holiday weekend in August 2008.

The safe sun message is also a key part of the brand's strategy, which positions St.Tropez as the fashionable and safe tan, alongside the message that it is not fashionable to sit in the sun. The brand recently staged an event to raise the profile of Sun Awareness Week which saw 30 models 'sunbathe' in St Pancras station in the middle of the day.

www.st-tropez.com

Future Plans

To lead the category on a global basis with particular attention to North America.

To collaborate with ITEC to create the first internationally recognised tanning qualification, due to launch in September 2008. This will go a long way to help raise standards within beauty salons.

To act as a leading beauty brand and roll out a counter concept in leading department stores.

To repackage its retail products in early 2009 to express the premium nature of the brand.

To build on the notion that its products can boost self esteem, by supporting charities that work with women around the issue of self esteem.

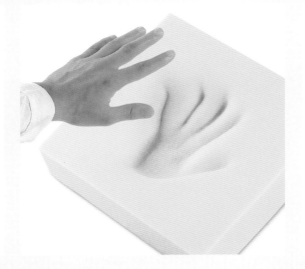

THE *ONLY* MATTRESS AND PILLOW RECOGNIZED BY **NASA** AND CERTIFIED BY THE SPACE FOUNDATION ✦

As the world leader in premium mattresses and pillows and the only manufacturer to be endorsed by NASA, TEMPUR® has revolutionised sleep technology. It is committed to improving the lives of its users by not only providing a comfortable sleep experience, but also preventing and relieving the pain and frustration of many common medical conditions such as arthritis, sciatica and back pain.

Brand Overview

TEMPUR Products are made from a unique, proprietary, open celled, temperature sensitive material that adapts to and supports the individual user by evenly distributing body weight.

The basis for the TEMPUR Pressure Relieving Material was originally developed in the 1970s by NASA to protect astronauts against G Forces during lift off and re-entry to the earth's atmosphere. TEMPUR scientists realised the enormous potential of this material and began experiments in the early 1980s to perfect it for consumer use. After millions of pounds in research, the TEMPUR Material was developed. It remains the only producer of mattresses and pillows worldwide to be endorsed by NASA and certified by the Space Foundation.

On conventional mattresses the body needs to adjust during the night. This is due to unrelieved pressure, which restricts blood flow and results in the build up of pressure, causing pain and forcing the body to reposition. TEMPUR Mattresses, on the other hand, mould to the exact shape and position of the body giving the neck, back, shoulders and feet the comfort and support they need. Pressure is evenly distributed thus reducing pressure points, practically eliminating the need for tossing and turning and helping to prevent and relieve chronic pain conditions such as sciatica and arthritis.

Since its launch in Sweden in 1991, TEMPUR Products have been recommended by more than 30,000 medical professionals worldwide. It has also experienced high levels of customer satisfaction. A recent independent survey showed that 95 per cent of TEMPUR customers recommend the products and 65 per cent have recommended TEMPUR Products up to five times.

TEMPUR Mattresses and pillows have also been clinically proven to reduce tossing and turning by up to 83 per cent in tests carried out by the Institution for Clinical and Physiological Research at the Lillhagen Hospital in Gothenburg, Sweden.

The brand has also been endorsed by a host of celebrities and sports stars who claim that they have found the perfect sleeping partner in TEMPUR. Supporters include Jane Seymour, The England Rugby Team, Sir Paul McCartney, David Blaine, Kyran Bracken, Charlie Dimmock and Susan Hampshire.

Marketing and Communication

TEMPUR's communications strategy integrates advertising, PR and marketing campaigns to successfully communicate the benefits of its products via TV, press, direct mail, websites and point of sale promotion.

Since TEMPUR Products are proven to be particularly beneficial for improving quality of sleep and helping to relieve back pain, sciatica and arthritis, TEMPUR targets potential

consumers who would benefit from the unique pressure relieving properties of its range. Marketing activity focuses on offering education, advice and support for sufferers of all sleep-depriving health conditions.

TEMPUR's NASA heritage is also widely used in marketing activity to communicate TEMPUR's position as the only producer of mattresses and pillows worldwide to be endorsed by NASA and certified by the Space Foundation.

www.tempur.co.uk

Future Plans

To remain a growth-oriented organisation dedicated to improving the quality of life for people around the world by providing innovative personal comfort and medical products made with the revolutionary TEMPUR Pressure-Relieving Material.

To be the global leader in the bedding market.

To continue to dominate within the bedding category and render 'old' technologies obsolete.

The **co-operative**
good for everyone

The Co-operative Group has 2.5 million members, 87,000 employees, 4,000 branches across 12 businesses with a £9 billion turnover. It is the world's largest consumer co-operative and has been around for some 160 years. Run by its members, 'doing the right thing' has always been at its heart.

Brand Overview

The challenge for the Co-operative movement, which has never had a unified brand, has been how to bring together its wide variety of businesses and numerous Co-operative societies. The Co-operative Group operates food retail, online electrical, pharmacy, funeral services, travel, property and farming businesses as well as a recently launched legal services business. It is also the parent organisation of The Co-operative Bank, Insurance and Investments, along with its internet bank, Smile. The scale of the Group can't be underestimated; it is the UK's third largest pharmacy chain, largest independent travel agency, biggest funeral services business, the UK's largest farmer and the leading convenience retailer.

Following The Co-operative Group's merger with United Co-operatives in 2007, huge investment was made in refitting and rebranding branches, as well as implementing brand standards to unite all the businesses and deliver a consistently good customer experience.

The Co-operative Group is in the unusual position of being owned and democratically run by its members. Just £1 allows anyone to join and each member has an equal say in how the business is run and how it achieves its social goals. Every year members receive a share of the profits, in the form of dividends, that they helped to create. The Co-operative returned over £38 million of its 2007 profits to individual members.

The Co-operative sees itself as a challenger brand – operating in a sustainable way and trading ethically are key principles. Since 2005, 98 per cent of the electricity supplied to the Group has been obtained from renewable sources and the Group has committed to reduce its electricity consumption by 25 per cent by 2012. Being responsible for making the Fairtrade phenomena mainstream, it is the UK's leader in this area, with the largest number of Fairtrade products. It also has a strong stance against animal testing. In 2008, The Co-operative Group's family of businesses received top ratings in the Good Shopping Guide, which is recognised as the leading reference book for ethical consumers.

Its care for the environment encompasses issues such as climate change, waste, loss of biodiversity and the use of chemicals. The Group has offset more than 300,000 tonnes of CO_2 since 2000 through renewable energy, energy efficiency and rainforest reforestation projects in the developing world.

The Group's principles have led to a long list of accolades including the Most Trusted Brand, the Greenest Supermarket and the Most Ethical Brand for the second year running. Furthermore, The Co-operative has gained two listings in the annual independent Ethical Reputation Index (ERI) top 10 for the second year running.

Another of the brand's guiding principles is community, epitomised by its long running community investment programme. In 2006 it launched a Group-wide community and campaigns strategy focusing on climate change, social inclusion, tackling crime and food ethics. In 2007 the Group contributed £10.4 million to the community, including a project to install solar panels at 100 UK schools, with more planned in 2008. Hence the use of the endline 'Good for everyone' to sum up the brand's proposition.

Marketing and Communication

The relaunch of The Co-operative brand will see at least 70 per cent of outlets rebranded by spring 2009. Not just a new look, it is a commitment to delivering excellent customer experience standards – all outlets must pass a rigorous mystery shopper programme before they can take the brand. Brand standards are benchmarked against leading competitors in each sector and monitored regularly.

The Co-operative is also working to ensure consumers know that The Co-operative is a family of businesses – not just a food store or a bank. It will also be communicating its principles: from the use of its wind farm – which opened in 2006, with two more planned – to Fairtrade, ethics and climate change.

Extensive media activity is planned for the second half of 2008 to support this, while master brand TV advertising will launch in 2009.

www.co-operative.coop

Future Plans

To develop the membership base, which is currently 2.5 million, to use as a platform for cross-selling between the family of businesses.

To focus on engaging with employees across all businesses.

To communicate the organisation's co-operative difference through the way it trades and what it does with its profits.

Charities supported by the Superbrands

On the pages that follow you will find details of some of the charities supported by the Superbrands featured in this publication.

BBC Children in Need
www.bbc.co.uk/pudsey/
Freephone: 0845 733 2233
Registered Charity No: 802052

BBC Children in Need helps disadvantaged children and young people in the UK. Some have experienced domestic violence, neglect, homelessness or sexual abuse, and others have suffered from chronic illness, or have had to learn to deal with profound disabilities from a very young age.

Many organisations supported by the charity aim to create a lasting impact on children's lives. Some offer low achieving children from areas of deprivation a chance to develop their educational skills and ambitions and others create opportunities for young people who are homeless or socially excluded, to enable them to move forward and secure a fulfilling future.

The charity offers grants to voluntary groups, community groups and registered charities around the UK that focus on improving children's lives. Grants are targeted on the areas of greatest need and money is allocated geographically to ensure that children in all corners of the UK receive a fair share of what is raised.

Supported by: BT

Breakthrough Breast Cancer
www.breakthrough.org.uk
Tel: 08080 100 200
Registered Charity No: 1062636 (England & Wales) and SC039058 (Scotland)

Breakthrough Breast Cancer is the UK's leading charity committed to fighting breast cancer through research, campaigning and education. In 1999, Breakthrough set up the UK's first dedicated breast cancer research centre, in partnership with The Institute of Cancer Research. There are now over 120 scientists working in collaboration at the centre to find out more about the causes, treatment and prevention of breast cancer, the most commonly diagnosed cancer in the UK.

Breakthrough's vision is a future free from the fear of breast cancer and the charity needs to raise at least £25 million each year to fund its vital research, campaigning and education work, including the work that takes place at its centre in London and its new research units in Edinburgh, London and Manchester.

Breakthrough also campaigns for better services for people affected by breast cancer as well as promoting breast awareness amongst the general public, policy makers, health professionals and the media.

Supported by: Avon

Breast Cancer Care
www.breastcancercare.org.uk
Tel: 0845 092 0800
Helpline: 0808 800 6000
Registered Charity No: 1017658 (England & Wales) and SC038104 (Scotland)

Breast Cancer Care is here for anyone affected by breast cancer. We bring people together, provide information and support, and campaign for improved standards of care. We use our understanding of people's experience of breast cancer and our clinical expertise in everything we do.

Every year over 44,000 people discover they have breast cancer. We aim to be there for every one of them as well as their family and friends. We offer the chance to talk to someone who has been there and has experienced breast cancer themselves. Our highly specialised team provides all the latest knowledge through our helpline and website along with booklets and factsheets that help people to understand their diagnosis and the choices they have.

Anyone with breast cancer or breast health concerns can call our helpline free on 0808 800 6000 or visit our website.

Supported by: Highland Spring and Royal Doulton

Cancer Research UK
www.cancerresearchuk.org
Tel: 020 7242 0200
Registered Charity No: 1089464

Cancer Research UK is the world's leading independent organisation dedicated to cancer research. We carry out scientific research to help prevent, diagnose and treat cancer, and we ensure that our findings are used to improve the lives of all cancer patients.

We have discovered new ways of treating cancer that together have saved hundreds of thousands of lives across the world and we work in partnership with others to achieve the greatest impact in the global fight against cancer.

We help people to understand cancer by providing life-changing information to patients, their families and friends, and we run cancer awareness campaigns to help people reduce their risk of the disease.

One in three of us will get cancer at some point in our lives. Our ground-breaking work, funded almost entirely by the general public, will ensure that millions more people survive.

Supported by: Superbrands (UK) Ltd

Caudwell Children
www.caudwellchildren.com
Tel: 01782 600812
Registered Charity No: 1079770

Caudwell Children makes direct donations of specialist equipment, treatments, and therapies to sick and disabled children throughout the UK. The Charity also organises yearly holidays for children with life limiting and terminal illnesses.

The Charity provides: specialist equipment to provide disabled children with mobility and independence, supporting social interaction and enhancing their lives; life changing treatments, that can improve quality of life and in some cases increase survival rates; pioneering therapies (e.g. UK Caudwell Autism Initiative) giving parents the tools to understand autism, unlocking their children's lives, helping them achieve their potential; and the Annual Destination Dreams Programme – giving families with children fighting life threatening conditions, desperately needed magical memories on a holiday of a lifetime.

Since the Charity was registered in 2000 it has provided over £5 million worth of practical support and has been formally acknowledged as the third largest provider of specialist equipment across the UK.

Supported by: Wedgwood

ChildLine
www.childline.org.uk
ChildLine helpline: 0800 1111
Registered Charity No: 216401

ChildLine, a service provided by NSPCC, is the free and confidential 24-hour helpline for children in trouble or danger across the UK. Trained volunteer counsellors comfort, advise and protect children and young people who may feel they have nowhere else to turn.

Since it was launched in 1986, ChildLine has saved children's lives, found refuge for children in danger on the streets, and given hope to thousands of children who believed no one else cared for them. ChildLine has now counselled over two million children and young people.

Children call ChildLine about a wide range of problems, but the most common problems are abuse (both sexual and physical), bullying, serious family tensions, worries about friends' welfare and teenage pregnancy.

Supported by: BT

Comic Relief
www.comicrelief.com
Tel: 020 7820 5555
Registered Charity No: 326568

Comic Relief was launched from the Safawa refugee camp in Sudan, on Christmas Day 1985, in response to crippling famine in Africa. The aim was to take a fresh and fun approach to fundraising and, through events like Red Nose Day, inspire those who hadn't previously been interested in charity to get involved.

Comic Relief has worked with some of the biggest names in entertainment, sport and business and tackles some of the biggest issues facing people across the world. Its work ranges from supporting projects that help children who are living rough in India to community programmes helping the elderly across the UK. A number of high profile partnerships have brought in millions of pounds to help reach these aims but the biggest group of supporters remains schools, with over 60 per cent taking part in Red Nose Day 2007.

Supported by: BT

Community Links
www.community-links.org
Tel: 020 7473 2270
Registered Charity No: 1018517

Community Links is an innovative charity running community-based projects in east London. For 30 years we have helped thousands of children, young people, adults and older people in deprived neighbourhoods. Our programme of national work shares the local lessons across the country to widen the impact of our projects and generate lasting social change.

Supported by: Tate & Lyle Cane Sugar

Community Network
www.community-network.org
Tel: 020 7923 5250
Registered Charity No: 1000011

Community Network provides a telephone conference call service to other charities and not-for-profit organisations. As the pioneers of social telephony, the emphasis is on creating opportunities for social inclusion, breaking down the isolation many people suffer through age, frailty, mobility, location, transport or caring responsibilities. Community Network creates 'virtual' communities of interest using user-friendly, affordable, accessible technology – no special equipment is required, just a phone.

Working in partnership with other agencies, including local government, Community Network has developed projects such as: FriendshipLink, 'bringing' friends to your home by phone; FaithLink, allowing people to 'attend' religious services from their homes; telephone group book clubs; and 'respite care' groups for carers.

Supported by: BT

Diabetes UK
www.diabetes.org.uk
Tel: 020 7424 1000
Register Charity No: 215199

Diabetes UK is the largest organisation in the UK working for people with diabetes, funding research, campaigning and helping people live with the condition.

There are over two million people in the UK living with diabetes and more than 500,000 who have the condition but don't know it. If not managed effectively diabetes can lead to complications including blindness, kidney failure and heart disease.

Diabetes UK's mission is to improve the lives of people with the condition by providing practical support, information and safety-net services to help people manage their diabetes. Therefore the work of Diabetes UK is vital.

Supported by: Specsavers

Everyman
www.everyman-campaign.org
Tel: 0800 731 9468
Registered Charity No: 534147

Everyman is the UK's premier male cancer campaign, funding the world's first dedicated male cancer research unit at The Institute of Cancer Research.

Scientists at The Everyman Centre are undertaking vital research into prostate and testicular cancer, two diseases that have historically been under-funded

A key research objective is to identify the causes of prostate cancer, the most common cancer in men. This includes trying to establish how prostate cancer develops and how to distinguish between aggressive and non-aggressive forms of the disease.

Another key area of research is inherited gene mutations for testicular cancer. Research has found that having a first degree relative (father, brother or son) suffering from the disease is one of the strongest risk factors.

One man dies from prostate cancer every hour in the UK. Everyman is striving to develop more effective treatments and early detection screening to bring an end to these needless deaths.

Supported by: Cosmopolitan

Fight for Sight
www.fightforsight.org.uk
Tel: 020 7929 7755
Registered Charity No: 1111438

Fight for Sight is the UK's leading charity dedicated to funding world-class research into blindness and eye disease.

The charity's current research programme of over £5 million is supporting research into a wide range of eye diseases including age-related macular degeneration, glaucoma, cataract, diabetic retinopathy and many inherited conditions.

The charity is proud of its many achievements, which include providing £1 million towards a state-of-the-art research unit in the new Children's Eye Centre at London's Moorfields Eye Hospital and funding the research team at Moorfields Eye Hospital, responsible for the recent breakthrough in gene therapy to treat Leber's congenital amaurosis.

It's only thanks to the generosity of our supporters that major medical advances have been made possible in eye research. The fight against eye disease is far from over, however.

Supported by: Specsavers

Habitat for Humanity
www.habitatforhumanity.org.uk
Tel: 01242 264240
Registered Charity No: 1043641

Habitat for Humanity's vision is of a world where everyone has a safe decent place to live. In over 90 countries Habitat for Humanity is working to make poverty housing a thing of the past. We bring people in severe housing need together with the resources they require, and help them build, repair or renovate safe, decent places to live.

We give people a hand up rather than a hand out, and since 1976 we have provided the means for people from all backgrounds to come together to build a better world. To date this has seen over 260,000 families helped out of poverty and able to look forward to a future of hope and opportunity.

Supported by: Whirlpool

Hearing Dogs for Deaf People
www.hearingdogs.org.uk
Tel: 01844 348100
Registered Charity No: 293358

Hearing Dogs for Deaf People selects and trains dogs to respond to everyday household sounds such as the alarm clock, doorbell, telephone, cooker timer, baby cry and smoke alarm.

The dogs alert the deaf person by touch, using a paw to gain attention and then lead them back to the sound source. For sounds such as the smoke alarm and fire alarm, the dogs will lie down to indicate danger.

Most dogs are chosen from rescue centres, giving unwanted dogs useful and happy lives to the benefit of deaf people, and the size and breed of dog is usually unimportant.

The practical value is obvious, but the therapeutic value should not be underestimated. Many recipients find their increased confidence and independence encourages them to go out and participate in activities which they previously avoided.

The Charity celebrated its 25th anniversary in 2007 and has placed more than 1,450 hearing dogs since its inception in 1982.

Supported by: Specsavers

In Kind Direct
www.inkinddirect.org
Tel: 020 7714 3930
Registered Charity No: 1052679

In Kind Direct re-distributes new goods donated by some of Britain's best-known manufacturers and retailers to thousands of voluntary organisations working at home and abroad. Founded in 1996, In Kind Direct became operational in 1997 and has since gone on to assist over 5,000 charities, working with over 700 donor businesses and funders. Our network of voluntary organisations represents every kind of cause – family welfare, sickness and disability, homelessness, emergency relief, environment, ethnic support and community groups. In Kind Direct is proud to be one of The Prince's Charities.

Supported by: Kickers

Make-A-Wish Foundation® UK
www.make-a-wish.org.uk
Tel: 01276 405060
Registered Charity No: 295672 (England & Wales) and SCO37479 (Scotland)

Make-A-Wish Foundation UK grants magical wishes of children and young people fighting life-threatening illnesses.

Make-A-Wish has no cures to offer and all too often some of our endings are sad, but during desperate times when there seems to be no hope, Make-A-Wish steps in to provide positive and uplifting relief. Most of all, a wish granted brings a time of magic and joy for the special children and families that we serve. Over 4,800 special wishes have been granted since 1986.

Supported by: Fairy

Marie Curie Cancer Care
www.mariecurie.org.uk
Tel: 0800 716 146
Registered Charity No: 207994 (England & Wales) and SCO38731 (Scotland)

Marie Curie Cancer Care provides free, high quality nursing to give terminally ill people the choice of dying at home, supported by their families.

Every day, 410 people will die of cancer in the UK. Most (around 70 per cent) want to be cared for in their own homes, close to the people and things they love, with a sizeable minority opting for hospice care. However, more than 50 per cent of cancer deaths still occur in hospital, the place people say they would least like to be.

Marie Curie Cancer Care is campaigning for more patients to be able to make the choice to be cared for and die at home.

This year, Marie Curie Cancer Care expects to care for more than 27,000 terminally ill people in the community and in its 10 hospices. But for every family the charity helps there are always others that it can't. Marie Curie Cancer Care wants to reach all of these families – making choice a reality for them all.

Supported by: Yellow Pages

Mencap
www.mencap.org.uk
Tel: 020 7454 0454
Registered Charity No: 222377

Mencap is the UK's leading learning disability charity. Everything we do is about valuing and supporting people with a learning disability, and their families and carers.

We work with people with a learning disability across England, Wales and Northern Ireland to change laws and challenge prejudice. The services we provide, in areas such as housing, employment, education and personal support, give thousands of people the chance to live their lives as they choose.

People with a learning disability are among the most excluded people in today's society. Our vision is a world where they are valued equally, listened to and included. We want everyone to have the opportunity to achieve the things they want out of life.

Every person with a learning disability – no matter how severe their disability – can make choices about how they want to live. They just need the right support. That's why Mencap is here. We are the voice of learning disability.

Supported by: Nokia

National Children's Bureau
www.ncb.org.uk
Tel: 020 7843 6000
Registered Charity No: 258825

National Children's Bureau (NCB) promotes the voices, interests and well-being of all children and young people across every aspect of their lives and is dedicated to working with and for them to ensure that their voices are heard wherever and whenever it counts. As an umbrella body for the children's sector in England and Northern Ireland, we provide essential information on policy, research and best practice for our members and other partners. Always working from an evidence-informed perspective, and actively promoting collaborative working across the sector, NCB influences and informs policy, practice and service developments.

Supported by: Nokia

For women and children.
Against domestic violence.

Refuge
www.refuge.org.uk
National Domestic Violence Helpline
(Refuge and Women's Aid): 0808 2000 247
(24-hour freephone)
Registered Charity No: 277424

Refuge opened the world's first refuge in 1971 and works with women and children who have experienced domestic violence. It is the country's largest single provider of specialist accommodation, practical and emotional support to women and children escaping domestic violence. Refuge is a national 'lifeline' for up to 80,000 women and children every year.

Refuge provides safe, emergency accommodation through a growing countrywide network of refuges and runs the National Domestic Violence Helpline in partnership with Women's Aid. Refuge also offers services for children, individual and group counselling for abused women and community based outreach services for women including specialist services for minority ethnic communities. Meanwhile, its growing team of independent domestic violence advocates support woman through the criminal justice system.

Supported by: Cosmopolitan

Richard House Children's Hospice
www.richardhouse.org.uk
Tel: 020 7511 0222
Registered Charity No: 1059029

Richard House is a purpose-built children's hospice in east London.

Our core purpose is to accompany families with children and young people with life-limiting and life-threatening conditions, during the child or young person's journey through life to death, creating positive experiences along the way which become good memories for the future.

Our services are wide-ranging, completely free to families and tailored to our multi-cultural community. We need to raise £1.8 million in 2008/09 to keep Richard House open.

Supported by: Tate & Lyle Cane Sugar

The Commonwealth Society for the Deaf

Sound Seekers
www.sound-seekers.org.uk
Tel: 020 7233 5700
Registered Charity No: 1013870

Sound Seekers helps children who are deaf or have a hearing problem in developing commonwealth countries. We target children in areas where access to hearing assessment and treatment is difficult or non-existent. Some 60 million children throughout the world suffer from preventable hearing impairment. Malaria, measles, lassa fever and meningitis can all lead to deafness, as can HIV/AIDS.

We work in partnership with the host government and key NGO's to develop hospital-based audiology services, and community outreach via a HARK! mobile clinic. Training of key personnel in-country to conduct hearing assessments, fit hearing aids, advise on ear care and to look after and maintain equipment, is integral to each project.

Sound Seekers' mobile clinics provide outreach services to children in Uganda, Namibia, South Africa, Lesotho, Sierra Leone, India and The Gambia. We also support schools for deaf children and are currently planning major new projects in Tanzania, India, Zambia and Ghana.

Supported by: Specsavers

The
Meningitis
Trust

The Meningitis Trust
www.meningitis-trust.org
Tel: 01453 768000
Registered Charity No: 803016 (England & Wales) and SC037790 (Scotland)

The Meningitis Trust – the UK's longest established meningitis charity – helps anyone who has been affected by meningitis and meningococcal septicaemia. With as many as 500,000 people living in the UK who have had either viral or bacterial meningitis and up to one adult in every four knowing someone who has had the disease, the charity's ongoing work is much-needed.

Most people survive meningitis, but many are left with debilitating after-effects, including deafness, blindness, limb loss (where septicaemia has been involved), learning difficulties, memory issues and behavioural problems.

We provide ongoing practical and emotional support to families and individuals through free services, including a 24-hour nurse-led helpline, financial support grants, counselling, home visits and family days.

The Trust is committed to raising awareness of the signs and symptoms of meningitis. We rely on voluntary donations and partnerships with businesses to continue our vital work.

Supported by: Silver Cross

The National
Autistic Society

The National Autistic Society
www.autism.org.uk
Tel: 020 7833 2299
Helpline: 0845 070 4004
Registered Charity No: 269425

The National Autistic Society (NAS) is the UK's leading charity for people affected by autism. We champion the rights and interests of all people with autism and aim to provide individuals with autism and their families with help, support and services that they can access, trust and rely upon and which can make a positive difference to their lives. Over half a million people in the UK have autism, which is a serious, lifelong and disabling condition.

We were founded in 1962, by a group of parents who were passionate about ensuring a better future for their children. Today we have over 17,000 members, 80 branches and provide a wide range of advice, information, support and specialist services to 100,000 people each year. A local charity with a national presence, we campaign and lobby for lasting positive change for people affected by autism.

Supported by: LEGO®

Variety Club Children's Charity
www.varietyclub.org.uk
Tel: 020 7428 8100
Register Charity No: 209259

For more than 50 years Variety Club Children's Charity has been helping sick, disabled and disadvantaged children up to the age of 19 years.

We are best known for our Sunshine Coaches but Variety Club helps children in many other ways including building and equipping children's hospitals, taking some 100,000 children each year on exciting outings, providing specially tailored electric wheelchairs through our EasyRider programme, training paediatric nurses and obtaining items for individual homes to help children and their carers.

All of this is made possible because volunteers from many walks of life give generously of their time and money, supported by a galaxy of celebrities from show business and sport. Our volunteers' hard work keeps costs to a minimum and ensures that for every pound raised a very high percentage goes straight to the children. So, when you support Variety Club, you can be sure that your contribution is making a real difference to the lives of the children we help.

Supported by: Thomas Cook

Vision Aid Overseas

Vision Aid Overseas
www.vao.org.uk
Tel: 01293 535016
Registered Charity No: 1081695

Vision Aid Overseas (VAO) is a charity dedicated to helping people in the developing world whose lives are blighted by poor eyesight, particularly where spectacles can help. Over 300 million people in the developing world need spectacles to live an ordinary life due to poverty, lack of facilities and long distances between optical service providers.

VAO works by sending abroad teams of volunteer optometrists and dispensing opticians who set up clinics, screen large number of patients and provide appropriate spectacles. In addition, it establishes workshops and trains nurses in eye testing skills with the aim of developing long term optical services in its target countries. Founded in 1985, Vision Aid Overseas has transformed over 375,000 lives with a pair of spectacles and is continuing to have a significant impact in its target countries.

Supported by: Specsavers

WOODLAND
TRUST

Woodland Trust
www.woodland-trust.org.uk
Tel: 01476 581111
Registered Charity No: 294344 (England) and SC038885 (Scotland)

The Woodland Trust is the UK's leading woodland conservation charity, owning more than 1,000 woods which are open free of charge for the public to enjoy. Our vision is to protect what we have, restore what has been spoilt and create new woods for the future, to make our countryside friendlier for people and wildlife.

The UK has only 12 per cent woodland cover compared to a European average of 46 per cent. To tackle this, the charity works with communities to plant millions of trees throughout the UK. It also campaigns for better protection of ancient woodland which is the UK's most precious wildlife habitat and home to threatened species such as the dormouse and red squirrel. Trees and forests also stabilise the soil, generate oxygen, store carbon, transform landscapes and provide one of the richest habitats for flora and fauna.

Supported by: Yellow Pages

Advocacy Builds Superbrand Status

By Colin Byrne
CEO
Weber Shandwick, UK & Ireland

When my wife had a new baby recently, she didn't turn to baby magazines or adverts to decide what buggy to buy or what baby food to consider. She turned to friends and other new mums in her online and personal networks for recommendations. People she knows, whose views she would respect as informed and independent. Advocacy in action.

Advocacy is the positive recommendation of a brand or idea by a trusted independent third party. Every time a category expert posts a positive review in an online forum it is also advocacy in action.

Whereas 15 years ago companies saw advocacy as a positive but elusive benefit to their business, today Superbrands are actively trying to shape and drive positive conversations. Analysis from Bain and Associates has closed this virtuous circle,

showing that positive recommendation is predictive of a brand's revenue growth. Reicheld's oft-quoted book 'The Ultimate Question: Driving Good Profits and True Growth' suggests that whether or not a customer recommends a brand is the most important metric.

Unsurprisingly then, Superbrands enjoy far higher levels of positive recommendation than competitors in their category. Weber Shandwick's own consumer research across Europe identified that brands such as Sony, Bombay Sapphire, Honda, Audi and Nokia each enjoy twice as many promoters as detractors. They far outstrip competitors in their categories, some of whom have serious negative word-of-mouth challenges – 'badvocacy' – to deal with, typically resulting from poor product and service experiences or unethical activities.

Our research involved 4,000 consumers in Germany, the UK, Spain and Italy, across five product categories: cars, spirits, televisions, PCs and mobile phones. The research identified that advocacy drives customer acquisition. Over one third of consumers said a positive recommendation had driven them to try a brand.

We also discovered that 50 per cent of European consumers felt that their own positive endorsement of a brand had driven a friend to try it for the first time. Intuitively, of course, it makes sense. Who buys a car without first asking an existing owner how it drives? But word-of-mouth recommendations are not limited to high value purchases. In the spirits category, positive recommendation was a big driver of trial, perhaps because the perceived 'costs' of trying a new drink (and not liking it) are fairly low.

Time and again, research from surveys undertaken on behalf of our clients demonstrates that friends, colleagues and category experts are up to five times more influential than advertising in driving purchase decisions. While advertising has an undeniable role in helping shape brand perceptions and raising awareness of offers, when it comes to the crunch,

a personal recommendation is simply more effective. But what are those personal recommendations built upon? Our research showed that typically, a product or service experience that surpassed expectations was the catalyst for a positive recommendation. The old axiom of 'surprise and delight' holds true.

Our research also demonstrated that, on average, 20 per cent of a brand's customers would be willing to recommend

it but are not currently doing so. In other words, they are inactive advocates. This reinforces the case for building proactive advocacy initiatives to unlock the potential of these customers.

So how can brands use advocacy to build Superbrand status? We have identified five key themes:

1. Advocates take a share in brand development

Superbrands put advocates at the heart of product and service development right from the start. We're not just talking about the odd focus group; rather the principle is to co-create new sources of value with the brand's dedicated fan base.

Superbrands realise that by seeing their customers as a community with vested interests, not just a source of revenue, they can actually build better experiences and more value for all parties. Google Labs, Dell's Ideastorm and 'MyStarbucksIdea' invite advocates to beta-test, shape and propose new products and services to take the brand onwards.

Organisations that successfully link their customers with the production process can successfully unleash a powerful form of advocacy. Dole, Tesco and Timberland are all working to provide customers with a clear line of sight into the production and transportation process. In an age where the carbon footprint has become a

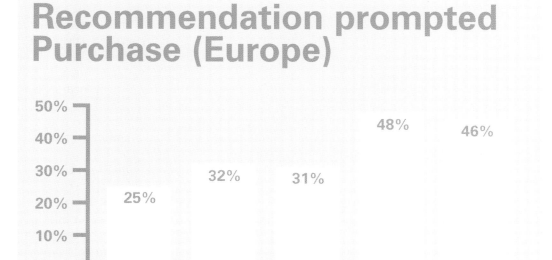

Recommendation prompted Purchase (Europe)

(Source: Weber Shandwick Pan-European survey, 4,000 consumers, November 2007)

household term, people want to know exactly what the environmental and social impact of their buying behaviour is. Superbrands know that there is no need to be defensive; rather this interest presents an opportunity to build stronger advocacy.

2. Advocating a cultural idea

Superbrands act as the stewards of big, shared cultural ideas and they nurture their growth amongst a community of like-minded advocates. Superbrands are cultural icons that rise above a mere product benefit. They appreciate that sometimes people recommend a brand not just because of the product but simply because they like it. So, creating advocacy can be more than just beating product and service expectations.

Apple is not just a great consumer electronics business, whose products have clear functional and aesthetic benefits; rather it is a cultural icon. Why? Because it promotes the idea of independent creative thinking. For Apple, technology is a vehicle for creativity rather than a more efficient way to re-engineer a production line. People who share these values are willing advocates of a shared cultural idea. Superbrands actively engage their advocates: asking them to champion the brand, teasing them with snippets of product news, fostering creativity.

3. Advocacy re-orientates marketing communications

Superbrands rely on advocacy to drive awareness and consideration far more than traditional paid media. Google, eBay and Facebook all built their brands and large customer communities on the back of word-of-mouth between peers long before investing in advertising in the old-fashioned sense. Rather than reaching for the TV scripts, Superbrands build initiatives to drive word-of-mouth. To some extent, they cede control over marketing content but gain influence by sharing marketing responsibility with their passionate advocates. Offering customers a chance to shape the brand and its communications is simply more inclusive. This is Opensource marketing and it makes sense; after all,

people share the things they have had a hand in shaping. Microsoft successfully launched software products for the design community by offering the community itself the chance to devise the launch party, a conference and speakers of their choice. Superbrands do not jealously guard their brand; rather they understand that its very popularity means it will become part of today's mash-up culture.

4. Advocacy starts from within

Superbrands unlock the passions of their staff, turning them from employees into champions. They build their brands from the inside out, empowering staff to carry the vision and passion of the business with them wherever they go. Enlightened businesses not only invest sufficient time and effort in driving the internal understanding of the brand vision and values but also invite their employees to identify product and service issues and then empower them to develop the solutions. DeLaRue's 'My Contribution' programme delivered £38 million in productivity gains by acting upon staff suggestions for operational improvements, in order to deliver the new brand vision.

But Superbrands do not simply stop at high quality internal feedback; they also enhance the reach of their staff advocates by providing platforms for staff to share their stories with friends and peers. The theory goes that however niche an employee's interests are, someone somewhere in the world will want to join that conversation. Whether providing a blog for every employee, encouraging staff to post their views online, or simply opening special offers to friends and family, Superbrands will fuel employee conversations.

5. Advocacy is built on compelling stories

A positive recommendation is one thing, but it is the content of that recommendation where the new frontier of Advocacy lies. Our research initiatives now look at what topics and themes come up in conversation

and what brands can do to encourage them. People tell stories and stories are an oral tradition as old as mankind itself.

Have you heard the story about the dustbins placed beside the innocent drinks stall at Glastonbury? Customers were prompted to throw their bottle in one or the other depending on whether they thought the innocent team should give up their day jobs and turn innocent into a real business. This is a great example of a story, (which may not even be true), that continues to circulate. Superbrands are adept at telling stories about themselves. They understand that iconic brands have to perform universally understood myths that help us make sense of our world. The longstanding Virgin 'feud' with British Airways is a salient example of performing a heroic adventure myth. Stories need heroes too and Richard Branson or Steve Jobs are classic examples of the visionary character that makes a story interesting.

In conclusion, Superbrands have Advocacy as part of their DNA. They listen to their customers; they invite them into the brand as part-owners. They also foster a set of shared cultural values. But rather than leaving it to chance, Superbrands not only put advocacy initiatives into their marketing communications but right at the heart of their entire operations.

WEBER SHANDWICK

Advocacy starts here.

Weber Shandwick is one of the world's leading PR and creative ideas agencies. Its roots in the UK go back to the early 1970s, and in its newest incarnation celebrated its sixth anniversary in 2007. Part of The Interpublic Group, it puts its creative talent, communications expertise and specialist teams to work on award-winning campaigns for some of the biggest companies and most innovative brands around the world.

Weber Shandwick UK & Ireland has six specialist practice teams in technology PR, healthcare PR, financial communications, corporate communications, consumer marketing and public affairs and also offers cross-practice consultancy within broadcast, CSR, digital, multi-cultural and internal communications.

Weber Shandwick is part of a global network with a strong presence across Europe. In the UK alone, the company employs 350 people across its London, Manchester, Leeds, Glasgow, Edinburgh, Aberdeen, Inverness and Belfast offices.

www.webershandwick.co.uk

Don't think big. Think brave.

By Raoul Shah
CEO
exposure

By definition, a Superbrand conveys scale, power, influence and excellence. To attain such status represents widespread recognition and an achievement that is the privilege of the few. But beyond this, although many might debate and review which brands are worthy of the accolade, there is an almost intangible formula for success that runs deeper – a unique blend of commercial business principles with a creative magic that ensures the brand stands apart and ahead in its category.

At exposure we believe that, of the four defining criteria above, it is influence above all that is the key to the success of brands. Influence brought about by the integration and expert execution of a clear creative vision. Beyond wonderful products and successful distribution strategies, it is the influential power of this creative essence that separates the good from the 'super'. This is the currency of the future.

Creativity is the generation and development of ideas – it is about thought leadership. Looking at the brand listings, it is the 'thinking brands', not the ones that simply react to the market, that are

ranked highest. Each one has a strong creative vision, built around a clear and often extremely simple idea. A true belief in creativity must exist in a brand's DNA in order to create the differentiation that makes the best brands virtually untouchable. That special 'something', or unique idea, ensures the emotional value a brand needs to take it beyond just a functional product offer.

The generation of an idea is not a one-time project. It is a continuum that requires constant updating, review and reinvention. The most successful brands demonstrate a belief and loyalty to an overarching 'big idea' – the essence of the brand – but, below this, each one is constantly developing a series of new ideas that embrace change and ensure continued relevance to the brand's audience. Good ideas are not a stop sign. They are a signal to say "Keep going", "Give us another". At the point when we are starting to get too comfortable, let's change and create a new idea.

Ideas are a business culture, not a marketing tactic. Superbrands allow the culture of creativity and ideas to permeate

through the business at every level. From the boardroom to the personal experience of engaging with a particular product, a successful brand's 'big idea' acts as a roof, holding together everything that plays out below it. This roof allows flexibility, adaptation and scope, while also providing a framework within which other ideas and brand developments can be nurtured.

The business of ideas also requires more than just the ability to commit ideas to paper and business plans – a company needs the bravery and vision to make ideas happen. To see them through to fruition. To sometimes step into the unknown. To take a risk. So, if you don't like risk, don't look to build a Superbrand. In the words of Renzo Rosso, founder of Diesel, success shines on "Only the Brave".

Sony BRAVIA™ became famous due to an outstanding TV advert, but this brand's success was due to much more than that. It reflected a product truth in an engaging and entertaining way, while also delivering a creative 'magic' that probably seemed crazy in the early stages of its evolution. Sony has a history of making great ideas happen. In

1979, Akio Morita chose to ignore market research going against the proposed concept of a personal stereo with in-ear headphones. The Walkman went on to sell 100 million units. The Sony PlayStation was launched using very unconventional tactics back in the early 1990s. The influence generated through the integration of PR, product placement, word-of-mouth and smart media partnerships contributed in large part to making the PlayStation the rock-and-roll leader in gaming. Different. Alternative. Challenging. And suddenly a cool product that appealed to children and adults alike. A simple idea combined with the ability to execute this creative vision resulted in Morita appearing in the Time 100 'builders and titan' category as one of the most important people of the century. His view was that "a company without borders is one without limit".

So where do great ideas come from? Is there a secret formula to ensure successful creative development? The simple answer is no, there is not a ready-made package that brands can buy in to. The ideas involved in the building of Superbrands come from a clear vision and true belief – from the inside out – embracing the creative process in order to respond to cultural shifts and ensure continued relevance. Creativity is not simply a recruitment challenge. It is a subtle management of the tension that exists between commercial gain and creative stand-out. A stagnant business is unlikely to notice great ideas – until it decides to place creativity at the heart of everything it does. From the reception (and receptionist), to the paper towels and choice of hold music, focus on (and be passionate about) the detail not just the obvious big stuff like the chairman's office.

Google represents everything a Superbrand should stand for – which has emanated from an initial great idea that is just over 10 years old. Google's approach is a great example of how to embrace creativity within a business culture. The brand encourages every employee to commit 20 per cent of their work time to developing new innovations – labelled 'Innovation Time Off'. Apparently 50 per cent of all Google's new product launches have originated from this time allocation.

Another process through which brands can ensure relevance is to listen and respond to the social conscious and attune to or even influence cultural movements. Facebook was an idea that was fuelled by people power. Was the idea the winner? Or was it simply good timing – a zeitgeist moment? I would argue that currently the idea is Facebook itself; it has certainly influenced a step change in social behaviour, although the brand has yet to establish true 'brand' credentials beyond being a social network.

Product Red is a simple idea that has created a cultural shift in how consumers choose products, based on a visible charitable impact. Similarly, in the ethical and organic products category, many brands are built around a single good idea (innocent, Green & Blacks) that has touched the public conscience. These examples demonstrate an empowering of the social conscience to spark a popular movement. On a different level, Ocado represents a simple idea that has revolutionised the traditional shopping movement – taking us from the supermarket aisles to the mouse on our kitchen table. And Nike, a brand surrounded by some of the best creative brains in the world, has an amazing ability to produce ideas that seem effortless, simple and inclusive. Run London is such an example; a mass run across the capital that has made the concept of running cool, fun and approachable. A movement for everyone to join.

While Apple has no doubt been uniquely responsible for evolving the concept of personal entertainment into a global movement, its ubiquitous white headphones are a brilliant branding device that signify membership of an exclusive club. This 'exclusive' member is seen in every street, subway and departure lounge on the planet.

Cultural relevance is key to great ideas becoming catalysts for brand adoption and celebration. Chanel's recent Mobile Art initiative (pictured above left) is a fantastic new example of how a brand has tapped into something culturally rich in order to bring the brand to an audience that is as interested in challenging architecture, design and art, as it is in beautiful bags. On a different level, the street artist Banksy has created arresting and often beautiful images seen from Disneyland to the West Bank, a Britney album to the Tate. Culturally relevant. Creative. And now worth a lot of money! Superbrand or just super clever?

The overarching ideas that have fuelled these movements have contributed in a large part to all these brands being defined as Superbrands – more than just the power of any large advertising campaign or shiny flagship store. And thus, one can conclude that successful ideas are not necessarily fuelled by big budgets alone. Ideas, and the influence of creative vision, are a currency in themselves.

☐ exposure

exposure is a communications agency providing integrated marketing and creative solutions for lifestyle brands.

In a competitive market, exposure maintains its edge through its grasp of the zeitgeist – a deep understanding of social and cultural influences that is passed on to clients. Tuned into what's happening in the world's most vibrant cities, exposure sees what's coming early, and uses this perspective to create groundbreaking ideas for its clients – ideas to make them famous and adored.

www.exposure.net

The Age of Trialogue

By Andrew Walmsley
Co-Founder
i-level

This year's Superbrands top 500 list is topped by two of the titans of the digital world – Google and Microsoft® – locked in combat for the lucrative leadership position. The youngest two companies in the top 10, together they've been leading the digital revolution, creating and developing new spaces to build brands.

They play in a sector which has fundamentally shifted the basis of brand success. It's not just that advertising and distribution have changed since the internet appeared – there's something more profound afoot.

So what does it take to create brand power in the digital age?

When Moses climbed the mountain to collect a set of tablets, he wasn't expecting a consultation exercise. No focus groups had been conducted, and no quantitative research. The tablets came with commandments on them, and there was a certain amount of implied definitiveness that came with that term.

And media's been pretty much like that for most of the several thousand years since then. A small number of people told a large number of people what they thought, and there was little opportunity for the mass to respond – and if they did, it was subject to the editorial control of those in power.

Which is why when the web appeared in 1994, people started getting excited. A new paradigm was emerging, they said. In the future, where there previously had been a monologue, there will be a dialogue. Consumers will be able to respond to communications just as easily as they can receive them, and the implications for brands are enormous.

I went to a conference in Edinburgh in 1996, where hundreds of marketing and media folk debated hotly the exciting opportunity this new world of dialogue would bring their brands. We spent three days talking about how brands would be able to have a dialogue with consumers, and that this would be a more powerful means of communication because of the level of consumer involvement.

Throughout the debate it was clear what benefits a dialogue with consumers could have for brands. The trouble was, there wasn't much in it for consumers. Speaking for myself, I don't really want to have a dialogue with Persil, or Sainsbury's or Yoplait. I don't even want to have a dialogue with Audi or Vodafone or Selfridges, in which I would normally be expected to be considerably more interested.

Ultimately I want them to get on with being them. Make my clothes clean, connect my calls – the hygiene factors are important, but the emotional elements are just as much theirs too, and I either buy into them or I don't.

So the ability to create real, meaningful dialogue often ended up being too costly, too difficult and often simply too much work for the value generated.

But emerging over the last few years has been a new dynamic, infinitely more powerful than the dialogue ever promised to be, more threatening, more revolutionary and more valuable.

When we look back in another 10 years, we will see that the true impact of digital media was not to find new ways to connect brands to consumers, but in connecting those consumers (or 'people' as they like to refer to themselves) to each other.

This simple fact has created a new ecosystem.

Now, people collaborate together to create software, releasing it back onto the web where it outperforms the 'commercial' competition. They share information about medical conditions, challenging the authority of the medical establishment. They co-operate to drive down fuel prices, publishing the cheapest price for your postcode. And they join forces to bring down brands who let them down, publishing videos of underperforming products.

The age of the Trialogue has arrived.

The challenge this poses for brands is that they're no longer handing down the tablets. Their consumers have relegated them to the position of supplier, and are talking about them, not to them.

While this is a threat to brands who adhere to the status quo, it's an opportunity for those who can reinterpret themselves as facilitators. They recognise that the bulk of the discourse will be between consumers, and their role in this is to enable, empower, listen and just occasionally, talk.

The trialogue will influence every aspect of marketing, from product design (threadless.com) through to product recommendation (tripadvisor.com), and its potency derives from the opportunity that brands now have, not to talk at people, but to be a small part of billions of their conversations.

This is the point where user-generated content meets brands, and it is an area fraught with difficulty for the unwary but rich with opportunity for the creative.

Most of the focus on user-generated content has been on the media phenomenon it has created. Google buying YouTube for £850 million was the richest of a series of UGC media brand acquisitions that included Flickr (bought by Yahoo!), MySpace (NewsCorp) and Last.fm (CBS).

Other media owners have watched with envy as audiences have flocked to these sites, and brands have looked on perplexed – knowing the value of that audience (they're hard to find elsewhere) but conscious that this isn't simply a medium in which you can just advertise.

And while some have exported familiar techniques from the traditional armoury, running quizzes and competitions on MySpace, others have taken a radical approach, building the trialogue into the very fabric of their products. The products I've chosen here are about as far from having digital roots as it's possible to be – you don't need to be virtual to take advantage of the trialogue.

When I was a kid, LEGO® was a fantastically creative toy that inspired endless innovation – you could build anything, as long as it was essentially square. But now LEGO have built the trialogue into their brand. LEGO Factory allows web users to design their own kits and order the parts, even customising the packaging. But it also lets them share their designs and discuss them, building a community that helps LEGO to stay close to its enthusiasts.

While running is a competitive sport, most training is done alone. But Nike+ has turned a solo activity into a social phenomenon. A sensor placed in your shoe sends data on your run to your iPod, which shows your distance run, calories burned and so on. But when you synchronise the iPod with your computer, it uploads those details to the website, where it's shared with thousands of other runners.

When I looked last night, more than 35,000 runs had been recorded in the past 24 hours, and people were mapping their routes, challenging each other and competing in their own 10km runs across the globe. As you'd expect, music is integral to the experience, and the iTunes playlists of top athletes can be bought from the store, while charts are compiled from runners' favourite powersongs.

Any retailer will tell you how hard it is to predict demand for individual lines. Despite the sophistication of predictive models, trend-spotters and other sooth-sayers, there are always things you thought would shift like hot cakes but instead just take up shelf space. Less frequently, but just as frustrating, are those at the other end of the scale – surprise hits that customers just can't get enough of, and inevitably are on a six-week lead-time from the Philippines.

How great it would be if you just sold things that people like. Better still, if you only made things people like, and knew they'd buy them. Threadless, the online t-shirt store, carries only designs its users have uploaded – and manufactures only those that get a critical mass of votes. You won't see them having sales to shift that unmovable stock.

A clothing brand, a sports shoe, a toy. Each has empowered a community of its consumers, and by connecting them together has itself benefited. But these aren't just 'soft' benefits. They're driving new revenue streams, repeat purchase and real engagement – consumer relationships whose strength is founded not in the transient moment of a product need, but in the enduring nature of humans to be social animals.

This is what we mean by empowering consumers. When we talk about giving over control to consumers, it's often interpreted as abrogating responsibility – something marketers are rightly suspicious of. But none of these brands have 'given control' – instead, they've entered into a new, mature relationship with their customers, letting them shape product, service and delivery to their demands.

The trialogue has fundamentally altered consumers' expectations of brands, and their power to influence the public perception of them. Brand strength in the digital age will derive not just from listening and responding, but from recognising and celebrating consumers' participation in the creation of great brands for the digital age.

i-level was founded in 1998. With annual billings in excess of £100 million, and a staff of 160, i-level plans and buys digital media for a wide range of blue chip clients. It has been profitable in each year since its formation and has been voted Agency of the Year eight times. Indeed, since launch it has won more than 40 industry and national awards.

In 2007, i-level won the prestigious Queen's Award for Enterprise: Innovation, while the care of its staff has been recognised by i-level's inclusion, for three consecutive years, in The Sunday Times Best Small Companies to Work For list.

www.i-level.com

Expert Council 2008/09

Wayne Arnold
Founder &
European CEO
Profero

Wayne is one of the digital industry's most experienced practitioners, having co-founded Profero with his brother in 1998.

Recently changing roles from UK managing director to European CEO, Wayne has successfully supervised UK and pan European campaigns for an enviable client list including Apple, AstraZeneca, Channel 4 and MINI. He has expanded the Profero client base, by carefully positioning Profero as the only full-service agency of its kind, with offices across Europe and Asia.

Wayne is also chairman of the IPA's Digital Marketing Group.

Vicky Bullen
CEO
Coley Porter Bell

Vicky has built her career in the design industry, joining Coley Porter Bell from Graphique (now Vibrandt) where she worked on brands such as Persil, Coral and Robin from the Unilever detergent portfolio.

Joining Coley Porter Bell as an account director, Vicky was promoted to client services director, then to managing partner and finally to chief executive in September 2005.

During her time at Coley Porter Bell, Vicky has led some of the agency's largest business, working with companies such as MasterFoods, Cadbury Trebor Bassett and Kimberly-Clark. Coley Porter Bell's clients include Nestlé, Pernod Ricard and Coca-Cola.

Highlights for Vicky include winning a Design Effectiveness Award and a Marketing Grand Prix for Kotex, while also getting into the D&AD book, as well as relaunching the Coley Porter Bell identity in 2007.

Vicky also sits on the Ogilvy UK Group Board.

Hugh Burkitt
Chief Executive
Marketing Society

Hugh has been responsible for the launch of the Marketing Society's 'Manifesto for Marketing', introduced the Marketing Leaders Programme for potential marketing directors and established the Panoramic Group, which has created a new forum where the UK's leading marketing organisations have agreed to work together to promote marketing.

He began his own career as a Unilever trainee at Birds Eye Foods and progressed via the Manchester Business School to Collett Dickenson Pearce in 1972. He spent the next 30 years in advertising, founding the agency Burkitt Weinreich Bryant in 1986, and leaving in 2002 as chairman of Burkitt DDB.

He is co-author with John Zealley of Marketing Excellence – a review of the lessons to be learned from the winners of the Marketing Society's Awards for Excellence.

Alison Burns
CEO
JWT London

Alison began her career at BMP DDB, then BBH working on accounts such as Channel 4, the Guardian and Nestlé. After 10 years in London she was lured to the US where she spent three years as vice president of marketing for PepsiCo working on the global Pizza Hut and the domestic Fountain Beverage divisions.

After a brief 'baby break', she returned to the world of work in spectacular style as the president of Fallon New York, quadrupling the agency's revenues and winning some impressive pieces of business including L'Oréal, PepsiCo, Timberland, Starbucks and MTV Networks to name a few.

After five years at Fallon, Alison worked as a branding and communications consultant providing both agencies and clients with advice on brand development, positioning and marketing for brands including Kraft, Yahoo! and Motorola.

Alison returned with her family to London as JWT London CEO in February 2006.

Colin Byrne
CEO
Weber Shandwick,
UK & Ireland

Colin joined Weber Shandwick in 1995, rising to lead the public affairs practice in London in 1997 and is now CEO of the global agency's UK & Ireland region as well as a member of the global management team. Clients have included IKEA, BBC, CNN Europe, The Sutton Trust, Coca-Cola and the British Government.

Prior to this, in 1992 Colin became the first communications director of The Prince of Wales Business Leaders Forum, the international NGO founded and presided over by Prince Charles and supported by many leading international firms. He managed CSR communications for the Forum globally and worked with leading global firms on the communication of their own CSR activities.

Earlier in his career, Colin worked in the British Labour Party's communications team, rising quickly to head of press & broadcasting. He served as deputy to then communications director Peter Mandelson as well as press aide to Tony Blair, Gordon Brown, Jack Straw and other Labour leaders.

Leslie de Chernatony
Professor, Brand
Marketing & Director,
Centre for Research
in Brand Marketing
Birmingham University
Business School

With a doctorate in brand marketing, Leslie has written extensively for American and European journals and is a regular presenter at international conferences. He has written several books on brand marketing, the two most recent being Creating Powerful Brands and From Brand Vision to Brand Evaluation.

A winner of several research grants, his two most recent have supported research into factors associated with high performance brands and research into services branding. He has been the Visiting Professor at Madrid Business School and is currently Visiting Professor at Thammasat University, Bangkok and University of Lugano, Switzerland. Leslie is a Fellow of the Chartered Institute of Marketing and Fellow of the Market Research Society. He acts as an international consultant to organisations seeking more effective brand strategies and has run acclaimed branding seminars throughout Europe, Asia, the US and the Far East. He is also an experienced expert witness in legal cases involving branding issues in commercial and competition cases.

Tim Duffy
Chief Executive
M&C Saatchi

Tim graduated from King's College, Cambridge and in 1986 joined Saatchi & Saatchi, as a strategic planner. Rising to group account director, he was responsible for British Airways and Silk Cut.

In 1995 he left Saatchi & Saatchi, to help launch M&C Saatchi. Now a top five UK agency with 19 offices in 14 countries, clients include Scottish & Newcastle, Royal Bank of Scotland, Ladbrokes, GlaxoSmithKline, Halfords, Transport for London, The COI, DSGi and MFI. Tim was appointed managing director in 1997 and UK chief executive in 2004.

Stephen Factor
Managing Director –
Global Consumer
Sector
TNS

A graduate of the City University Business School, Stephen spent the early part of his career working with new product evaluation tools for leading manufacturers in the FMCG sector.

From 1986 to 1990, he was based in Paris and then Milan, as development director of the European Burke group.

Returning to London, he was appointed chief executive of Infratest Burke's UK business. Following acquisition, he took the same role for NFO and subsequently TNS. With the consolidation of the market research industry, he became an active participant in the acquisition and integration of marketing services organisations.

At the beginning of 2006, Stephen took over global responsibility for TNS' FMCG business, supporting the world's leading brand owners in 70 countries around the world.

With some 25 years of experience working in global market research agencies, he blends hands-on corporate management experience with a deep understanding of FMCG markets and brands.

Peter Fisk
Founder
Genius Works

Peter Fisk is an inspirational author, speaker and consultant – described as "one of the best new business thinkers" by Business Strategy Review. His best-selling book Marketing Genius explores how to combine a more intelligent and imaginative approach to customers and brands in order to deliver extraordinary results, and has been translated into 26 languages. His new book Business Genius is an inspirational guide to growth and innovation, whilst Green Business explores how to make money by doing the right thing.

Peter has managed or advised many of the world's leading brands including American Express and British Airways, Coca-Cola and M&S, Microsoft® and Vodafone, and was CEO of the Chartered Institute of Marketing. He created the Genius Works (www.thegeniusworks.com) to bring together the latest ideas and best practices in strategy and marketing, innovation and brands – in the form of high energy workshops and events, strategic consulting and development programmes.

Cheryl Giovannoni
Managing Director
Landor London

Cheryl joined Landor as managing director of the flagship London office in October 2005. She is passionate about the pivotal role that branding and design play in the health and long term growth of brands.

South African born, Cheryl moved to London in 1993 to join ad agency Ogilvy, working with Unilever, Mattel, SmithKline Beecham and BUPA, before moving to Lowe Howard-Spink to run the global Braun account.

In 2001 Cheryl changed direction to join brand design agency Coley Porter Bell as CEO, also leading the agency's accounts with Nestlé, GlaxoSmithKline and GE. She was also a member of the Ogilvy UK Group Board.

Landor was twice named Design Agency of the Year (Marketing 2001/2005) and has been Packaging Agency of the Year for an unprecedented two consecutive years (GRAMIA Awards 2005/2006). Landor's clients include BP, Citigroup, Diageo, Ernst & Young, Jet Airways, Kraft Foods, Morrisons, Nokia, Procter & Gamble, PepsiCo and Traidcraft.

David Haigh
Chief Executive
Brand Finance

David qualified as a chartered accountant with PricewaterhouseCoopers LLP in London. He worked in international financial management before moving into the marketing services sector, firstly as financial director of The Creative Business and then as financial director of WCRS & Partners.

He then left to set up a financial marketing consultancy, which was later acquired by Publicis, the pan European marketing services group, where he worked as a director for five years. David moved to Interbrand as director of brand valuation in its London-based global brand valuation practice, leaving in 1996 to launch Brand Finance.

David is a Fellow of the UK Chartered Institute of Marketing. He is the author of: Brand Valuation; Brand Valuation – a review of current practice; Strategic Control of Marketing Finance; and Marca Valor do Intangível.

Graham Hiscott
Deputy Business
Editor
Daily Mirror

Graham started his career as a reporter on the Cambridge Evening News before moving to a press agency in Birmingham called News Team International. Eighteen months after this, he joined the Press Association as a regional reporter covering the East Midlands. It was here that Graham developed his interest as a consumer affairs correspondent, which led to another move to the Press Association's HQ in London. From there he was appointed consumer editor of the Daily Express, in March 2005. In March 2008 he moved to the Daily Express as deputy business editor, covering City as well as consumer stories.

A string of exclusives earned Graham the London Press Club Awards' Consumer Journalist of the Year 2007 accolade. He was runner-up in the same competition in the two previous years' Awards.

Among the reasons for his nominations was breaking the Dasani bottled water story and a series of stories about soaring energy bills.

Mike Hughes
Director General
ISBA

Mike joined the Unilever graduate scheme in 1972 after leaving Hertford College, Oxford with a degree in PPE. He then joined Coca-Cola UK in 1980 as marketing director, where he launched diet Coke into the UK market, before moving to Guinness as worldwide brands director in 1984.

Following a five-year stint as CEO of Guinness' North American business, Mike returned to the UK in 1992 to become MD of Guinness Great Britain.

In 1998 he became CEO of HP Bulmer Holdings plc. Following its sale in 2003, he moved into new technology, where he was responsible for the development and sale of a number of ventures.

In 2007, Mike assumed his current role as director general of ISBA, The Voice of British Advertisers. A member of key industry bodies, Mike also sits on the Executive Committee of the Worldwide Federation of Advertisers.

Paul Kemp-Robertson
Editorial Director &
Co-Founder
Contagious

Paul started his career at corporate communications firm Maritz before helping to launch shots magazine in 1990. After a spell in commercials production, he returned to shots, becoming editor in 1994. Subscriptions trebled under his tenure.

In 1998 he succeeded Donald Gunn as Leo Burnett's worldwide director of creative resources in Chicago. Paul was responsible for the agency's Great Commercials intranet site and its quarterly creative councils, known as the Global Product Committee.

Paul left Leo Burnett in 2004 to co-found Contagious – a quarterly magazine and DVD reporting on future trends and non-invasive marketing techniques. A joint venture with Xtreme Information in London, Contagious sees Paul reunited with shots founder Gee Thomson.

Paul has written numerous articles for publications including Business 2.0, the Guardian, Hollywood Reporter and M&M Europe, as well as co-editing D&AD's The Commercials Book. He has appeared on BBC Radio 4's The Today Programme and Five Live's Wake Up To Money.

David Magliano
Non-Executive
Director
Dyson & Glasses Direct

David joined Glasses Direct in 2005 and Dyson in 2006 as non-executive director.

Prior to this, David was director of marketing for London 2012, the organisation which bid for the Olympic Games. He was responsible for building UK public support and presenting London's bid to the International Olympic Committee.

Before London 2012, David was sales and marketing director of two low-cost airlines: easyJet and Go (of which he was a founder). Prior to this, he spent 10 years at Imagination, Ogilvy and HHCL.

David was UK Marketer of the Year in 1999 and 2005, and Global CMO of the Year in 2006. He was awarded an MBE in 2006.

Mandy Pooler
Director
Kantar

After reading English at Jesus College, Oxford, Mandy had a rush of numbers to the head during two years spent in the marketing department of the International Thomson Organisation.

In 1982 she joined Ogilvy & Mather as a media planner, becoming media director in 1991 and managing director of O&M Media in 1994. Mandy was a founder of The Network, which launched Ogilvy's 26 media operations into a single European media organisation.

In 1998 she became the first CEO of MindShare UK and after three turbulent but rewarding years changed direction to launch another new venture. The Channel is a knowledge centre around media and communications and a focus for collaboration for the WPP Group and its clients. In July 2006 she became director for development at Kantar, the holding group for the research and consultancy businesses owned by WPP.

She is chairman of AGB Nielsen in the UK, a fellow of the IPA and a former Advertising Woman of the Year.

Raoul Shah
CEO
exposure

Raoul started his career at agnès b. in Paris, after graduating from UMIST with a degree in textiles, economics and management. He then spent five years at the Pepe Jeans Group where he developed his marketing skills in the UK and across Europe.

In October 1993 he launched exposure, a business built on the power of network and word-of-mouth communications. Today, exposure is a multi-disciplinary communications agency, which employs 150 individuals in London, San Francisco and New York.

Raoul's responsibilities include overseeing the two US offices and the company's new specialist division, Beauty Lounge PR. His portfolio of fashion and lifestyle clients includes Levi's, Umbro, Edun, Maharishi, Penguin Books, Coca-Cola, Nobu and Land Rover.

In 2007, Raoul was top of the Guardian's most influential ethnic minority in media. He is an avid collector of skateboards, Japanese toys and 'Do Not Disturb' signs.

Craig Smith
Communications
Director
Publicis UK

Craig leads external and internal communications across the Publicis, Publicis Modem and Publicis Dialog agencies. Prior to this Craig was marketing director for customer publishing agency Publicis Blueprint, for which he continues to consult on marketing and new business strategies.

A seasoned business journalist, he was formerly editor of Marketing magazine for seven years, gaining recognition for the title as Business & Professional Magazine of the Year at the industry-standard PPA Awards in 2005/06. Craig is author of Marketing For Dummies and a regular commentator on marketing and media issues to the national and broadcast media.

Linda Smith
CEO
Starcom MediaVest
Group UK

Linda graduated from Royal Holloway and Bedford College in 1984 with a degree in modern languages, before going on to spend her first nine years in media at ITV. Roles at Yorkshire TV, Thames TV and Carlton TV provided experience in agency, client and international roles.

In 1993 she joined Capital Radio's Radio Sales House as commercial marketing director, responsible for trade marketing, research, client development and sponsorship and promotions.

In 1997 Linda joined MediaVest as commercial director, with responsibility for new business, direct marketing and commercial revenue streams.

2000 saw Linda's return to Capital Radio where she was appointed to the plc Board as commercial director, responsible for all commercial income, HR and technology. Linda worked with the Board to bring about the GCap merger in 2005, formed by Capital and GWR.

She joined Starcom MediaVest Group in January 2006 and is responsible for all UK operations.

Mark Sweney
Advertising, Marketing
& New Media
Correspondent
MediaGuardian.co.uk

Mark graduated from Auckland University, New Zealand in 1997 with a double major in English literature and psychology. After time out to travel across Asia he began work at Haymarket Publishing in 1999 in the directories division, responsible for producing a range of supplements for the company's business title portfolio.

In 2000 he joined Revolution magazine, as editorial assistant and was rapidly promoted to news reporter, following its transition from a monthly to a weekly title, to cover the digital business and marketing economy during the first dot com cycle of boom and bust. In late 2002 Mark became a reporter on Campaign magazine then moved to Marketing magazine, as chief reporter in March 2004.

In March 2006 Mark joined Guardian Newspapers as advertising, marketing and new media correspondent at MediaGuardian.co.uk. He also writes occasional pieces for the weekly MediaGuardian supplement and the daily Guardian newspaper.

Alan Thompson
Founding Partner
The Haystack Group

Alan co-founded The Haystack Group in 2001 and has since built it into one of the most recognised consultancy led intermediaries in the country.

Following a degree in psychology at University College London, Alan embarked on a career in marketing communications that has led him to work in each of the major disciplines at the highest level, for some of the biggest brands both in the UK and globally. His career has seen him advise the likes of Daimler Benz, Ford, Unilever, Mars, The Daily Telegraph, BSkyB, Sainsbury's and Lloyds TSB.

Alan advises brands on how to structure and manage their marketing resources, both internally and through agency partners, and has been involved in some of the highest profile pitches in the business as well as working on discreet strategic projects with many major UK and global brands.

Suki Thompson
Founding Partner
Oystercatchers

Suki is a founding partner of Oystercatchers, a marketing practice helping clients turbo charge their marketing in the digital age. Launched in November 2007, she has been working with clients such as lastminute.com, McDonald's, Regus, Honda, Nationwide, Barnardo's and Lloyds TSB.

Prior to this, Suki set up and ran The Haystack Group for six years, placing on average £500 million of communications budgets annually. During this time the Group became the leading search, selection and evaluation agency in the UK working with clients such as BA, Sainsbury's, Digital UK, Weetabix, Muller® and Unilever.

Before Haystack Suki was an experienced agency director, running business development for London agencies, including Rapp Collins, Impact FCA! and TBWA as well as setting up headhunting company, Kendall Tarrant in Asia.

Suki is a regular conference speaker and comentator in the marketing press. She also owns a specialist gin company called Bunker Gin.

Lucy Unger
Managing Partner
EMEA
Fitch

Lucy's career began with sales and marketing roles in blue chip multinational companies such as Unilever, Colgate-Palmolive, Tesco and Coca-Cola.

In 1996 she made the change to the agency side, opening a brand communications consultancy in Australia. During this time she successfully led project teams working with Westpac Banking Corporation, SOCOG (the 2000 Sydney Olympics Organising Committee), Fox Studios, VISA, John Fairfax and Multiplex.

Lucy joined Fitch in 2001 as a client director and has been instrumental in directing the development of relationships and delivery of projects with Nissan Europe, Vodafone, HSBC, the BBC and the Hyundai Motor Company of Korea.

In May 2003 she was promoted to joint managing partner of Fitch's London studio and in July 2006 to managing partner of the EMEA region. In this role she continues to play an active role in London-based client and project work, and new business, in addition to overseeing Fitch's operations in the Middle East and Continental Europe.

Andrew Walmsley
Co-Founder
i-level

Andrew co-founded i-level in 1998 and the company has since won more than 30 awards. It has been Agency of the Year consistently for eight years and in 2007 became the first digital agency to win a Queen's Award for Enterprise.

Andrew is on the judging panel for several industry awards and is frequently quoted in the trade and national media, as well as writing a weekly column in Marketing magazine. Furthermore, Ernst & Young named him London Media Entrepreneur of the Year in 2006.

Andrew has an MBA from Kingston University, where his dissertation researched the impact of digital media on advertising agencies.

Mark Waugh
Deputy Managing
Director
ZenithOptimedia

When Mark joined the UK media planning fraternity from Oxford University, media was seen as a trading-based discipline that followed the strategic lead offered by the advertising agency. In the intervening 17 years Mark has been a key player in driving the strategic importance of media planning in the industry and at the age of 28 he became the youngest ever managing partner of Optimedia. Mark joined market leader ZenithOptimedia as deputy managing director in 2003.

In his career Mark has amassed experience across almost every market category, from motors to luxury goods and financial services to FMCG. This, coupled with his agency's £700 million UK media spend, allows him a uniquely scaled perspective on the behaviour of some of Britain's biggest brands. In 2007 Mark launched newcast, ZenithOptimedia's integrated communications unit, which develops and executes everything from experiential marketing to digital branded content. If anyone has an holistic approach to building Superbrand fame it should be Mark.

Stephen Cheliotis
Chairman
Superbrands
Councils UK
& Chief Executive
The Centre for
Brand Analysis

Stephen began his career at global brand valuation and strategy consultancy, Brand Finance, where he advised companies on maximising shareholder value through effective brand management. In addition he produced key studies, including comprehensive reports on global intangible assets. His annual study of City Analysts was vital in understanding the importance of marketing metrics in forecasting companies' performance.

In 2001 Stephen joined Superbrands UK, becoming UK managing director in 2003 and overseeing two years of significant growth. Given a European role in 2005, his expertise was used across 20 countries.

He has been a freelance consultant since 2006 and in 2008 set up The Centre for Brand Analysis, which is dedicated to understanding the performance of brands and is contracted to run the Superbrands selection process. Stephen chairs the three independent councils for Superbrands UK.

He speaks regularly at conferences and also comments for international media on branding and marketing, with frequent appearances on CNN, the BBC and Sky.

The YouGov Consumer Vote

YouGov – challenging research

YouGov is an international, full service research company primarily using online panels to provide quantitative and qualitative research across a range of specialisms. These include consumer markets, financial services, technology and telecoms, media and organisation (both employee and employer aspects). YouGov's full service offering spans added value consultancy, syndicated and product offers, omnibus and field and tab services.

YouGov is considered the pioneer of online market research. Through panel management expertise, flexibility and an innovative approach to recruitment, YouGov operates a quality panel of over 200,000 UK members representing all ages, socio-economic groups and other demographic types, with excellent response rates. YouGov also specialises in growing and maintaining dedicated panels of specialist consumer and professional audiences.

Based on its track record, YouGov has been acclaimed as the UK's most accurate opinion pollster and dominates Britain's media polling. YouGov is one of the most quoted agencies in Britain and has a well-documented and published track record illustrating the success of its survey methods and quality of its client service work.

YouGov and Superbrands

YouGov has worked with the Superbrands organisation over the past few years, conducting online elections for all three of its UK programmes – Superbrands, Business Superbrands and CoolBrands.

The survey that took place for Superbrands 2008/09 was conducted using an online interview system. This was administered to members of the YouGov GB panel of individuals who have previously agreed to take part in surveys for the company.

Online research has proved to be the best medium for quantifying the perception of Superbrands amongst consumers; the stimulating process is intuitive, so it can be quick and enjoyable for participants while also delivering extremely useful data. Online research is non-intrusive – as the questionnaires are completed by invitation – and is more cost effective than conventional research methods. It is representative as there are sufficient numbers of individuals online to compensate for any biases in the online community when sampling. The final responding sample for the Superbrands 2008/09 survey was 2,223 individuals.

When the online election has been completed the final scores are sent to Superbrands, to be incorporated with the scores given to the brands by the

Tim Britton
Chief Executive UK

Expert Council (see selection process details at the beginning of this publication).

YouGov has executives who are members of the Market Research Society and ESOMAR. YouGov is a member of the British Polling Council. YouGov is also registered with the Information Commissioner.

www.yougov.com
info@yougov.com
+44 (0)20 7012 6000

149

The Superbrands Results, 2008/09

By Stephen Cheliotis
Chairman, Superbrands Councils UK
& Chief Executive, The Centre for
Brand Analysis

Whilst I have chaired the Expert Council, that plays a role in selecting the UK's Superbrands, for many years this is the first year in which my company, The Centre for Brand Analysis, has been employed to independently oversee the entire selection process.

That task began in earnest in autumn 2007 when I, together with a team of researchers, started to compile the 'population' list of major consumer brands operating in the UK – brands do not apply to be considered by submitting an entry. From the thousands of brands that were identified we have slowly eliminated the majority, through a combination of analysing expert and consumer opinion, resulting in a list of the top 500. These brands are listed on page 156 and are deemed to be the UK's Superbrands for 2008/09.

It's the third year since the methodology for selecting Superbrands was modified in order to incorporate the views of UK

consumers. It is only fair that those individuals consuming the brands ultimately determine which are genuine Superbrands. This article aims to summarize those views as well as look briefly at the views of the experts surveyed through the process.

Top performers overall
This year we have a new number one Superbrand in the form of Google by virtue of it being the most highly regarded brand in the eyes of consumers. Google replaced Microsoft®, which was the number one brand in 2007/08. Both technology giants have, over recent years, come to dominate Superbrand surveys – in the Business Superbrands results announced in the spring of 2008, both brands also competed for the top slot with Google again just pipping Microsoft® to the number one position.

Clearly both brands have become highly influential. Whether we ask consumers, as

we did in this survey, or media & marketing experts and business professionals, as we did for the Business Superbrands survey, both brands have come up time and time again in the last couple of years. The fact that Google has continued to knock Microsoft® into second place must be an annoyance for the software giant, especially when one considers the more extensive marketing budget of the latter.

Established British brands continue to perform well in the rankings with the likes of the BBC, British Airways and Cadbury continuing to be well placed in the top 20 – albeit that the survey was conducted prior to the Terminal 5 debacle which I am sure will have impacted severely on the British Airways brand. Joining these British goliaths in the top 20 is a resurgent Marks & Spencer, as well as another UK icon, the ceramic and chinaware creator Royal Doulton. That said, British brands have not had it all their own way, with giants like BP falling outside of the top 20 after a difficult year. Guinness also fell from the top group finishing in 23rd place, down from last year's eighth position; this despite the positive impact of its creative campaign 'Tipping Point'. In April 2008 the drinks brand credited the ad with reviving its fortunes in its home market, with sales up six per cent in the UK and Ireland.

In total 10 of last year's top 20 remained in the upper echelon of the rankings, namely Google, Microsoft®, Mercedez-Benz, the BBC, British Airways, Nike, Coca-Cola, LEGO®, Cadbury and Hilton. Of the 10 brands falling out of the top 20, only three dropped significantly – i.e. below the top 50 – this time around.

Of the new entries to this year's top 20, most rose only slightly on last year's performance but two brands stand out – Thorntons, which rose from 81st place last year to 18th place and Royal Doulton, which rose from 60th place last year to take 6th position.

Experts vs consumers

The independent and voluntary Expert Council, consisting of media and marketing experts (full biographies on page 144) plays an important role within the selection process; it is their collective scores on the initial shortlist that determines the final 750 brands to be judged by UK consumers.

This system enables us to go back at the end of the process to compare how the experts' and consumers' views on the top brands differed, as they have historically done quite significantly.

This year the pattern of differing opinion is again evident. Last year we saw eight brands sit in both the council and consumer top 20s. This year both audiences again only agreed on eight brands, five

Superbrands Top 10

2007/08	2008/09
Microsoft®	**Google**
Coca-Cola	**Microsoft®**
Google	**Mercedes-Benz**
BBC	**BBC**
BP	**British Airways**
British Airways	**Royal Doulton**
LEGO®	**BMW**
Guinness	**Bosch**
Mercedes-Benz	**Nike**
Cadbury	**Sony**

of which were the same as last time. This collection of super Superbrands featured Microsoft®, Coca-Cola, Google, the BBC and Nike. The three new brands to feature in both the expert and consumer top 20s in 2008/09 were BMW, Apple and Marks & Spencer.

Generally notable differences exist between the experts and consumers. Brands rated by consumers but failing to capture the votes of the council include predominately large, established brands such as Royal Doulton, Duracell®, the AA, LEGO® and Cadbury. One might assume that the council do not see these brands as particularly innovative in marketing terms or as having momentum. Nevertheless their awareness, longevity, ubiquity and the reliability and trust they engender with the public ensures their continued top Superbrand status in the eyes of consumers.

Conversely the brands that the council are rating in their top 20, yet which fail to hit the same positions in the consumer vote, tend to be recognised for their distinctive and strong brand values and quality – they are perhaps more niche or polarising. Brands such as innocent, Green & Black's or Waitrose – i.e. brands that tend to be featured in every marketer's collection of best practice case studies – don't quite hit the top notes with all consumer groups. Of course they are not necessarily trying to do this, so for these brands a segmented analysis of their performance is perhaps more important than their overall performance.

Experts' top 10 year-on-year

Despite significant changes in council members this year, the year-on-year expert results were fairly consistent. Eleven of the brands the council placed in their top 20 in

2007/08 featured once again – the numbers could have been higher if it were not for brands that had either been added to the process for the first time (like Green & Black's) or deleted, such as iPod (where the decision was made to only keep the parent brand). It is clear that intelligent marketing and a strong positioning in comparison to competitors gives brands a lot of credibility with the experts.

Top performing categories

In total there are 42 categories represented by the top 500 brands. The 'Food' category, encompassing 41 different food brands, is by far the most successful in volume terms. Incredibly however only two of those brands feature in the top 100, with Kellogg's in 24th place and Heinz in 36th.

The second strongest sector, in terms of the number of brands featured in the top 500, is the 'Toiletries & Cosmetics' category with 33 brands. Dominated by aspirational brands such as Estée Lauder, Chanel and Clinique the category also features more mass market competitors such as No7 and Nivea. This sector, however, has an even weaker representation in the top 100 than the Food category. None of its 33 brands make that level, with Estée Lauder coming closest by finishing in 120th position. No other categories have more than 30 brands in the top 500 although the 'Retail – General' category has 28 brands, topped by Marks & Spencer in 17th place. Other retailers making the top 100 were Harrods (35th) and John Lewis (60th). Surprisingly none of the big four supermarkets made the top 100, with Waitrose in 179th place, Sainsbury's at 232, Tesco at 301 and ASDA in 439th position.

In fact, with 38 of the 42 categories represented in the top 100 alone you can see that the top brands really do represent quite an eclectic mix of sectors – from coffee shops to theme parks and from chocolate bars to banks.

Looking at another indicative measure of sector strength – the average position within the top 500 of brands from a given sector – the best performing category is 'Technology – Computer Hardware & Software'; its eight entries in the top 500 have an average position of 83rd place. The 'Drinks – Coffee & Tea' category comes second with an average position of 139th, with four of its seven entrants firmly established in the top 100. Two 'Leisure & Entertainment' sub-categories follow with 'Games & Toy' brands enjoying an average position of 141st and the 'Gambling' brands enjoying an average position of 152nd.

Comparative Top 10s

	2007/08 Results		2008/09 Results	
Rank	Consumers	Expert Council	Consumers	Expert Council
1	Microsoft®	Google	Google	Google
2	Coca-Cola	Apple	Microsoft®	Apple
3	Google	iPod	Mercedes-Benz	Nike
4	BBC	Mini	BBC	BMW
5	BP	eBay	British Airways	BBC
6	British Airways	BBC	Royal Doulton	innocent
7	LEGO®	Coca-Cola	BMW	Audi
8	Guinness	Red Bull	Bosch	Coca-Cola
9	Mercedes-Benz	Tesco	Nike	Marks & Spencer
10	Cadbury	Waitrose	Sony	Waitrose

Surprisingly, considering some of the negative press surrounding the sector both in terms of it environmental impact and allegations of profiteering, 'Oil & Gas' is the fifth best performing sector based on average brand position.

Battling brands

One indicator of brand strength is its relative performance versus that of its competitors. Looking at the gap in positions between first- and second-placed brands, a few direct competitors looking particularly strong include Thomas Cook beating its nearest rival Kuoni by 268 places (the biggest gap between first and second in a given sector); Starbucks beating Costa Coffee by 242 places; the Manchester United brand sitting 139 places above Liverpool FC; Hilton beating fellow and closest ranked hotelier Marriot by 105 places; the BBC outperforming Sky by 75 positions; and in a result unlikely to be repeated next year, British Airways beating Virgin Atlantic by 65 places.

In some of the tighter battles, Nike continues to outperform close rival adidas, albeit by just 35 positions. Thorntons beats its parent company brand, Cadbury, by a single place while Parker pens sits nine places above Sellotape. BP and Shell vie for the top position in the Oil & Gas category with only 12 places separating them in the top 500. In the extremely competitive field of alcoholic spirits, top brand Jack Daniel's has an increasingly aggressive Glenfiddich an uncomfortable 14 places below it. In the battle of the car manufacturers, two German brands unsurprisingly lead the field with Mercedes-Benz coming four positions ahead of BMW.

Top Categories 2008/09

Category	Entries in the top 500
Food	**41**
Toiletries & Cosmetics	**33**
Retail – General	**28**
Clothing & Footware	**26**
Technology – General	**23**

On the move

Whilst the rankings we produce for Superbrands represent a snapshot of consumer opinion, and therefore do not offer a detailed insight into each brand's underlying equity, movements in this table may represent an early indication that all is not well or that a brand is gaining momentum.

As we have consumer data from three years, it is sensible to compare not just year-on-year performance but a brand's ranking over all three years to reveal its broader direction. We could for example conclude based on the evidence of the survey results that adidas is increasingly getting it right, having moved from 153rd place in 2006/07, to 52nd place in 2007/08 and 33rd place this year – an overall gain of 120 positions. Equally BUPA has been steadily rising in the table going from 313th place in 2006/07 to 265th last year and now up to 133rd. Other brands on the rise range from Royal Doulton, which has gone from 63rd to 60th and finally sixth place this year, to Thomas Cook which has improved its standing from 110th two years ago to 83rd last year and finally 72nd this time around.

However, brands have also gone in the opposite direction. American Express has lost ground falling from 42nd in 2006/07 to 101st in 2007/08 and 159th this year. Price based retailers like ASDA and Argos also seem to be dropping – the former going from 92nd to 186th and finally this year to 439th; the latter went from 82nd to 146th and this year rests at 463rd. Yet it seems that the online retailers are not specifically stealing their thunder. One of its most famous representatives, Amazon had already dropped from 53rd to 174th and this year dropped again to 285th.

Some brands have, as one would expect, been yo-yoing up and down from year to year. This could be due to the influence of marketing campaigns or some positive or negative publicity on consumers. A consistent performance is the true sign of a genuine Superbrand. Here we can find many examples including some of those brands featured within this publication. For example Duracell® has remained within a window of 17 places for three years, starting in ninth place before dropping slightly and then rising back up to 12th this year. The BBC was second two years ago

The Sexes Speak: Female Rankings

Female ranking	Brand	Male ranking	Female/male difference	Overall rank
1	**Google**	2	+ 1	1
2	**Microsoft®**	1	– 1	2
3	**Mercedes-Benz**	3	none	3
4	**Royal Doulton**	20	+ 16	6
5	**British Airways**	6	+ 1	5
6	**Bosch**	15	+ 9	8
7	**AA**	27	+ 20	15
8	**Thorntons**	29	+ 21	18
9	**BBC**	4	– 5	4
10	**Nike**	12	+ 2	9

Male Rankings

Male ranking	Brand	Female ranking	Male/female difference	Overall rank
1	**Microsoft®**	2	+ 1	2
2	**Google**	1	– 1	1
3	**Mercedes-Benz**	3	none	3
4	**BBC**	9	+ 5	4
5	**BMW**	19	+ 14	7
6	**British Airways**	5	– 1	5
7	**Ordnance Survey**	51	+ 44	27
8	**Sony**	16	+ 8	10
9	**Michelin**	61	+ 52	30
10	**Apple**	17	+ 7	11

and has for the last two years resided in fourth place, while Sony was 10th two years ago and remains in exactly the same position in the latest survey.

The sexes speak
When we cut the data to view the opinions of a specific demographic we tend to see, as one might expect, some pretty significant changes, albeit not necessarily at the top of the table. If we look, for example, purely at the female rankings we can see that 15 of their top 20 brands are consistent with the overall top 20. The biggest mover compared to the overall results is Green & Black's, which sits in 53rd place in the overall rankings with men placing it 132 places lower than women. The other notable riser is Parker, which is in 34th place overall due to it being ranked 81 places lower by men, and Fisher-Price which sits in 28th place overall or 40 places lower if we looked at how the male respondents rated it.

Quite clearly if we look at the top 20 brands according to men, we again find a general consensus with the overall results – in fact, exactly 15 of the 20 brands can again be found in the overall top 20. Notably the top position changes with Microsoft® taking Google's crown. The significant outsiders in the male top 20 are Ordnance Survey, which men placed 51 positions ahead of women and BP, which they rated 60 places higher than the females surveyed.

What perhaps is most telling when trying to identify the difference between the brands men and women rate, is the number of positions between where the two sexes placed specific brands; in 69 cases, there is a difference of 100 places between the male and female rankings.

Women ranked many lifestyle brands higher, particularly in the Clothing and Toiletries & Cosmetic categories – the biggest difference being seen in the Champneys brand, which was placed a staggering 312 places higher by women than men.

Some of the brands are clearly marketed specifically to women but other brands could and perhaps should see this gap between the sexes as a worrying issue; for example, what can the FAIRTRADE Mark, which was rated 220 places higher by women than men, do to make itself more relevant to men. Is the significantly better performance of innocent drinks amongst women a chink in the armour? Are those marketers that use it as an example of a brand with genuine consumer engagement – achieved through its use of more personal and friendly language – highlighting not only its strength but its weakness?

Brands more highly rated by men than women are, on the whole, as one might expect: such as all four football clubs in the top 500 and two shaving brands, Wilkinson Sword and Gillette. More surprisingly, both Facebook and YouTube are placed higher by men with the former 238 places higher than women and the latter 273 places higher. Sainsbury's is ranked some 233 places higher by men – Jamie Oliver's charms seem to be having more of an effect on men than women!

Of course cutting the data in other ways also produces interesting findings be it the difference in opinion between those in the ABC1 social group and the C2DE social grouping, old and young consumers or those of different regions.

For example we can see that brands like innocent and Bombay Sapphire are placed more than 300 positions higher by those in the ABC1 grouping compared to those in the C2DE grouping. Other brands doing considerably better amongst the ABC1s include Bose, Samsonite and PIMM'S® – again for some of these brands that will be no surprise and fits their positioning but for others, inclusion in this gap table will be of concern.

Brand such as Xbox have faired much better with the C2DE grouping, being placed 167 positions higher by them than the ABC1s. Other brands north of 150 places according to the C2DE group include Halifax and Lloyds TSB as well as brands such as Kingsmill, Russell Hobbs and Umbro.

Conclusions

All the brands featuring in the top 500 have been through a rigorous and multi-layered process and deserve their Superbrand status. For most of the brands it is their inclusion in this elite group, from the thousands of brands first considered, that is the most important thing, rather than their position within it. Nevertheless hopefully this article has given a glimpse into some of the wider insights that have been gleaned from the process. In-depth conclusions on what the rankings mean for each brand require further analysis, however I hope that most brands will not be too surprised or indeed disappointed by where they were positioned.

If you have any questions or comments about the selection process (outlined on page 10) or the results contained in this article please do not hesitate to contact me.

stephen.cheliotis@tcba.co.uk

THE CENTRE FOR
BRAND
ANALYSIS

The Centre for Brand Analysis (TCBA) is dedicated to understanding the performance of brands. There are many ways to measure brand performance. TCBA do not believe in a 'one size fits all' approach, instead offering tailored solutions to ensure the metrics investigated and measured are relevant and appropriate.

Its services aim to allow people to understand how a brand is performing, either at a point in time or on an ongoing basis, as well gain insight into wider market and marketing trends. Services fall into three categories:

Brand perception – measuring attitudes amongst customers, opinion formers, employees, investors, suppliers or other stakeholders.

Market insight – providing intelligence, trends and examples of best practice.

Marketing analysis – reviewing brand activity, including: campaign assessment; image/brand language assessment; marketing/PR review; agency sourcing and roster review; and ROI analysis.

Working principally for brand owners, TCBA also provides intelligence to agencies and other organisations. It utilises extensive relationships within the business community and works with third parties where appropriate, to access pertinent opinions, data and insights.

www.tcba.co.uk

Qualifying Superbrands 2008/09

118 118
AA
Abercrombie & Fitch
Actimel
Adidas
Adobe
AEG
After Eight
Aga-Rayburn
Alka-Seltzer
Alpha Romeo
Alton Towers
Amazon.co.uk
Ambre Solaire
American Express
Anadin
Anchor
Andrex
Ann Summers
AOL
Apple
Argos
Ariel
Arsenal FC
ASDA
Audi
Autoglass
Avon
A-Z Maps
B&Q
Bacardi
Baileys
Bang & Olufsen
Barclaycard
Barclays
Bassett's
BBC
Beechams
Ben & Jerry's
Bendicks
Benylin
Berghaus
BIC
Birds Eye
Bisto
Black & Decker
BlackBerry
Blaupunkt
Blu-Tack
BMW
Bold
Bombay Sapphire
Bonjela
Boots
Bosch
Bose
BP
Brabantia
Branston
Braun
Brita
Britax
British Airways

British Gas
Brylcreem
BT
Budweiser
Bupa
Burger King
Buxton
Cadbury
Caffè Nero
Calpol
Calvin Klein
Canon
Carling
Carlsberg
Carte D'Or
Castrol
Cathay Pacific
Center Parcs
Champneys
Chanel
Channel 4
Chelsea FC
**Chessington World
  of Adventures**
Chivas Regal
Cif
Clarins
Clarks
Classic FM
Clinique
Coca-Cola
Cointreau
Colgate
Collins
Colman's
Comfort
Cosmopolitan
Costa
Courvoisier
Cow & Gate
Crabtree & Evelyn
Crayola
Crown
Cunard
Deep Heat
Dell
De'Longhi
Dettol
Diesel
Dior
Direct Line
Disneyland Paris
DKNY
Domestos
Domino's
Dove
Dr Martens
Dulux
Dunlop
Duracell
Durex
Dyson
E.ON

E45
Early Learning Centre
Eden Project
Elastoplast
Electrolux
Elizabeth Arden
Encyclopædia Britannica
Esso
Estée Lauder
Eurostar
Eurotunnel
Evian
Expedia
Facebook
Fairtrade
Fairy
Famous Grouse
Ferrero Rocher
Filofax
Finish
Fisher-Price
Flash
Flora
Ford
Foster's
Four Seasons Hotels & Resorts
French Connection
FT
Fuji
Galaxy
Gap
Garnier
Gaviscon
George
Gillette
Glenfiddich
Good Housekeeping
Goodyear
Google
Gordon's
Gossard
Grand Marnier
Green & Black's
Grolsch
Guinness
Häagen-Dazs
Habitat
Halfords
Halifax
Hamleys
Harpic
Harrods
Harry Ramsden's
Harvey Nichols
Heineken
Heinz
Hellmann's
Hennessy
Hertz
Hewlett-Packard
Highland Spring
Hilton
HMV

Holland & Barrett
Homepride
Honda
Hoover
Horlicks
Hornby
Hovis
HP
HSBC
Huggies
Hugo Boss
IBM
IKEA
Imodium
Imperial Leather
Innocent
Intel
ITV
Jack Daniel's
Jacob's
Jacob's Creek
Jaeger
Jaguar
Jameson Irish Whiskey
JCB
Jean Paul Gaultier Perfumes
Jiffy
John Lewis
Johnnie Walker
Kellogg's
Kenco
Kenwood
Kettle Chips
KFC
Kickers
Kingsmill
Kit Kat
Kitekat
Kleenex
Kodak
Kronenbourg 1664
Kuoni
Kwik-Fit
La Senza
Ladbrokes
Lancôme
Land Rover
Lastminute.com
Le Creuset
Lea & Perrins
Lego
Legoland
Lemsip
Lenor
Levi's
Lexus
Lindt
Liverpool FC
Lloyds TSB
London Eye
Lonely Planet
Longleat
L'Oréal Paris

Lucozade
Lufthansa
Lurpak
Lycra
Maclaren
Madame Tussauds
Maglite
Magners Irish Cider
Maltesters
Mamas & Papas
Manchester United FC
Mappin & Webb
Marks & Spencer
Marmite
Marriott
Mars
Martell
Martini
MasterCard
Max Factor
McCain
McDonald's
McVitie's
Mercedes-Benz
Michelin
Michelin Travel Guides & Maps
Microsoft
Miele
Milton
Mini
Miss Selfridge
Molton Brown
Monopoly
Monsoon
Mothercare
Motorola
Mr Kipling
Mr Muscle
Mr Sheen
MTV
Müller
National Express
National Geographic
Nationwide
NatWest
Neff
Nescafé
New Covent Garden Food Co
New Scientist
Newcastle Brown Ale
Next
Nicorette
Night Nurse
Nike
Nikon
Nintendo
Nivea
No7
Nokia
Norwich Union
Nurofen
O2
Odeon Cinemas

Olay
Olympus
Omega
Oral-B
Orange
Ordnance Survey
Oxford University Press
Oxo
Pampers
Panadol
Panasonic
Parker
Paul Smith
Pedigree
Pentax
Pepsi
Perrier
Persil
PG Tips
Philadelphia
Philips
Pimm's
Pioneer
Pirelli
Pizza Express
Pizza Hut
Play-Doh
Playstation
Pledge
Polyfilla
Post Office
Post-it
Pret A Manger
Pritt
Prudential
Puma
Qantas
Quaker Oats
Quality Street
RAC
Radio Times
Radox
Raleigh
Ralph Lauren
Ray-Ban
Reader's Digest
Red Bull
Reebok
Remy Martin
Rennie
Ribena
Robinsons
Rotary Watches
Rough Guides
Rowntree's
Royal Albert Hall
Royal Bank of Scotland
Royal Doulton
Russell & Bromley
Russell Hobbs
Ryvita
Saab
Saga

Sainsbury's
Samsonite
Samsung
Sandals
Savlon
Scalextric
Scholl
Schweppes
Scottish Widows
Seiko
Selfridges
Sellotape
Seven Seas
Sharwood's
Shell
Sheraton Hotels & Resorts
Shredded Wheat
Siemens
Silentnight Beds
Silver Cross
Silver Spoon
Sky
Slazenger
Smeg
Smirnoff
Sony
Sony Ericsson
Southern Comfort
Specsavers
Speedo
Stanley
Stannah Stairlifts
Starbucks
Stella Artois
Strepsils
Strongbow
Swarovski
Swatch
Swiss Army
TAG Heuer
Tampax
Tate & Lyle Cane Sugar
Tate Galleries
TCP
Ted Baker
Tefal
Tesco
Tetley
Texaco
The Body Shop
The Daily Telegraph
The Economist
The Guardian/The Observer
The Independent
The National Lottery
The North Face
The Times
Thermos
Thomas Cook
Thomson Local
Thorntons
Thorpe Park
Tiffany & Co.

Timberland
Tipp-Ex
T-Mobile
Toblerone
TomTom
Toni&Guy
Topshop
Toshiba
Toyota
Trivial Pursuit
Tropicana
Tupperware
Twinings
Ty.Phoo
Umbro
Uncle Ben's
Vanish
Vaseline
Velux
Vicks
Vidal Sassoon
Virgin Atlantic
Virgin Media
Virgin Mobile
Virgin Trains
Visa
Vodafone
Vogue
Volvic
Volvo
Wagamama
Waitrose
Walkers
Wall's
Warburtons
Waterford Crystal
Waterman
Waterstone's
Wedgwood
Weetabix
Wembley Stadium
Werther's Original
Which?
Whirlpool
Whiskas
Whittards of Chelsea
Who's Who
WHSmith
Wilkinson Sword
William Hill
Winalot
Wonderbra
Wrigley's
Xbox
Xerox
Yahoo!
Yakult
Yellow Pages
YouTube
Zanussi

QUALITY   RELIABILITY   DISTINCTION